Good Night, Hem

For Hubert.

Athos previously appeared in *The Last Musketeer* (2008). Hemingway previously appeared in *The Left Bank Gang* (2006).

Designer: Keeli McCarthy
Editor: Conrad Groth
Production: Paul Baresh and Christina Hwang
Publicity: Jacq Cohen
Associate Publisher: Eric Reynolds
Publisher: Gary Groth

Fantagraphics Books, Inc.
7563 Lake City Way NE
Seattle, WA 98115

www.fantagraphics.com
facebook.com/fantagraphics
@fantagraphics

ISBN: 978-1-68396-461-2
Library of Congress Control Number: 2021935348
First Fantagraphics Books edition: September 2021
Printed in China

GOOD NIGHT, HEM

by Jason

1

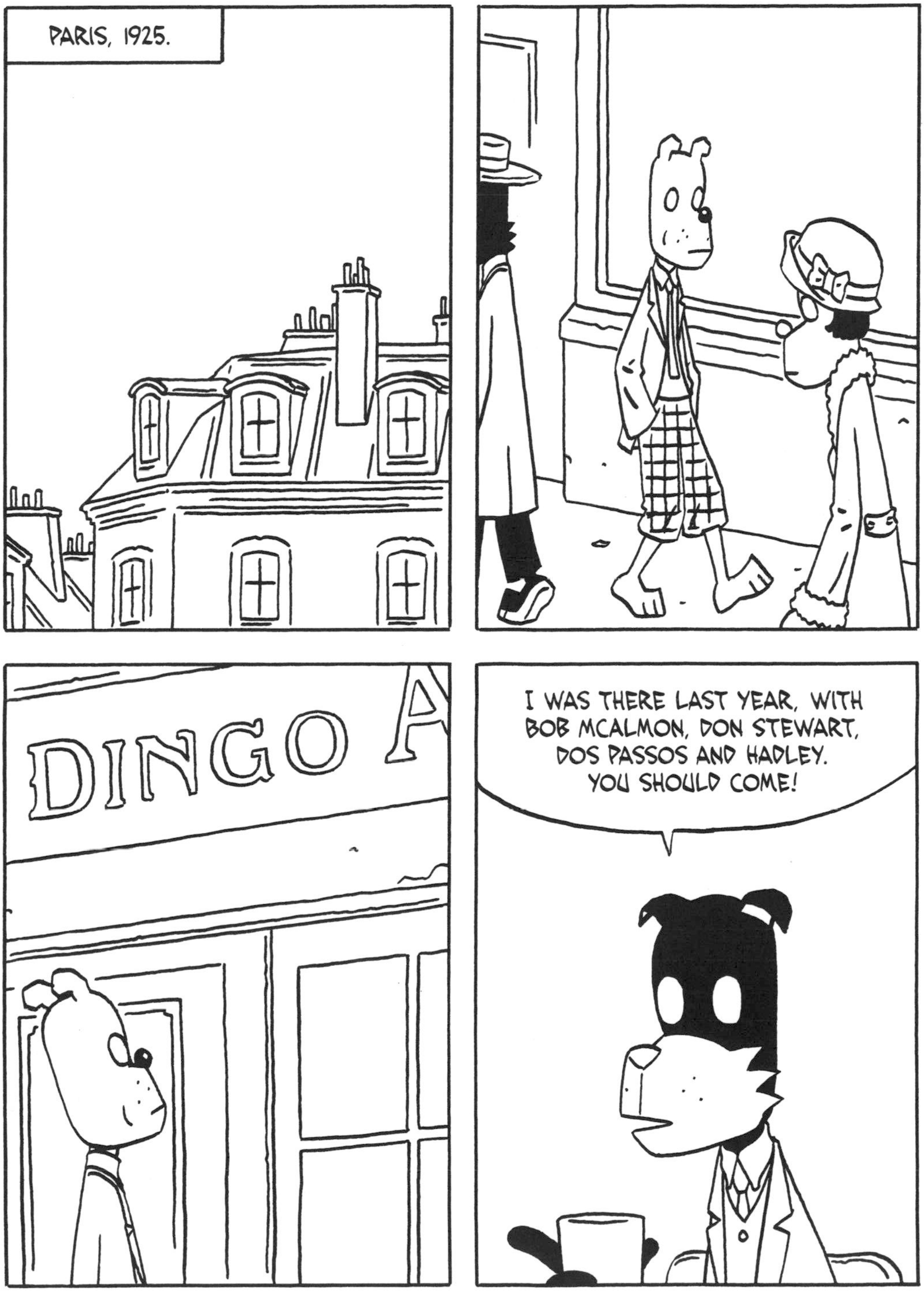
PARIS, 1925.
DINGO A
I WAS THERE LAST YEAR, WITH BOB MCALMON, DON STEWART, DOS PASSOS AND HADLEY. YOU SHOULD COME!

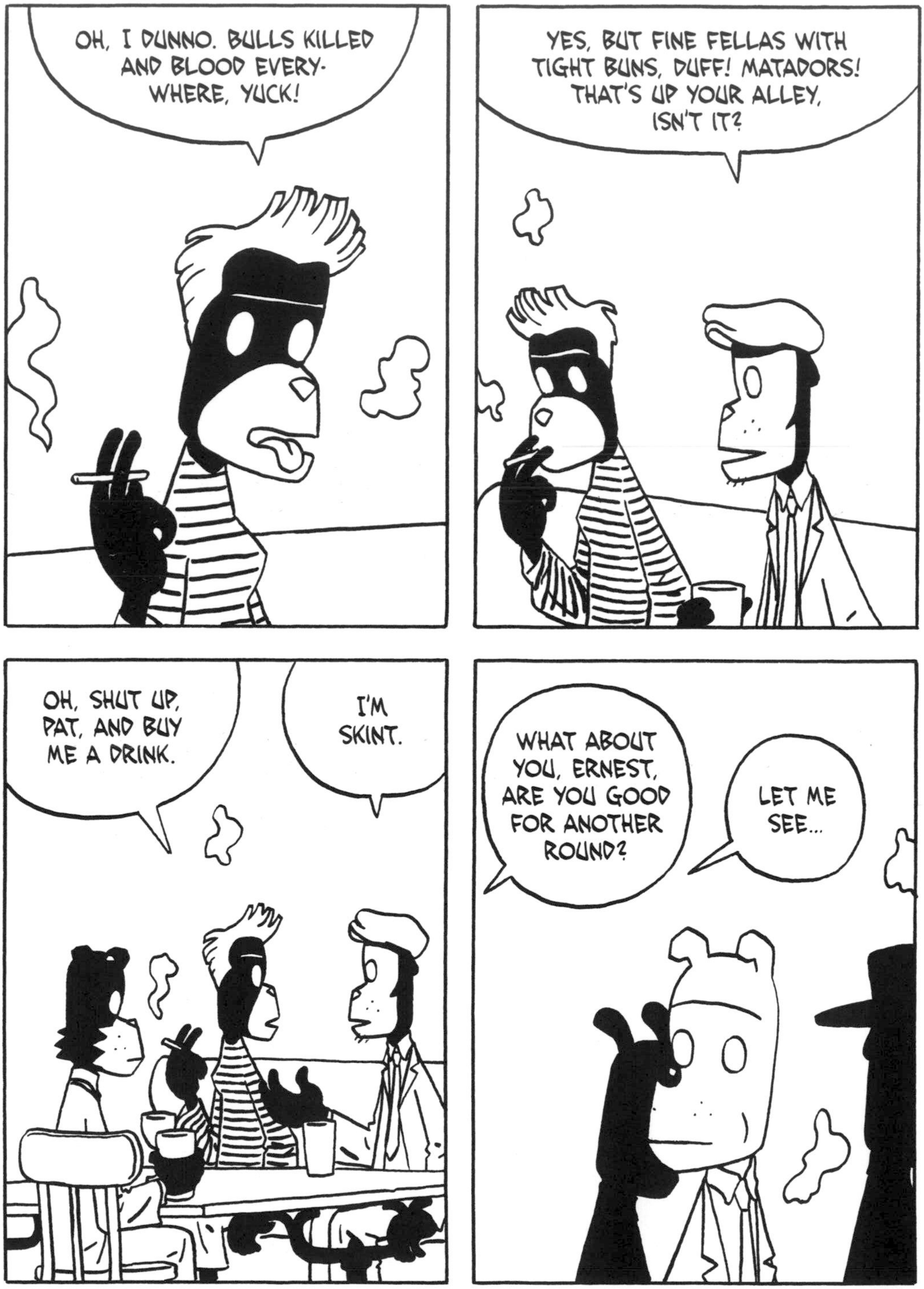
OH, I DUNNO. BULLS KILLED AND BLOOD EVERY-WHERE, YUCK!
YES, BUT FINE FELLAS WITH TIGHT BUNS, DUFF! MATADORS! THAT'S UP YOUR ALLEY, ISN'T IT?
OH, SHUT UP, PAT, AND BUY ME A DRINK.
I'M SKINT.
WHAT ABOUT YOU, ERNEST, ARE YOU GOOD FOR ANOTHER ROUND?
LET ME SEE...

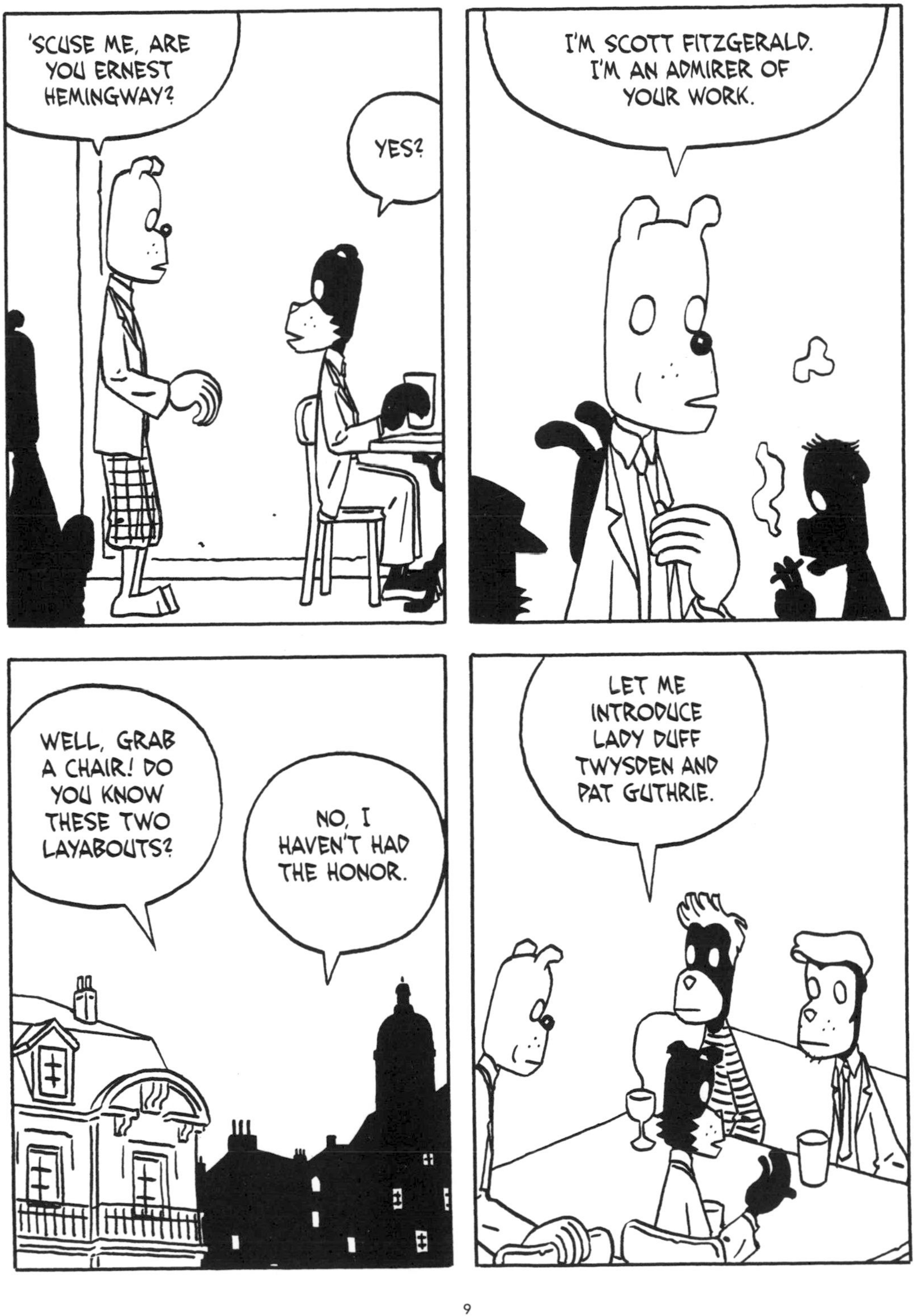
'SCUSE ME, ARE YOU ERNEST HEMINGWAY?
YES?
I'M SCOTT FITZGERALD. I'M AN ADMIRER OF YOUR WORK.
WELL, GRAB A CHAIR! DO YOU KNOW THESE TWO LAYABOUTS?
NO, I HAVEN'T HAD THE HONOR.
LET ME INTRODUCE LADY DUFF TWYSDEN AND PAT GUTHRIE.

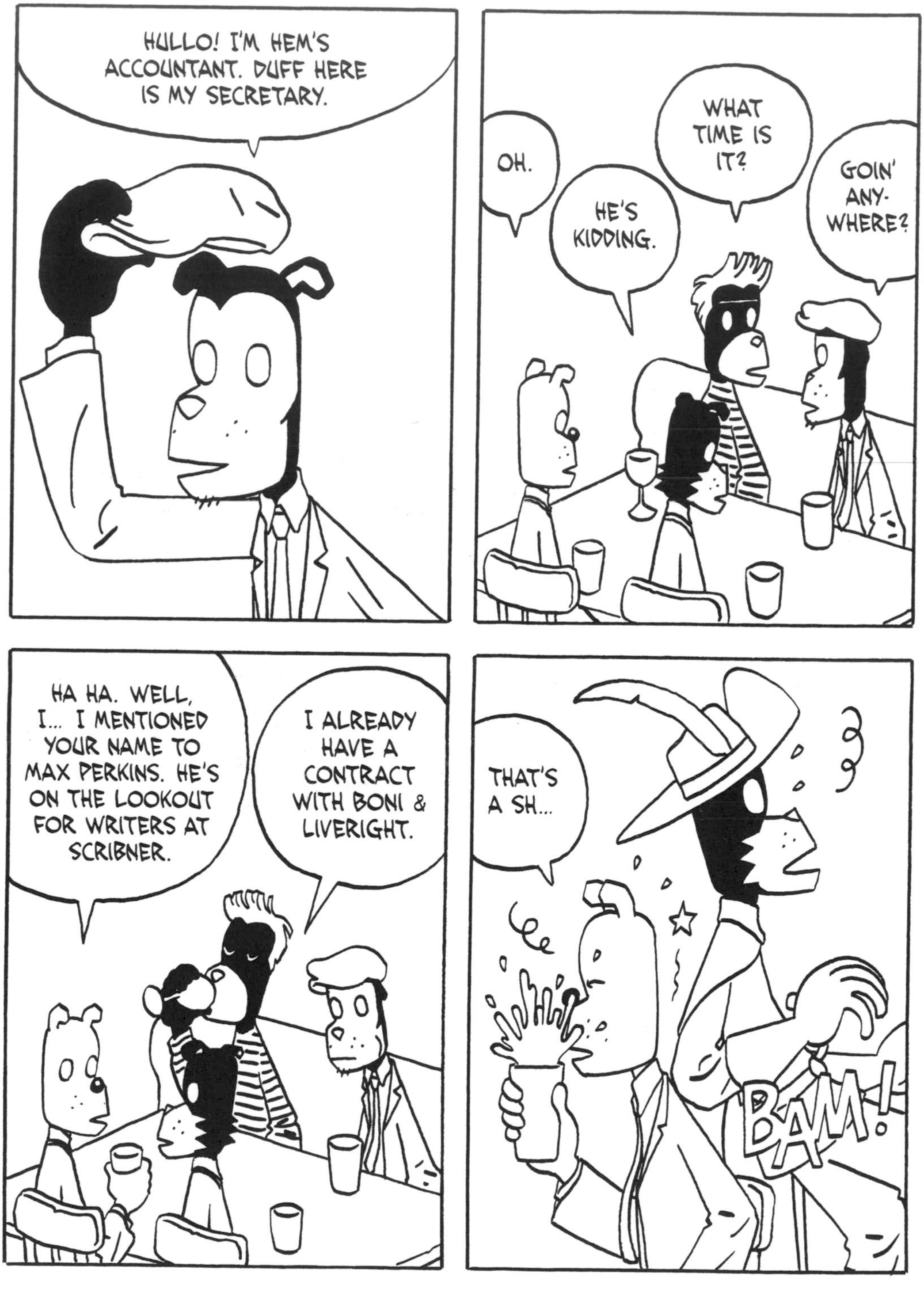
HULLO! I'M HEM'S ACCOUNTANT. DUFF HERE IS MY SECRETARY.
OH.
HE'S KIDDING.
WHAT TIME IS IT?
GOIN' ANY-WHERE?
HA HA. WELL, I... I MENTIONED YOUR NAME TO MAX PERKINS. HE'S ON THE LOOKOUT FOR WRITERS AT SCRIBNER.
I ALREADY HAVE A CONTRACT WITH BONI & LIVERIGHT.
THAT'S A SH...
BAM!

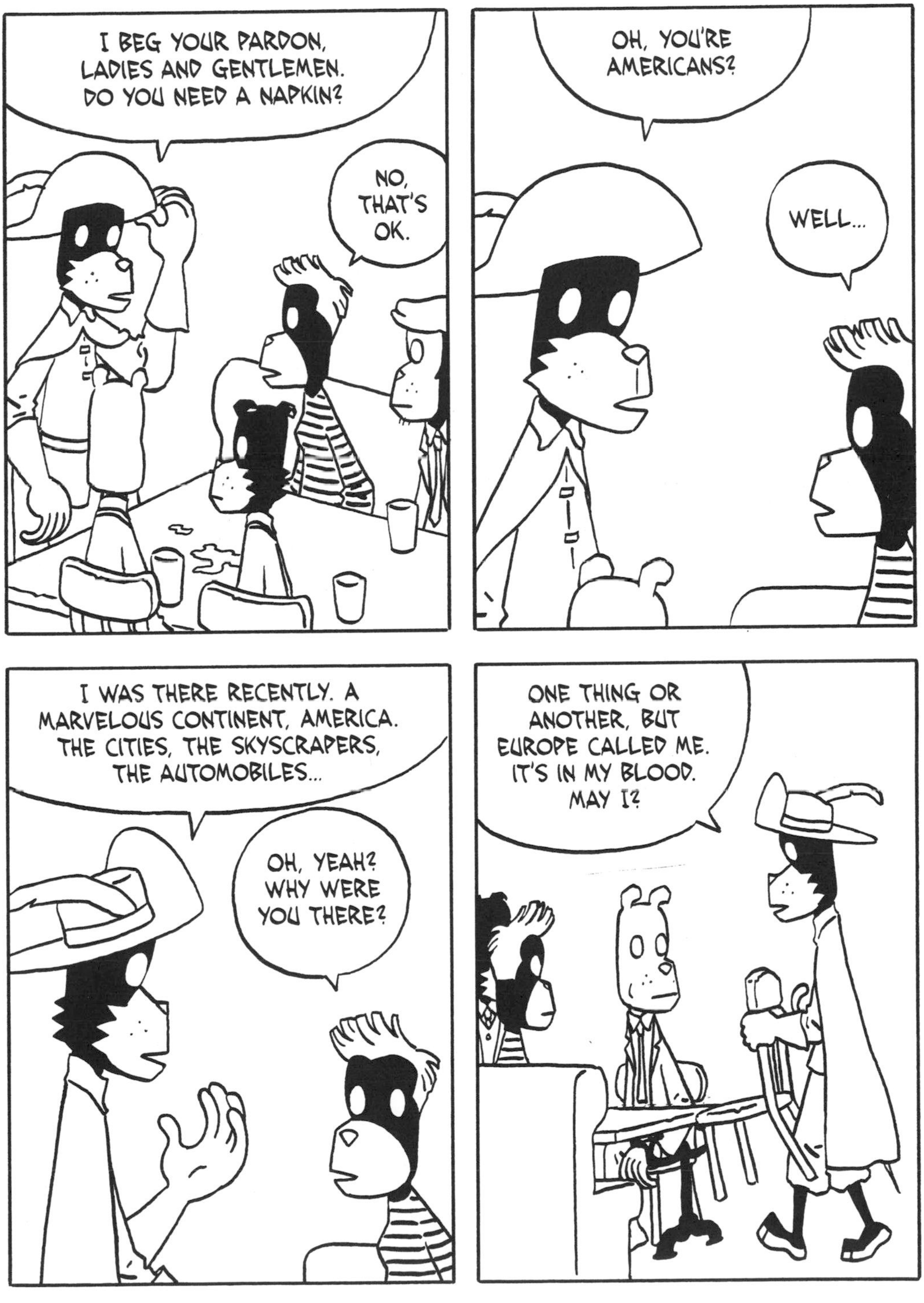
I BEG YOUR PARDON, LADIES AND GENTLEMEN. DO YOU NEED A NAPKIN?
NO, THAT'S OK.
OH, YOU'RE AMERICANS?
WELL...
I WAS THERE RECENTLY. A MARVELOUS CONTINENT, AMERICA. THE CITIES, THE SKYSCRAPERS, THE AUTOMOBILES...
OH, YEAH? WHY WERE YOU THERE?
ONE THING OR ANOTHER, BUT EUROPE CALLED ME. IT'S IN MY BLOOD. MAY I?

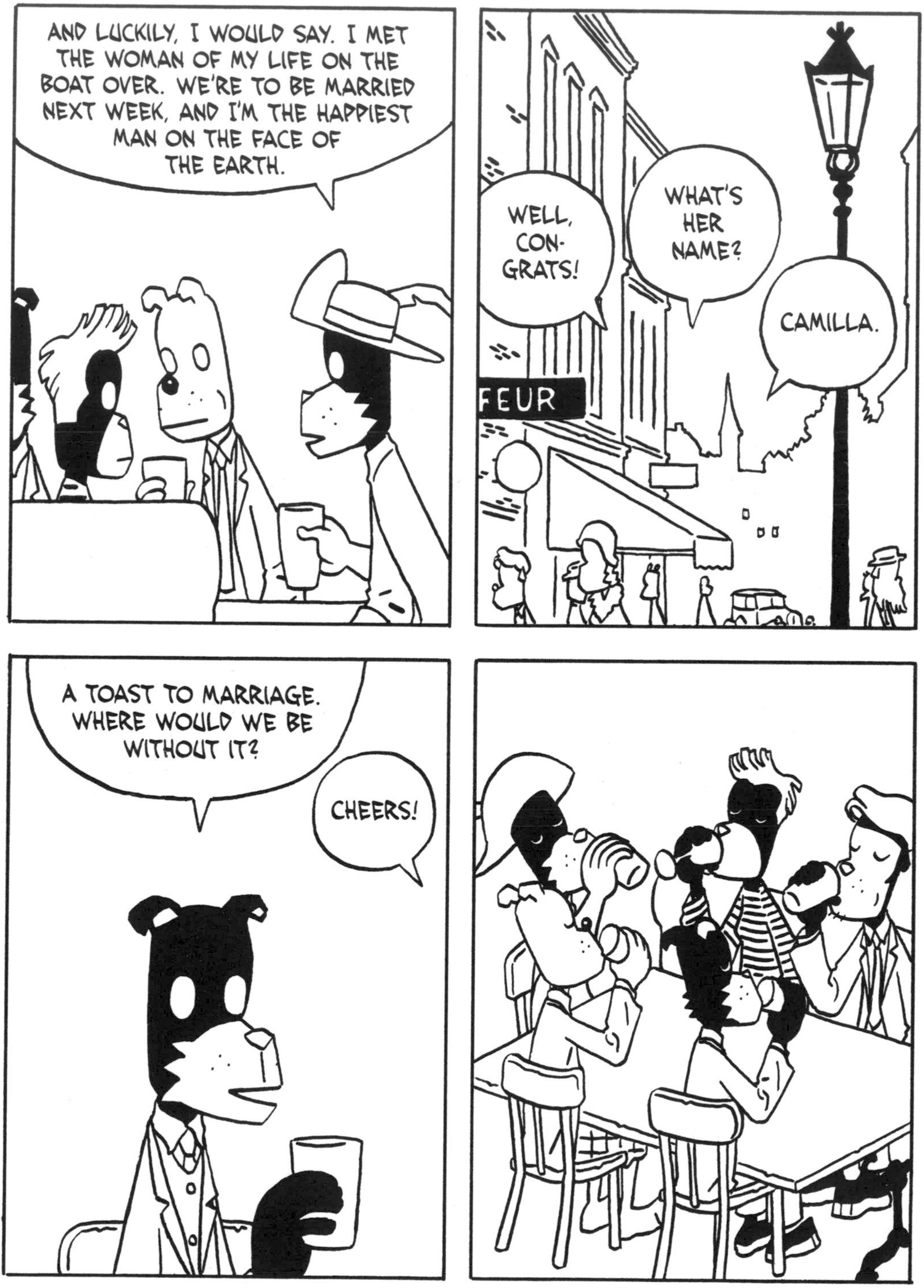
AND LUCKILY, I WOULD SAY. I MET THE WOMAN OF MY LIFE ON THE BOAT OVER. WE'RE TO BE MARRIED NEXT WEEK, AND I'M THE HAPPIEST MAN ON THE FACE OF THE EARTH.
WELL, CON-GRATS!
WHAT'S HER NAME?
CAMILLA.
FEUR
A TOAST TO MARRIAGE. WHERE WOULD WE BE WITHOUT IT?
CHEERS!

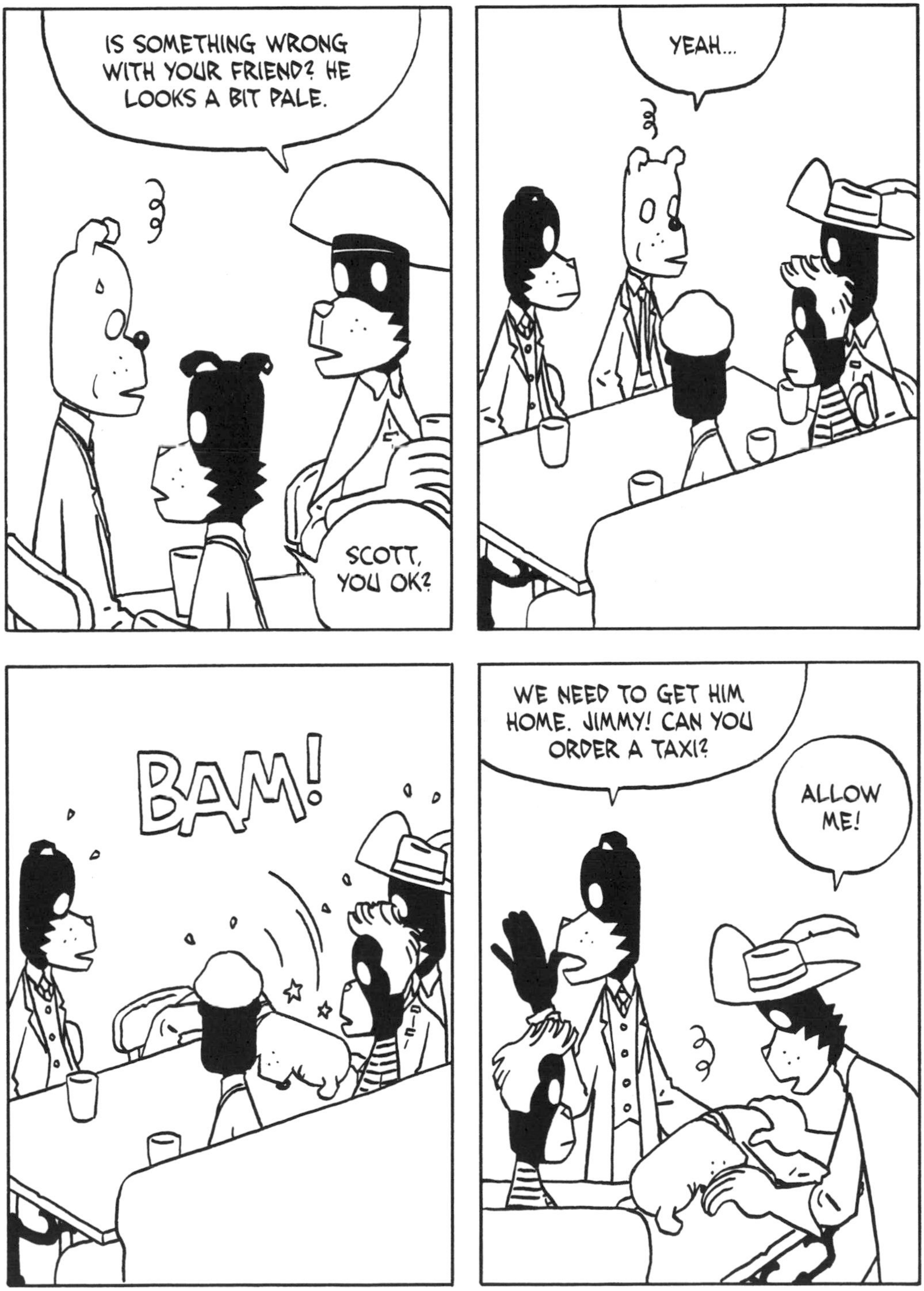
IS SOMETHING WRONG WITH YOUR FRIEND? HE LOOKS A BIT PALE.
SCOTT, YOU OK?
YEAH...
BAM!
WE NEED TO GET HIM HOME. JIMMY! CAN YOU ORDER A TAXI?
ALLOW ME!

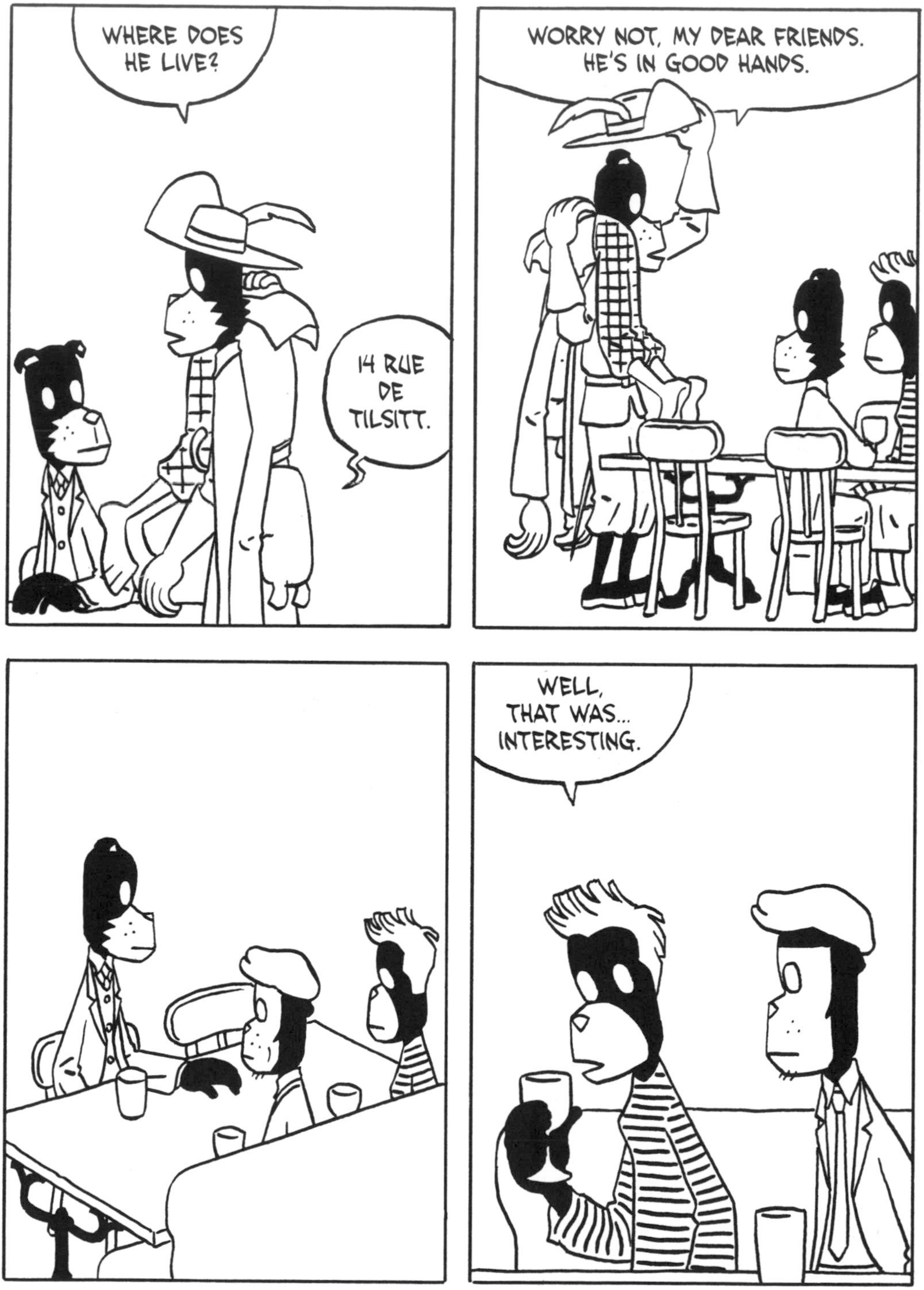
WHERE DOES HE LIVE?
14 RUE DE TILSITT.
WORRY NOT, MY DEAR FRIENDS. HE'S IN GOOD HANDS.
WELL, THAT WAS... INTERESTING.

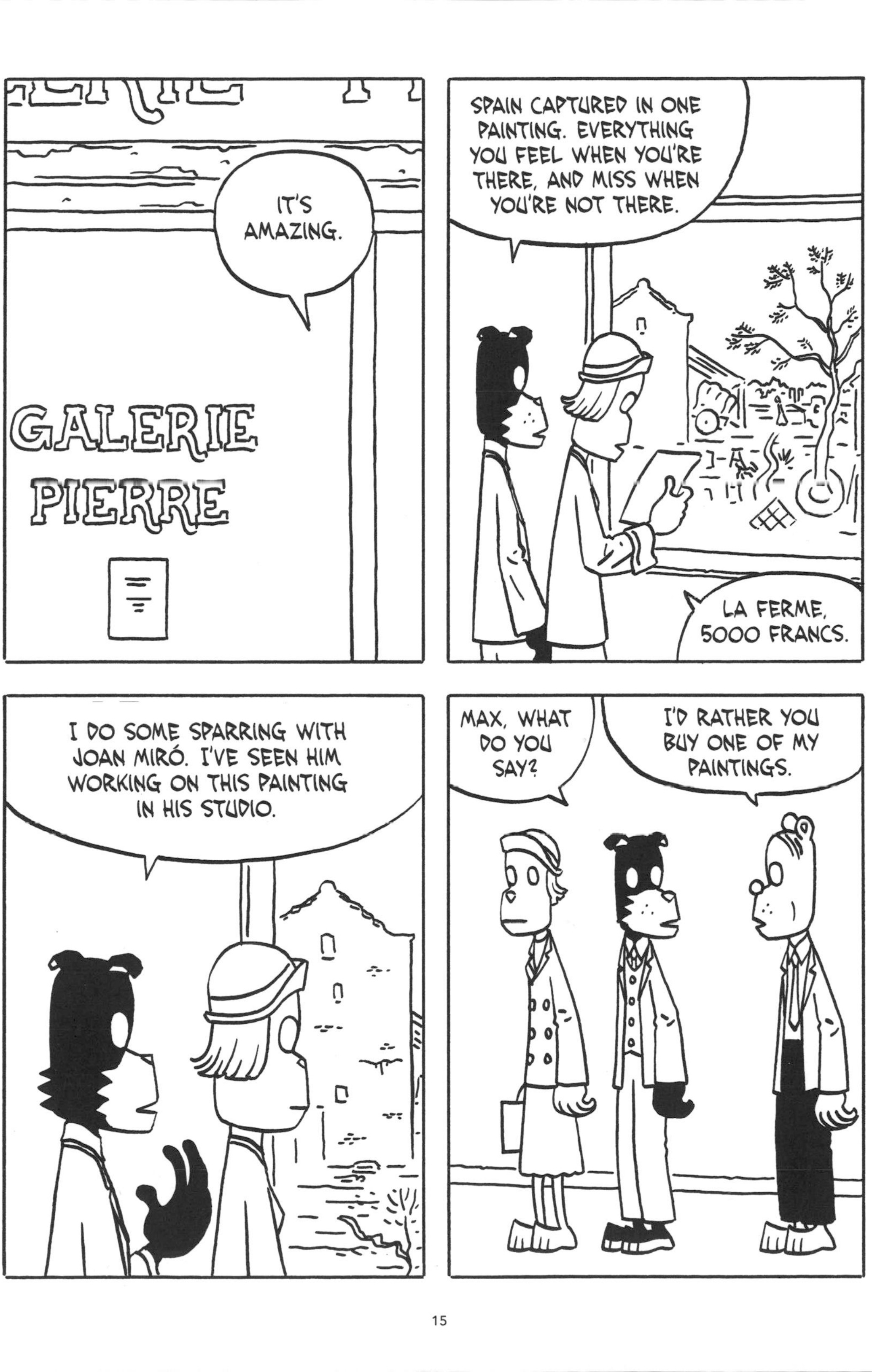
IT'S AMAZING.
GALERIE PIERRE
SPAIN CAPTURED IN ONE PAINTING. EVERYTHING YOU FEEL WHEN YOU'RE THERE, AND MISS WHEN YOU'RE NOT THERE.
LA FERME, 5000 FRANCS.
I DO SOME SPARRING WITH JOAN MIRÓ. I'VE SEEN HIM WORKING ON THIS PAINTING IN HIS STUDIO.
MAX, WHAT DO YOU SAY?
I'D RATHER YOU BUY ONE OF MY PAINTINGS.

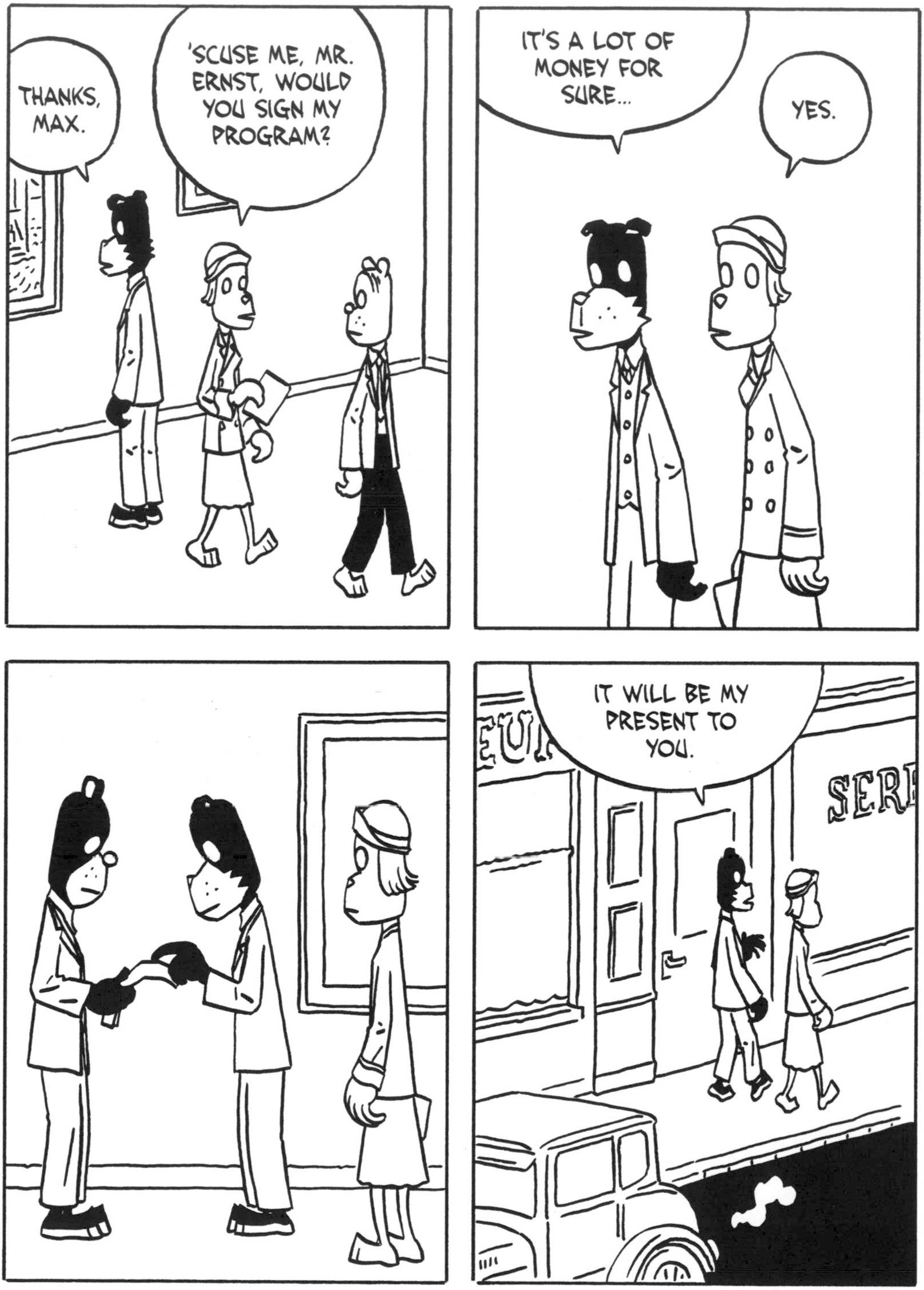
THANKS, MAX.
'SCUSE ME, MR. ERNST, WOULD YOU SIGN MY PROGRAM?
IT'S A LOT OF MONEY FOR SURE...
YES.
IT WILL BE MY PRESENT TO YOU.

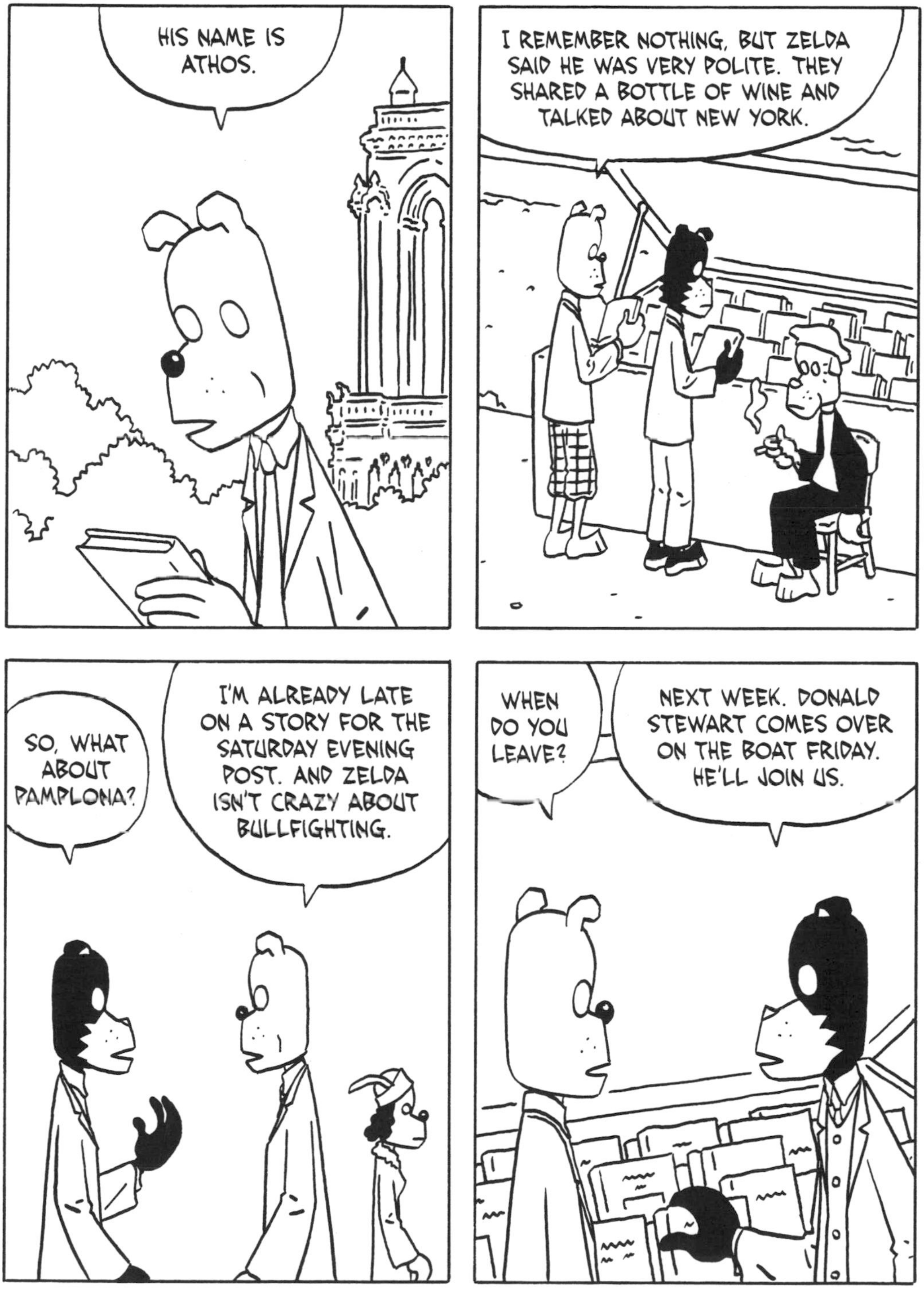
HIS NAME IS ATHOS.
I REMEMBER NOTHING, BUT ZELDA SAID HE WAS VERY POLITE. THEY SHARED A BOTTLE OF WINE AND TALKED ABOUT NEW YORK.
SO, WHAT ABOUT PAMPLONA?
I'M ALREADY LATE ON A STORY FOR THE SATURDAY EVENING POST. AND ZELDA ISN'T CRAZY ABOUT BULLFIGHTING.
WHEN DO YOU LEAVE?
NEXT WEEK. DONALD STEWART COMES OVER ON THE BOAT FRIDAY. HE'LL JOIN US.

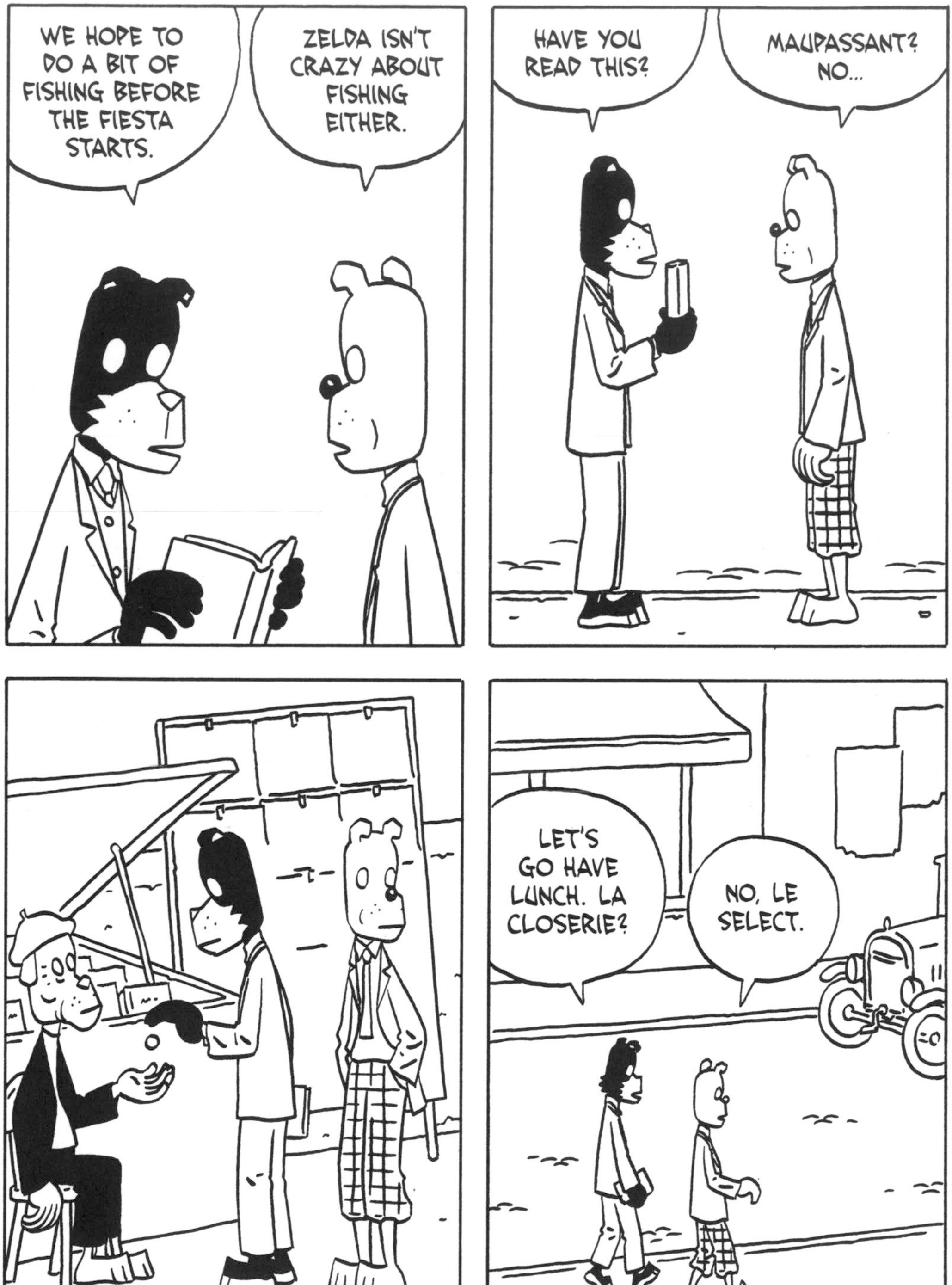
WE HOPE TO DO A BIT OF FISHING BEFORE THE FIESTA STARTS.
ZELDA ISN'T CRAZY ABOUT FISHING EITHER.
HAVE YOU READ THIS?
MAUPASSANT? NO...
LET'S GO HAVE LUNCH. LA CLOSERIE?
NO, LE SELECT.

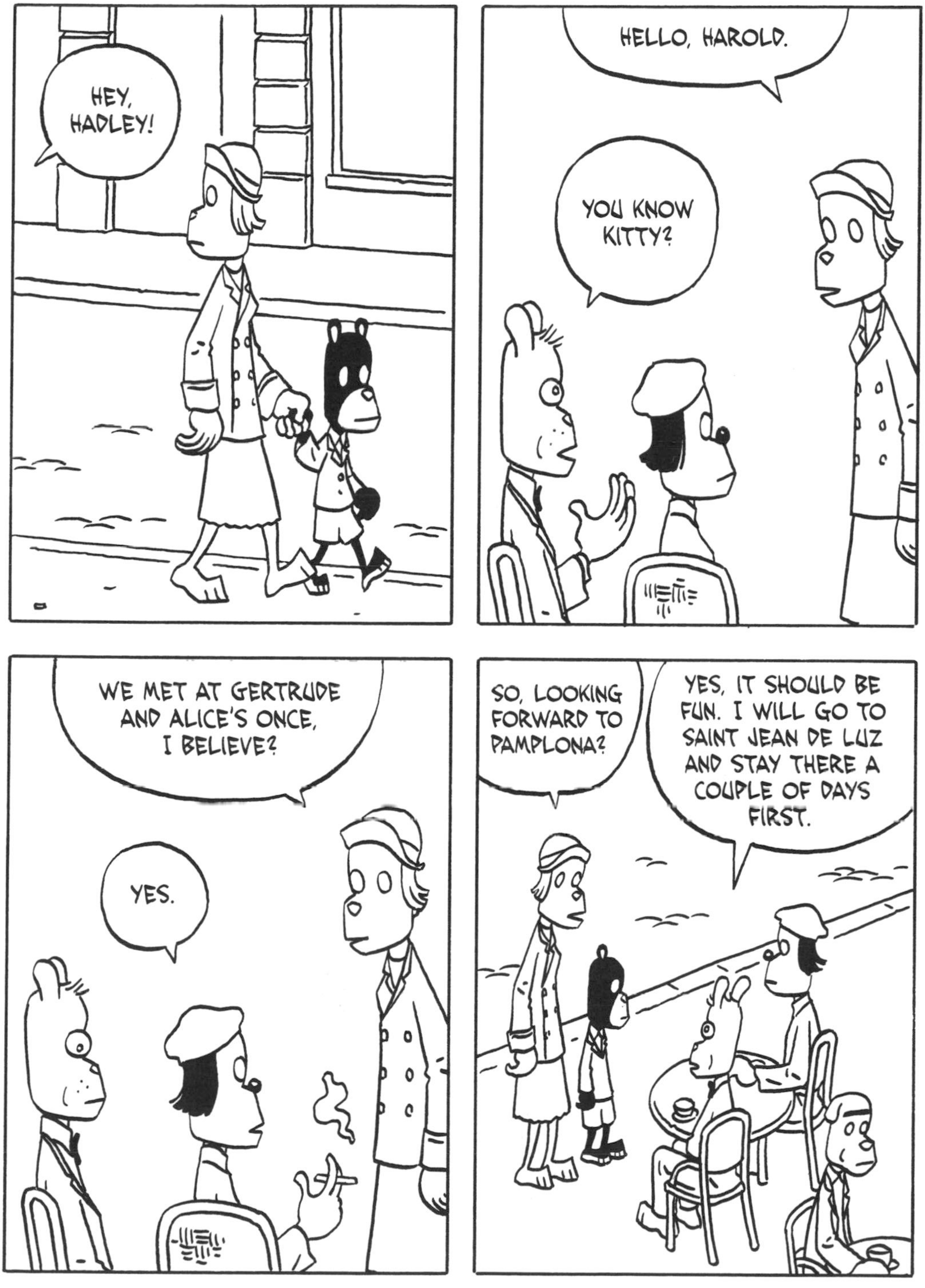
HEY, HADLEY!
HELLO, HAROLD.
YOU KNOW KITTY?
WE MET AT GERTRUDE AND ALICE'S ONCE, I BELIEVE?
YES.
SO, LOOKING FORWARD TO PAMPLONA?
YES, IT SHOULD BE FUN. I WILL GO TO SAINT JEAN DE LUZ AND STAY THERE A COUPLE OF DAYS FIRST.

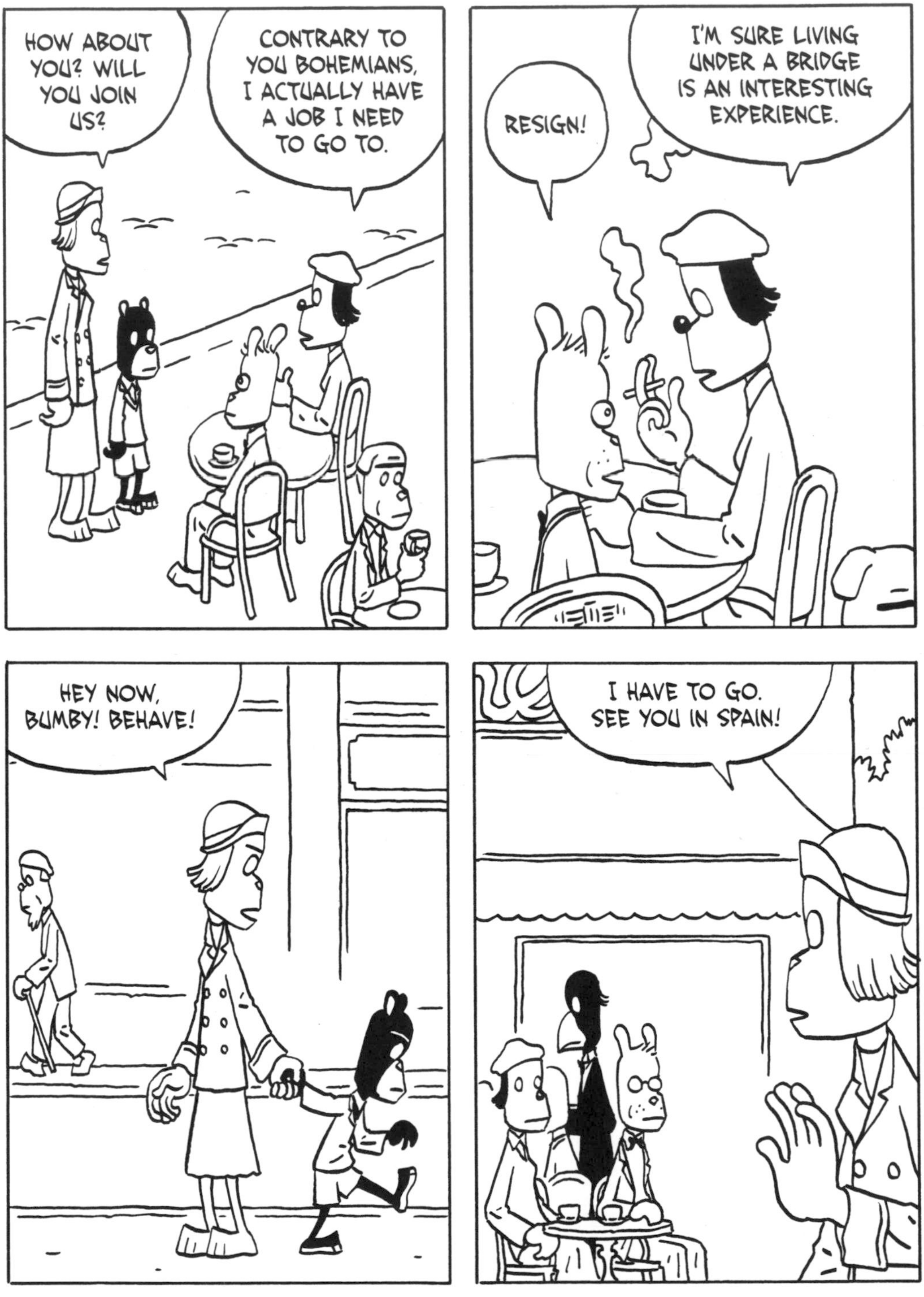

HOW ABOUT YOU? WILL YOU JOIN US?
CONTRARY TO YOU BOHEMIANS, I ACTUALLY HAVE A JOB I NEED TO GO TO.
RESIGN!
I'M SURE LIVING UNDER A BRIDGE IS AN INTERESTING EXPERIENCE.
HEY NOW, BUMBY! BEHAVE!
I HAVE TO GO. SEE YOU IN SPAIN!

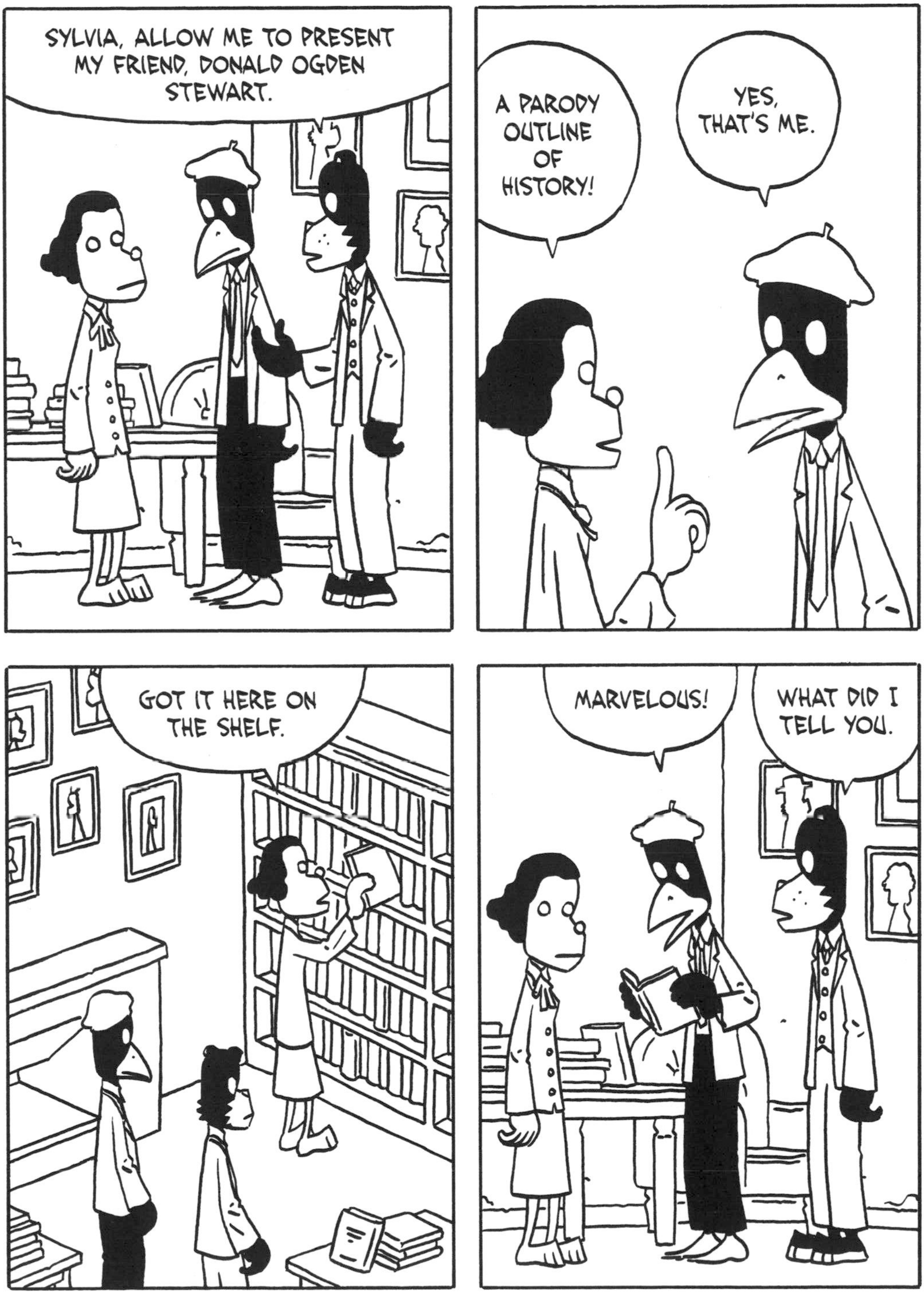
SYLVIA, ALLOW ME TO PRESENT MY FRIEND, DONALD OGDEN STEWART.
A PARODY OUTLINE OF HISTORY!
YES, THAT'S ME.
GOT IT HERE ON THE SHELF.
MARVELOUS!
WHAT DID I TELL YOU.

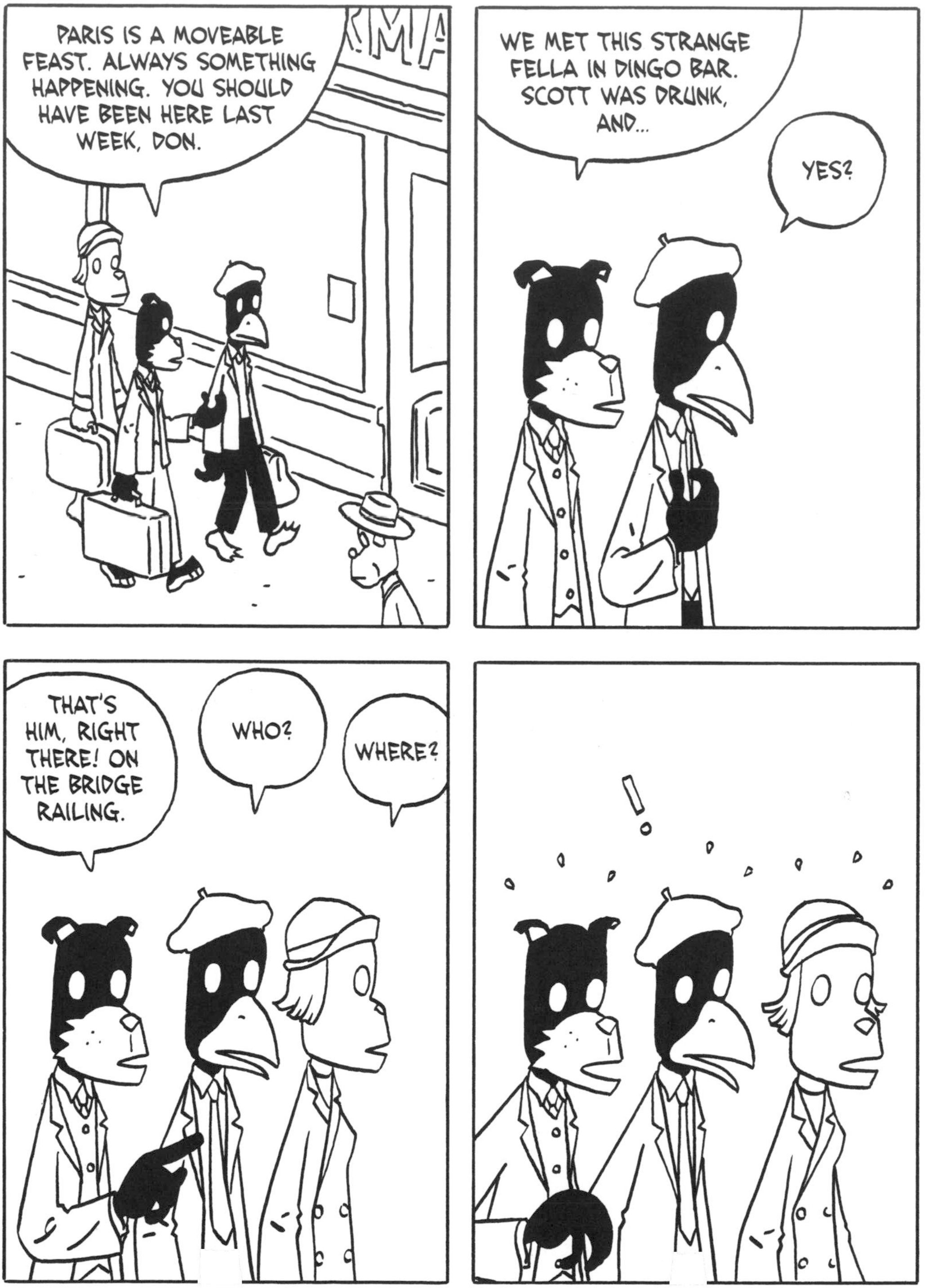
PARIS IS A MOVEABLE FEAST. ALWAYS SOMETHING HAPPENING. YOU SHOULD HAVE BEEN HERE LAST WEEK, DON.
WE MET THIS STRANGE FELLA IN DINGO BAR. SCOTT WAS DRUNK, AND...
YES?
THAT'S HIM, RIGHT THERE! ON THE BRIDGE RAILING.
WHO?
WHERE?
!

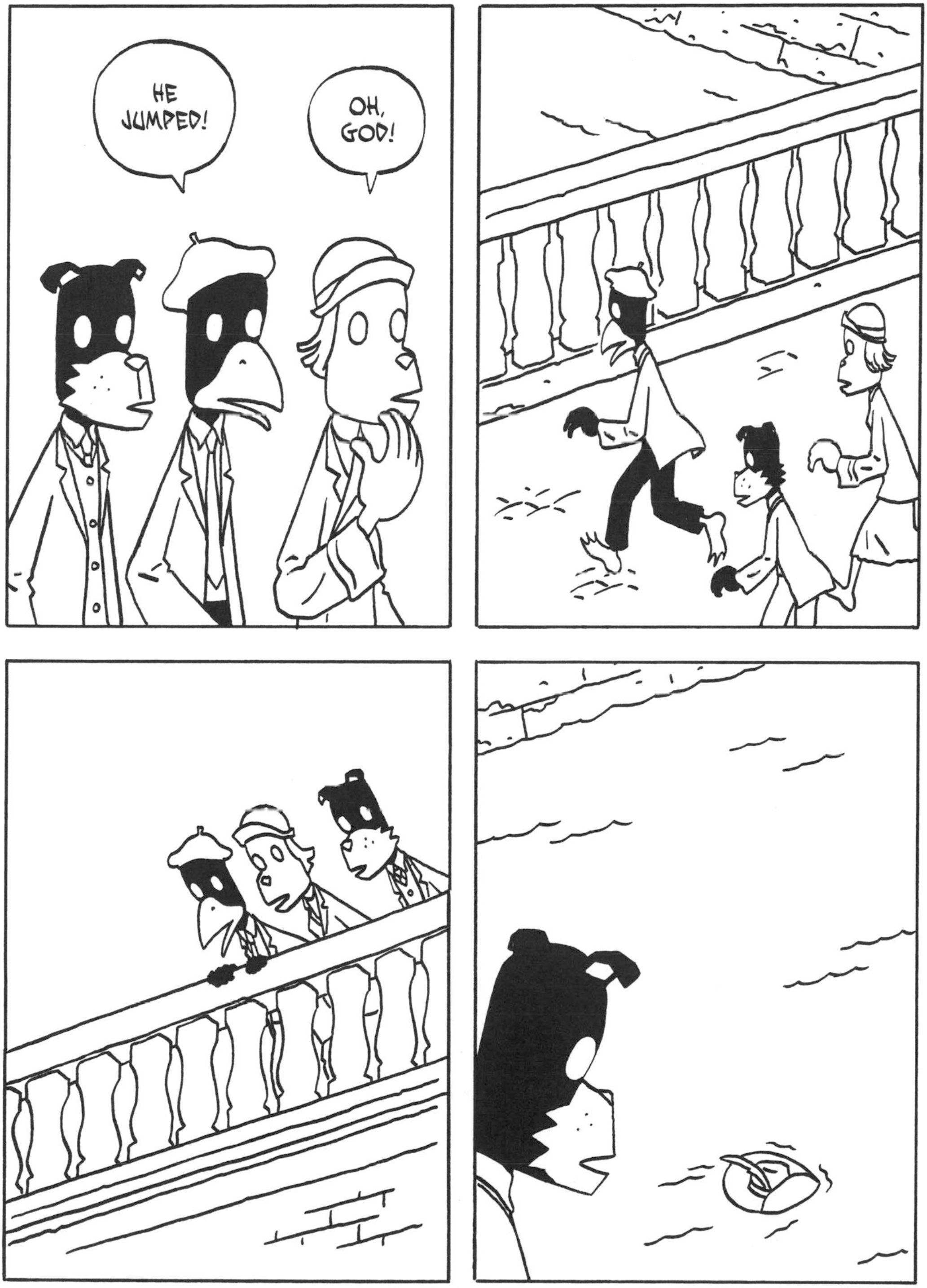
HE JUMPED!
OH, GOD!

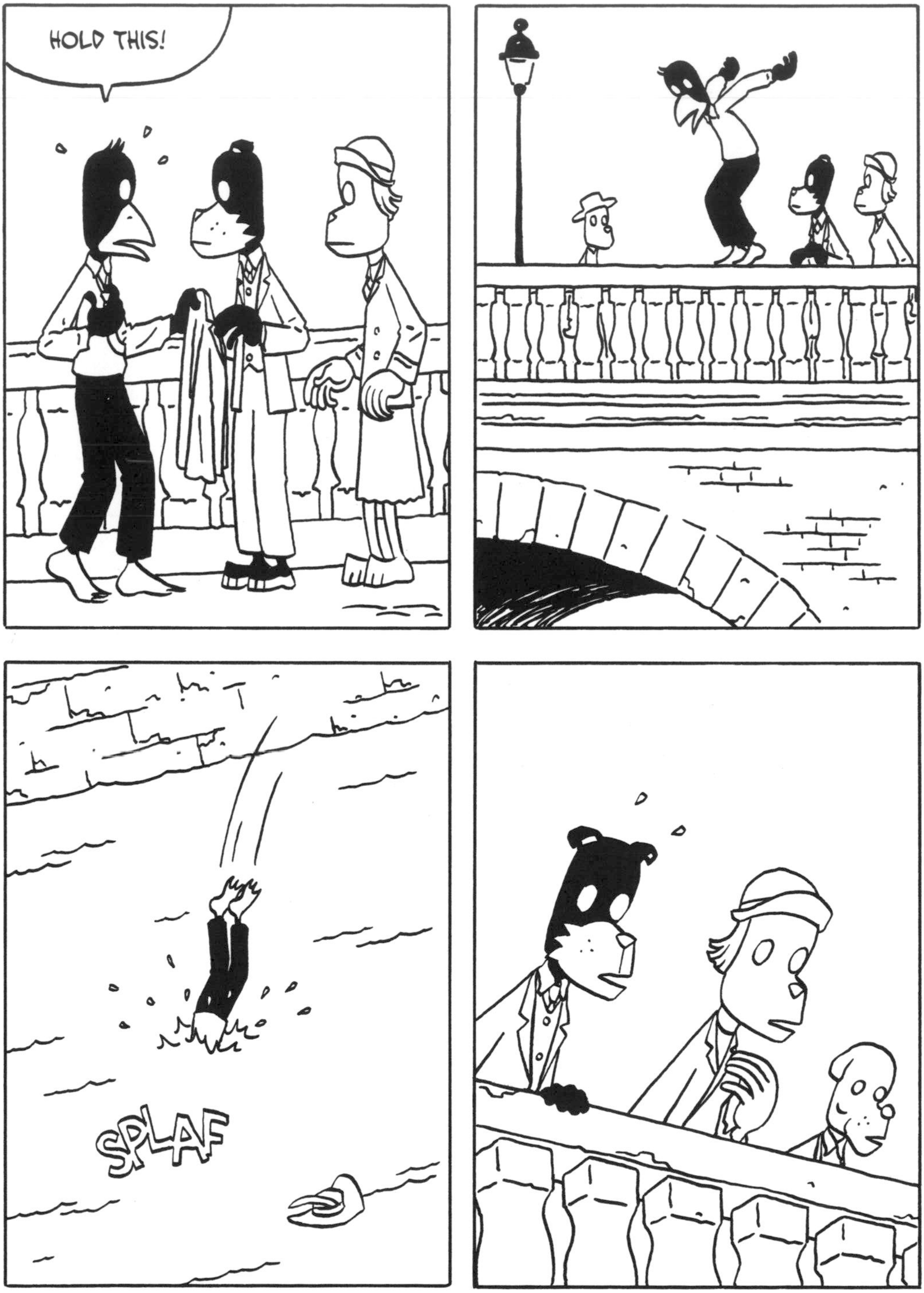
HOLD THIS!
SPLAF

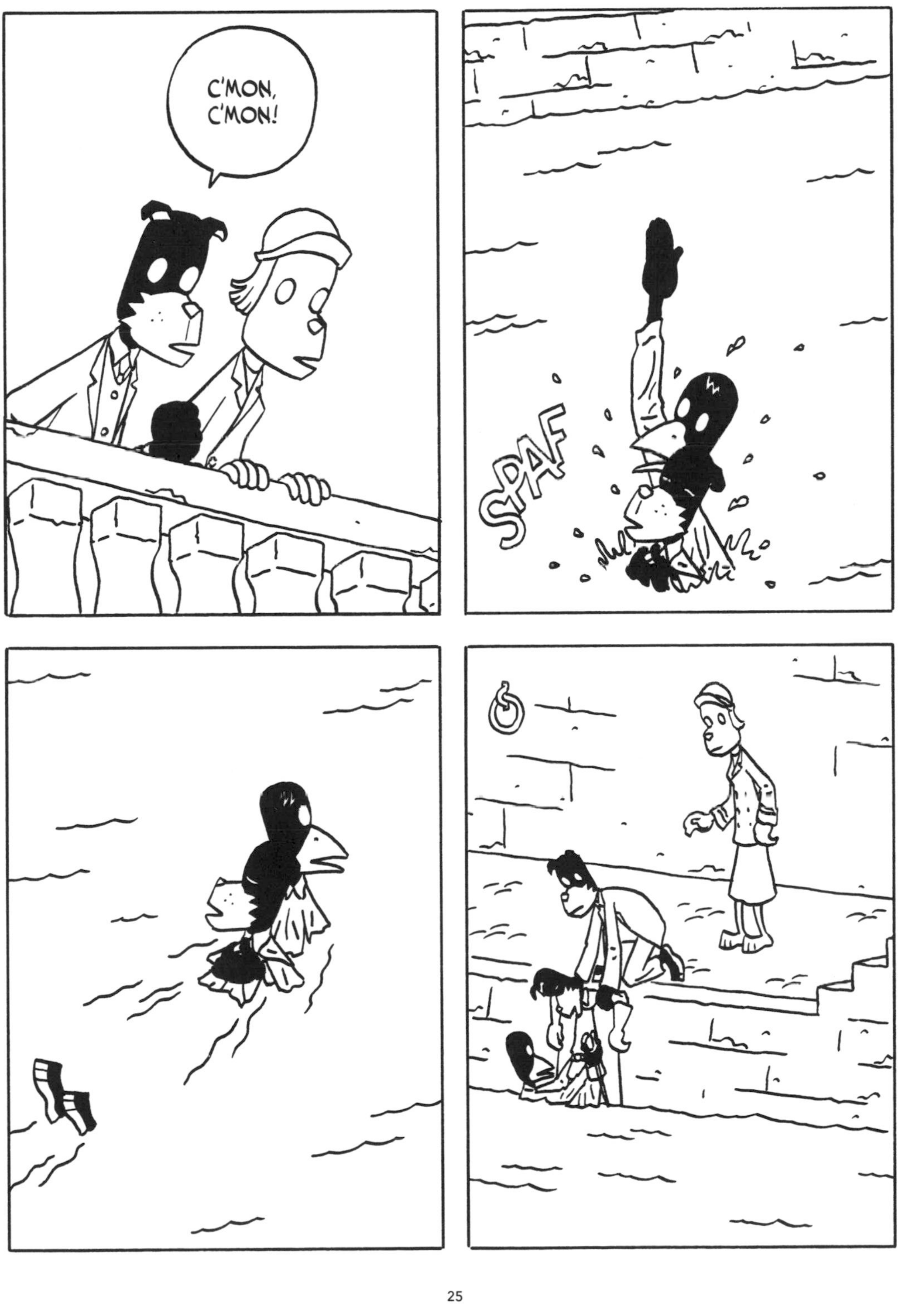
C'MON, C'MON!
SPAF

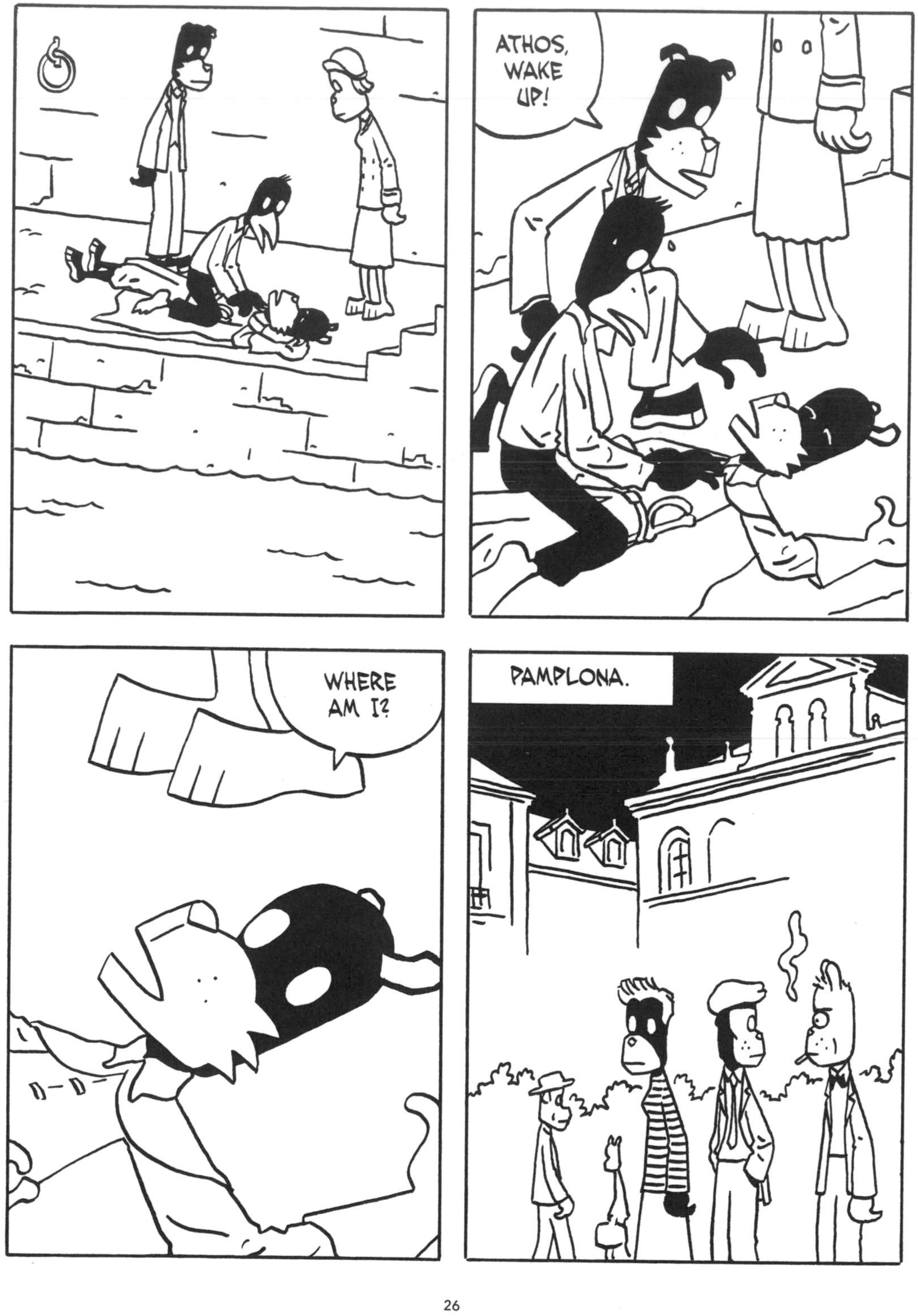
ATHOS, WAKE UP!
WHERE AM I?
PAMPLONA.

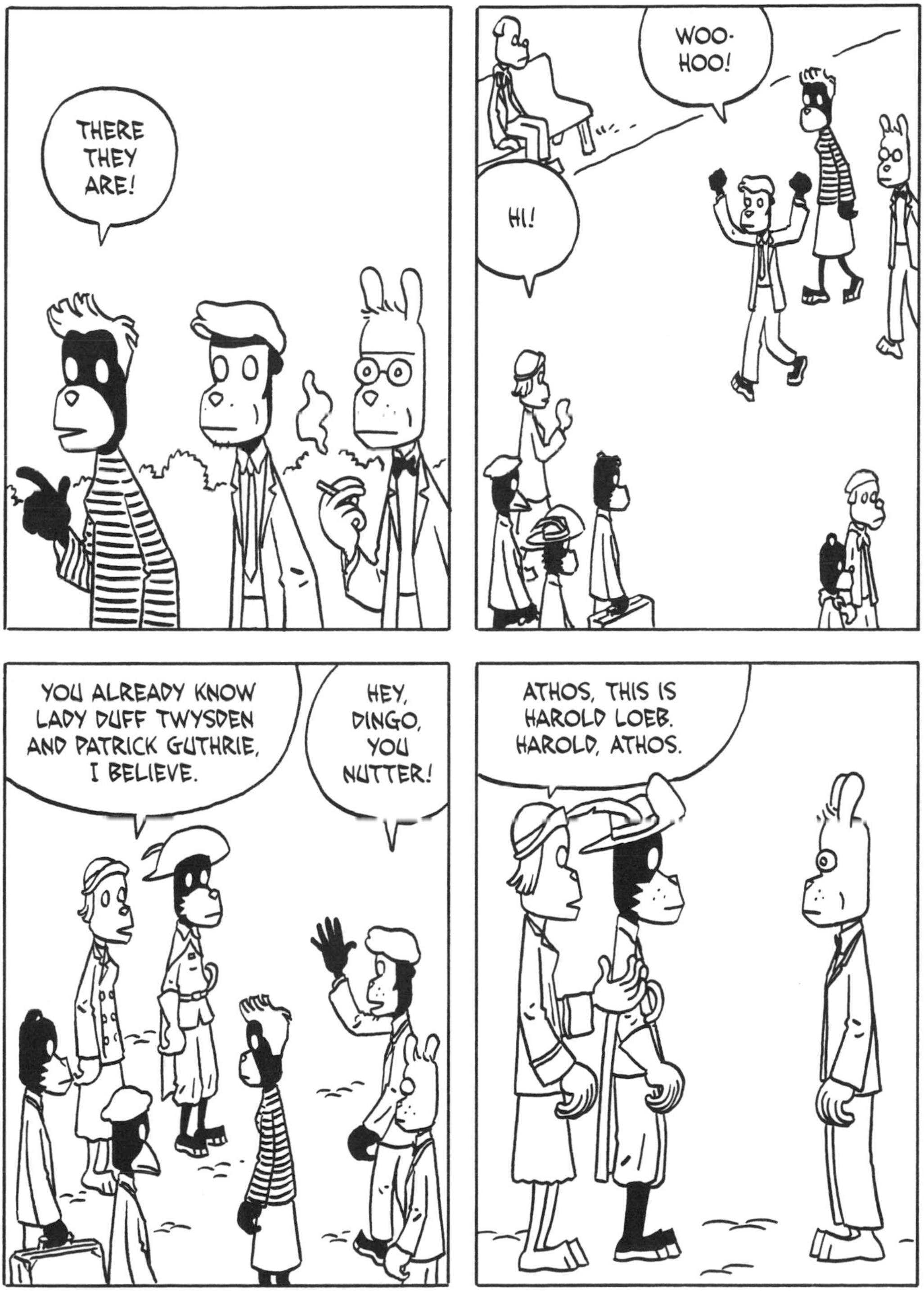
THERE THEY ARE!
WOO-HOO!
HI!
YOU ALREADY KNOW LADY DUFF TWYSDEN AND PATRICK GUTHRIE, I BELIEVE.
HEY, DINGO, YOU NUTTER!
ATHOS, THIS IS HAROLD LOEB. HAROLD, ATHOS.

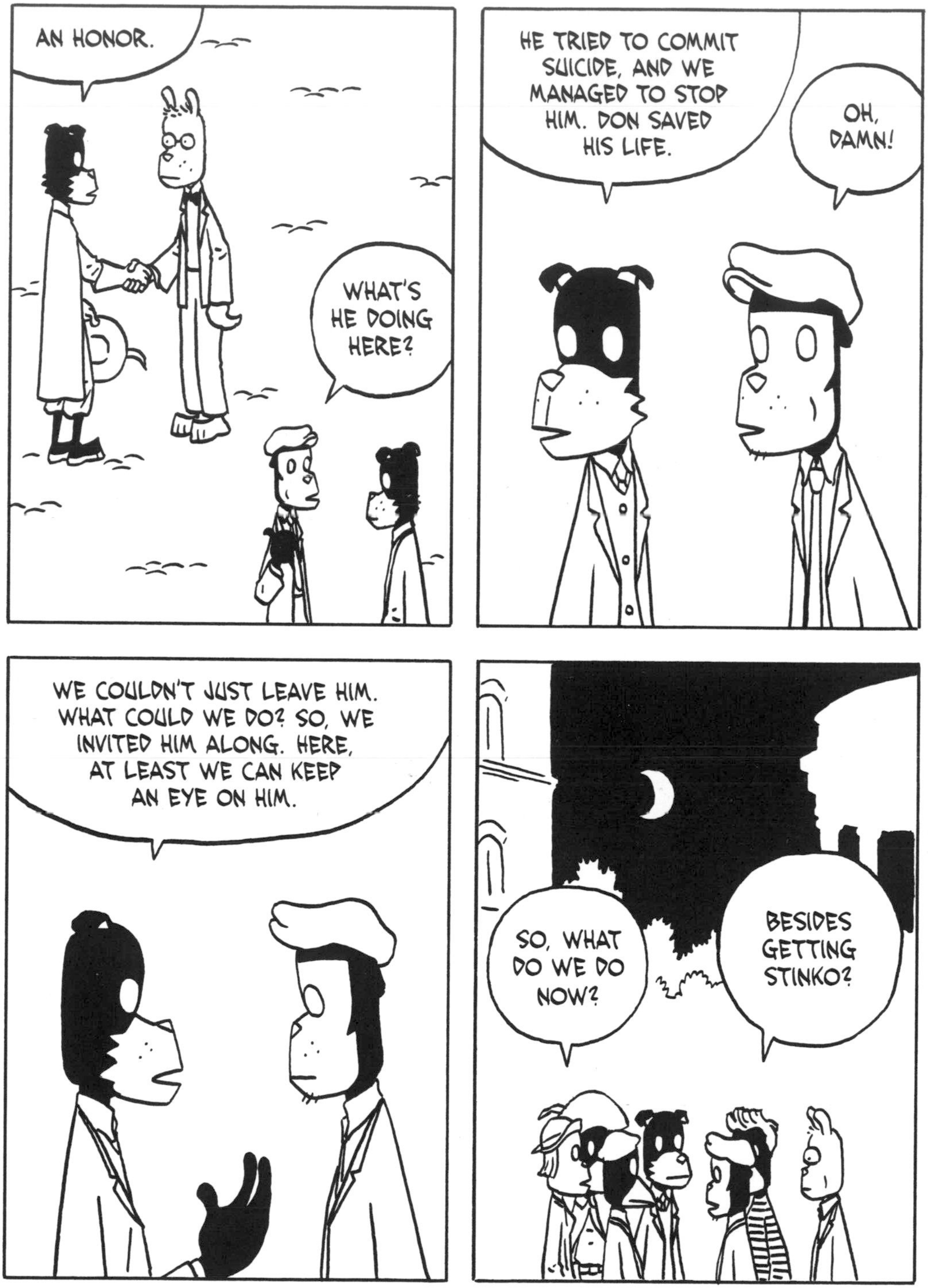
AN HONOR.
WHAT'S HE DOING HERE?
HE TRIED TO COMMIT SUICIDE, AND WE MANAGED TO STOP HIM. DON SAVED HIS LIFE.
OH, DAMN!
WE COULDN'T JUST LEAVE HIM. WHAT COULD WE DO? SO, WE INVITED HIM ALONG. HERE, AT LEAST WE CAN KEEP AN EYE ON HIM.
SO, WHAT DO WE DO NOW?
BESIDES GETTING STINKO?

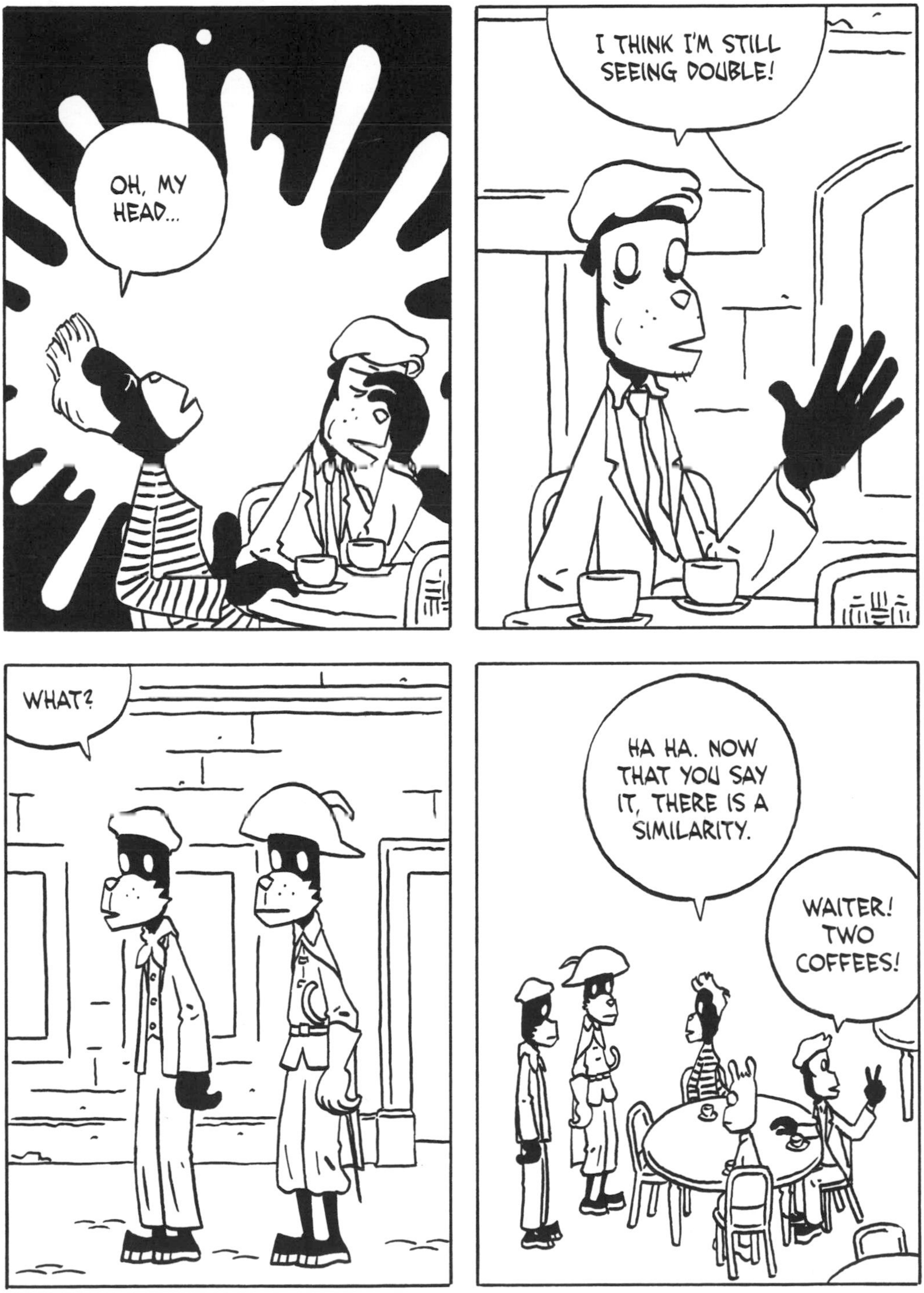
OH, MY HEAD...
I THINK I'M STILL SEEING DOUBLE!
WHAT?
HA HA. NOW THAT YOU SAY IT, THERE IS A SIMILARITY.
WAITER! TWO COFFEES!

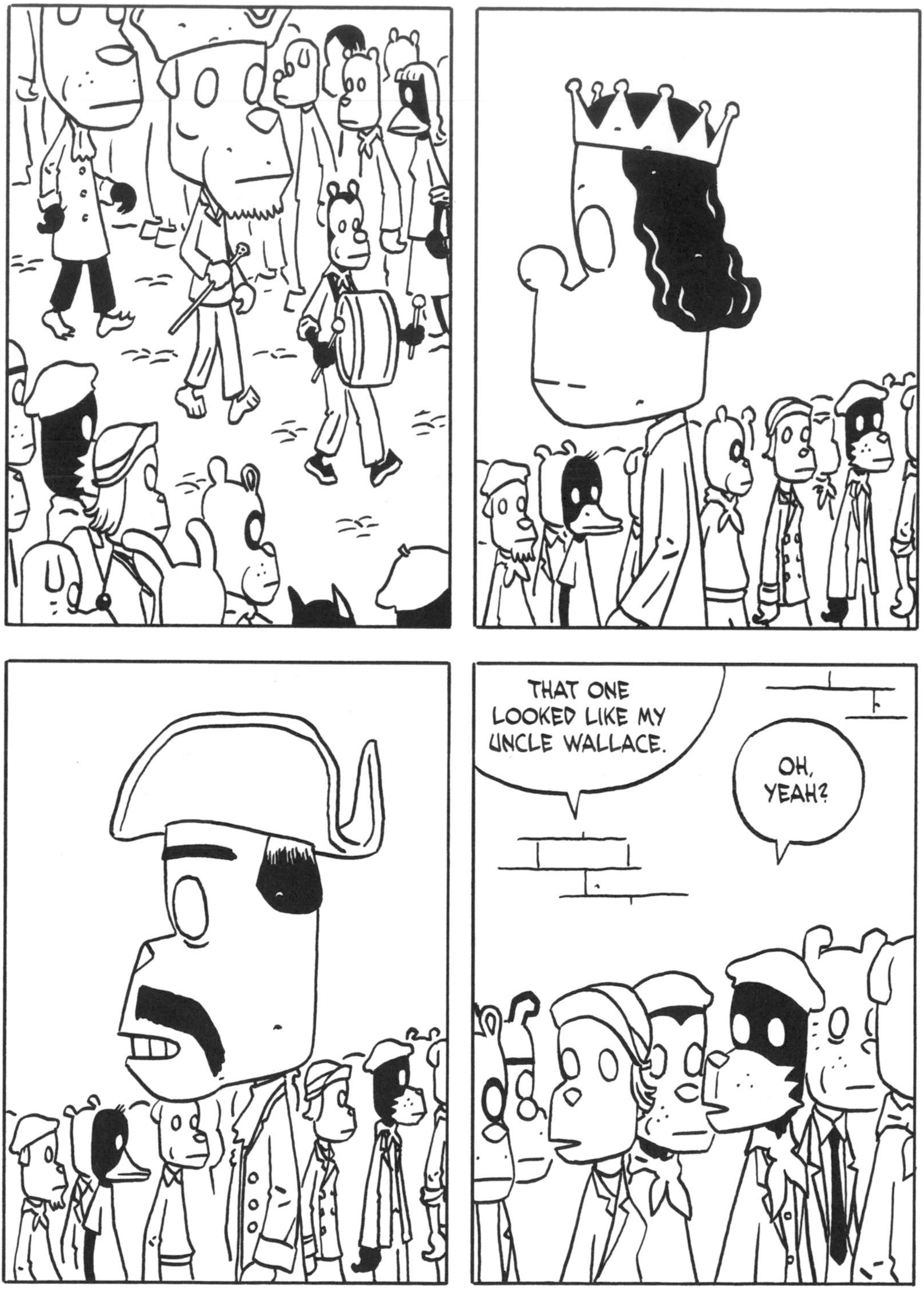
THAT ONE LOOKED LIKE MY UNCLE WALLACE.
OH, YEAH?

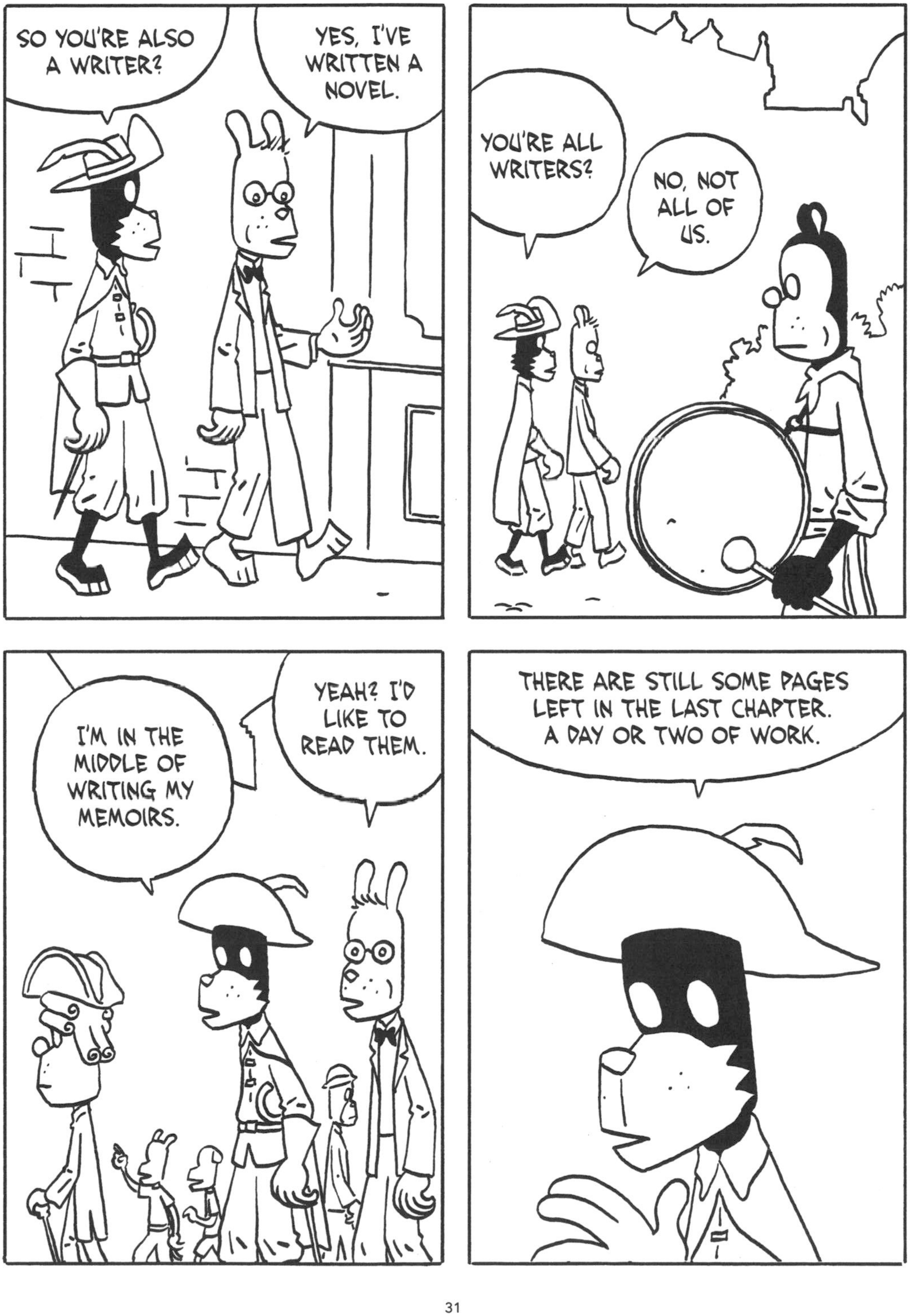
SO YOU'RE ALSO A WRITER?
YES, I'VE WRITTEN A NOVEL.
YOU'RE ALL WRITERS?
NO, NOT ALL OF US.
I'M IN THE MIDDLE OF WRITING MY MEMOIRS.
YEAH? I'D LIKE TO READ THEM.
THERE ARE STILL SOME PAGES LEFT IN THE LAST CHAPTER. A DAY OR TWO OF WORK.

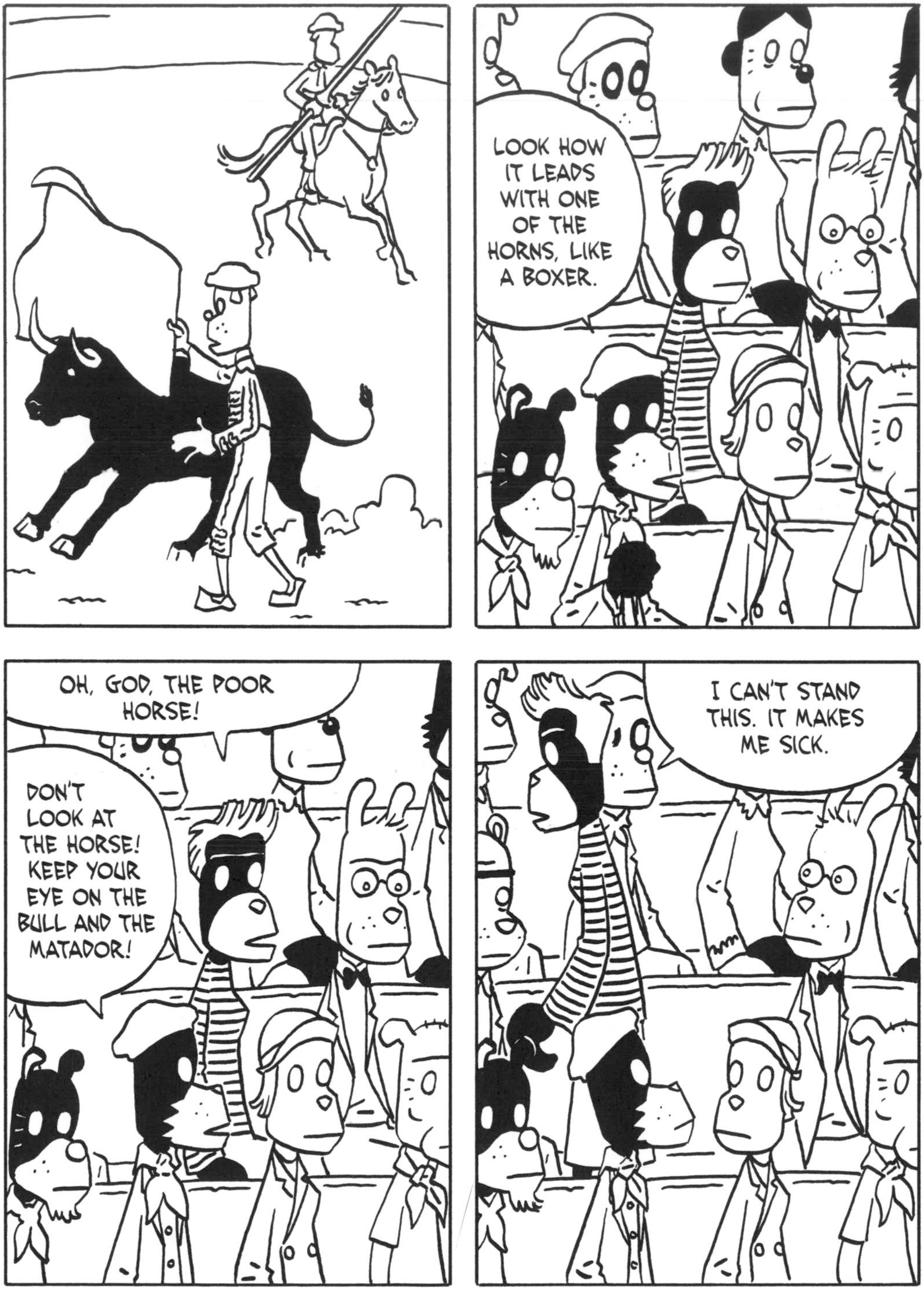
LOOK HOW IT LEADS WITH ONE OF THE HORNS, LIKE A BOXER.
OH, GOD, THE POOR HORSE!
DON'T LOOK AT THE HORSE! KEEP YOUR EYE ON THE BULL AND THE MATADOR!
I CAN'T STAND THIS. IT MAKES ME SICK.

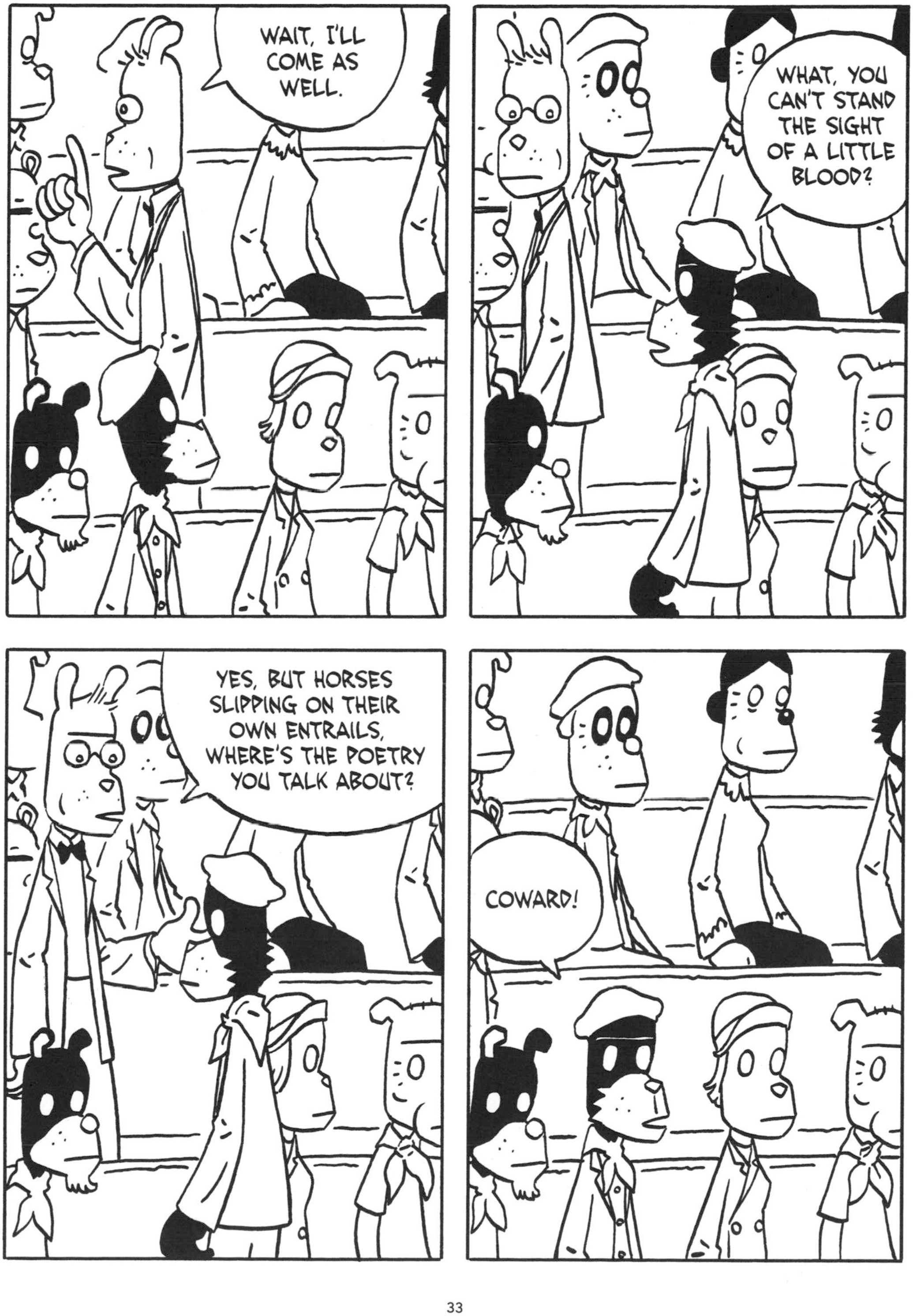
WAIT, I'LL COME AS WELL.
WHAT, YOU CAN'T STAND THE SIGHT OF A LITTLE BLOOD?
YES, BUT HORSES SLIPPING ON THEIR OWN ENTRAILS, WHERE'S THE POETRY YOU TALK ABOUT?
COWARD!

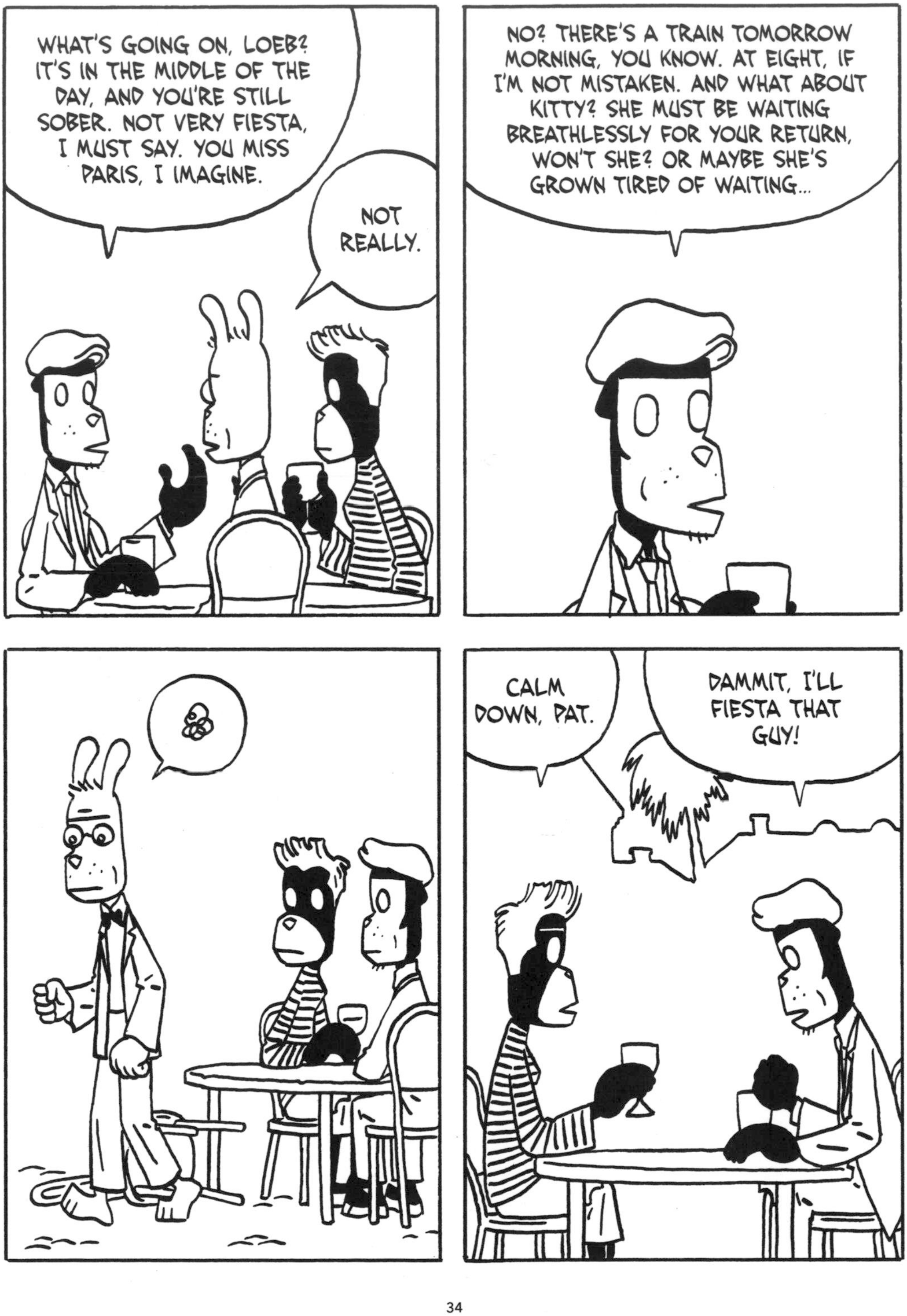
WHAT'S GOING ON, LOEB? IT'S IN THE MIDDLE OF THE DAY, AND YOU'RE STILL SOBER. NOT VERY FIESTA, I MUST SAY. YOU MISS PARIS, I IMAGINE.
NOT REALLY.
NO? THERE'S A TRAIN TOMORROW MORNING, YOU KNOW. AT EIGHT, IF I'M NOT MISTAKEN. AND WHAT ABOUT KITTY? SHE MUST BE WAITING BREATHLESSLY FOR YOUR RETURN, WON'T SHE? OR MAYBE SHE'S GROWN TIRED OF WAITING...
CALM DOWN, PAT.
DAMMIT, I'LL FIESTA THAT GUY!

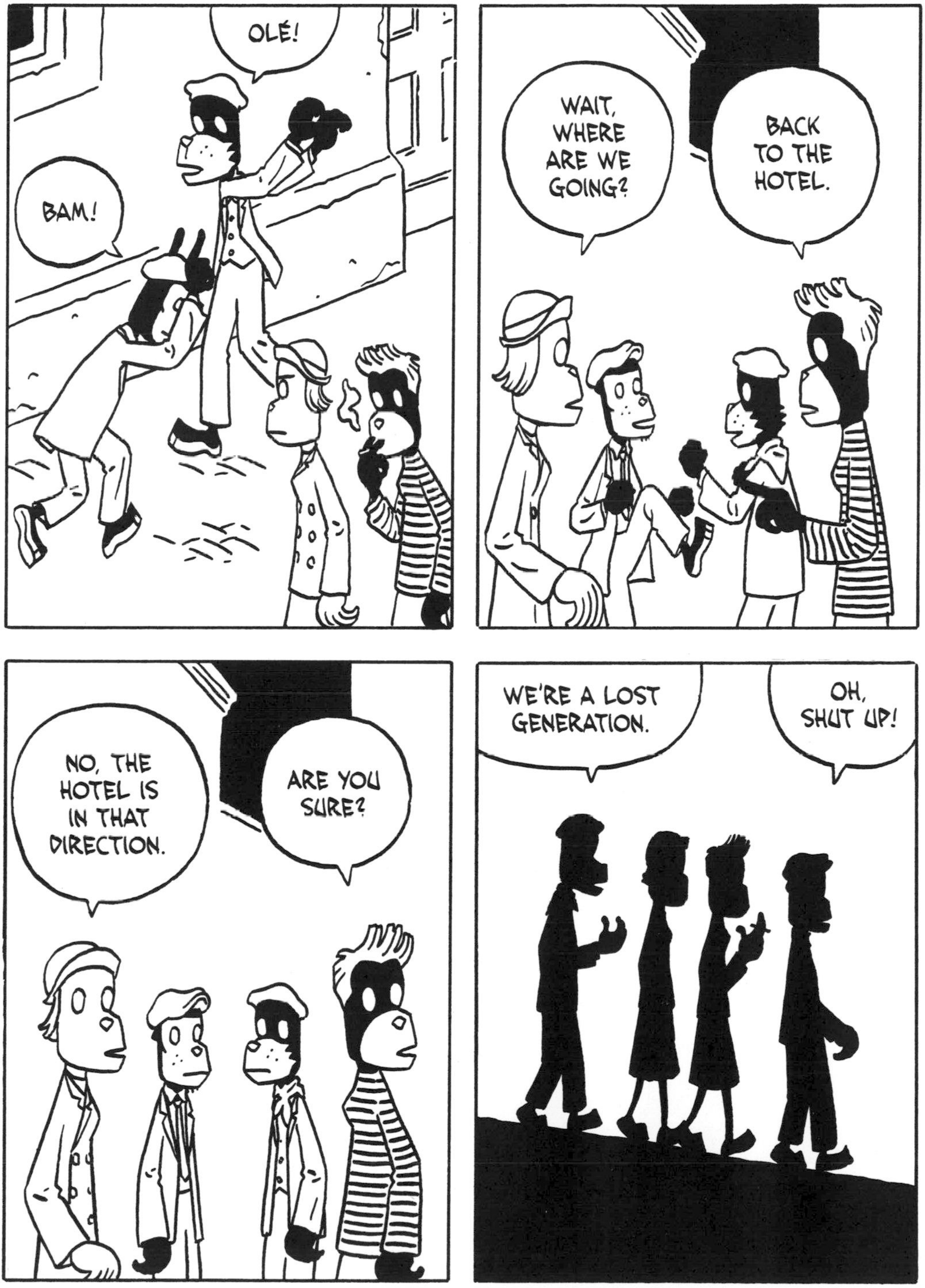
OLÉ!
BAM!
WAIT, WHERE ARE WE GOING?
BACK TO THE HOTEL.
NO, THE HOTEL IS IN THAT DIRECTION.
ARE YOU SURE?
WE'RE A LOST GENERATION.
OH, SHUT UP!

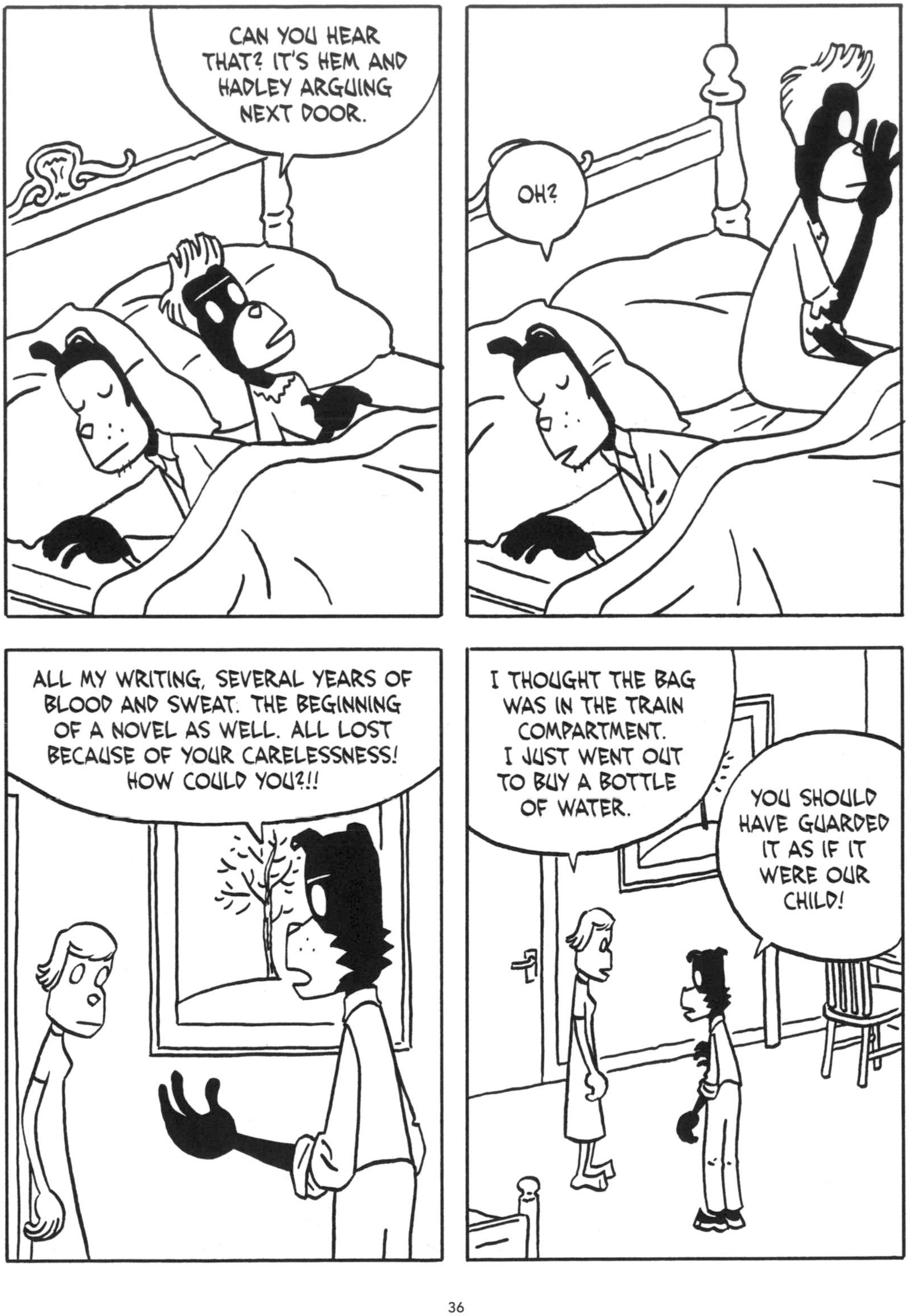
CAN YOU HEAR THAT? IT'S HEM AND HADLEY ARGUING NEXT DOOR.
OH?
ALL MY WRITING, SEVERAL YEARS OF BLOOD AND SWEAT. THE BEGINNING OF A NOVEL AS WELL. ALL LOST BECAUSE OF YOUR CARELESSNESS! HOW COULD YOU?!!
I THOUGHT THE BAG WAS IN THE TRAIN COMPARTMENT. I JUST WENT OUT TO BUY A BOTTLE OF WATER.
YOU SHOULD HAVE GUARDED IT AS IF IT WERE OUR CHILD!

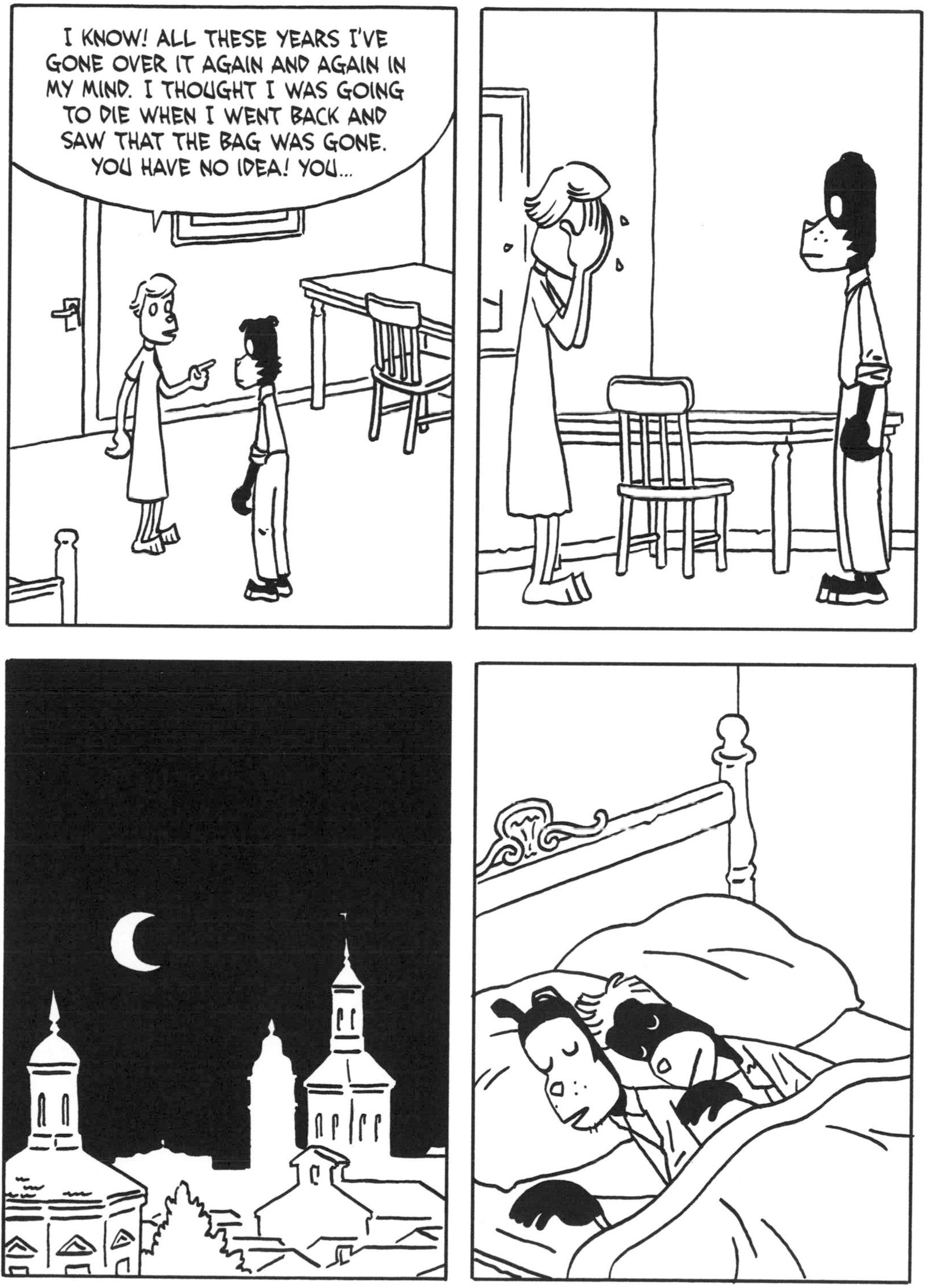
I KNOW! ALL THESE YEARS I'VE GONE OVER IT AGAIN AND AGAIN IN MY MIND. I THOUGHT I WAS GOING TO DIE WHEN I WENT BACK AND SAW THAT THE BAG WAS GONE. YOU HAVE NO IDEA! YOU...

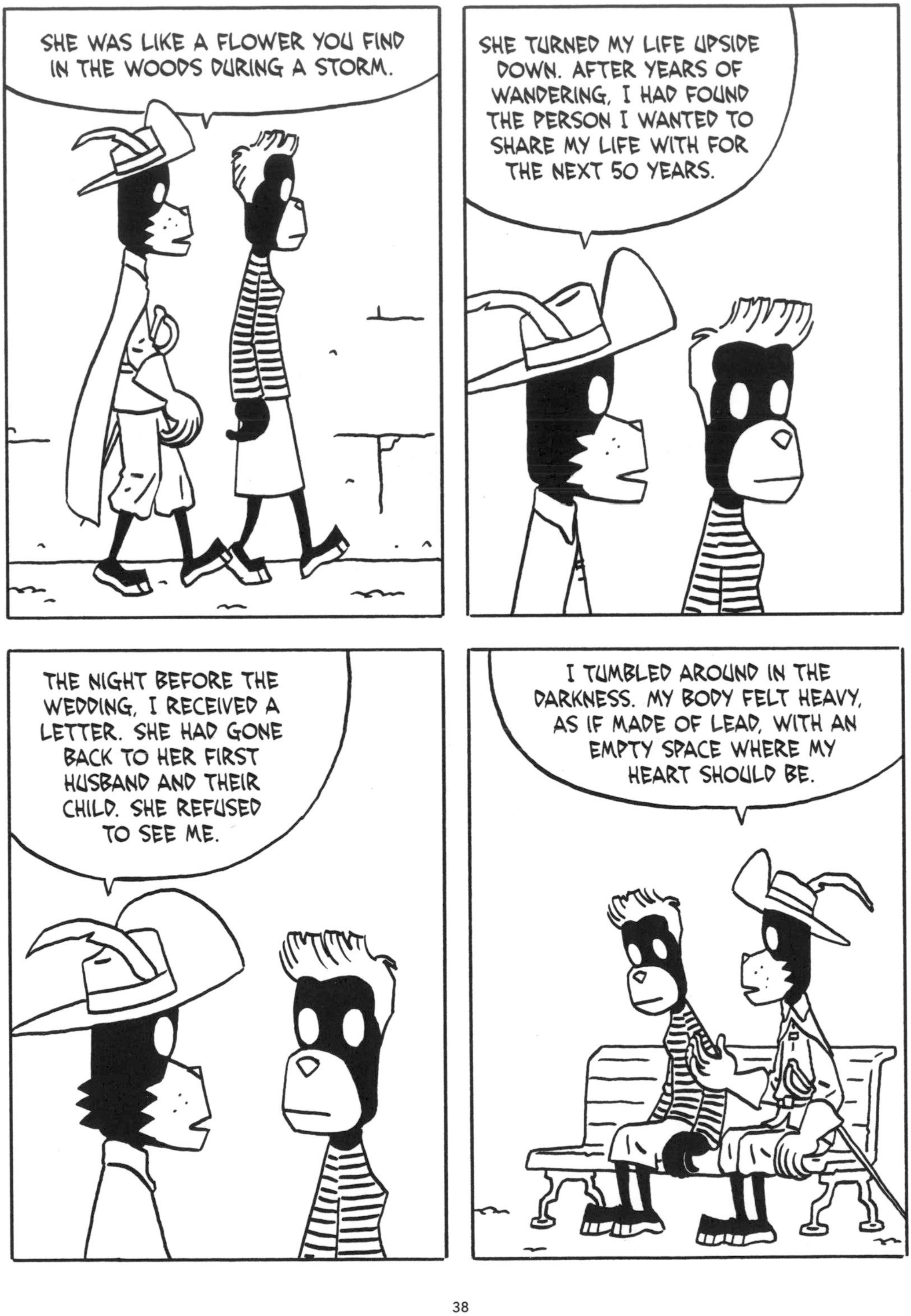
SHE WAS LIKE A FLOWER YOU FIND IN THE WOODS DURING A STORM.
SHE TURNED MY LIFE UPSIDE DOWN. AFTER YEARS OF WANDERING, I HAD FOUND THE PERSON I WANTED TO SHARE MY LIFE WITH FOR THE NEXT 50 YEARS.
THE NIGHT BEFORE THE WEDDING, I RECEIVED A LETTER. SHE HAD GONE BACK TO HER FIRST HUSBAND AND THEIR CHILD. SHE REFUSED TO SEE ME.
I TUMBLED AROUND IN THE DARKNESS. MY BODY FELT HEAVY, AS IF MADE OF LEAD, WITH AN EMPTY SPACE WHERE MY HEART SHOULD BE.

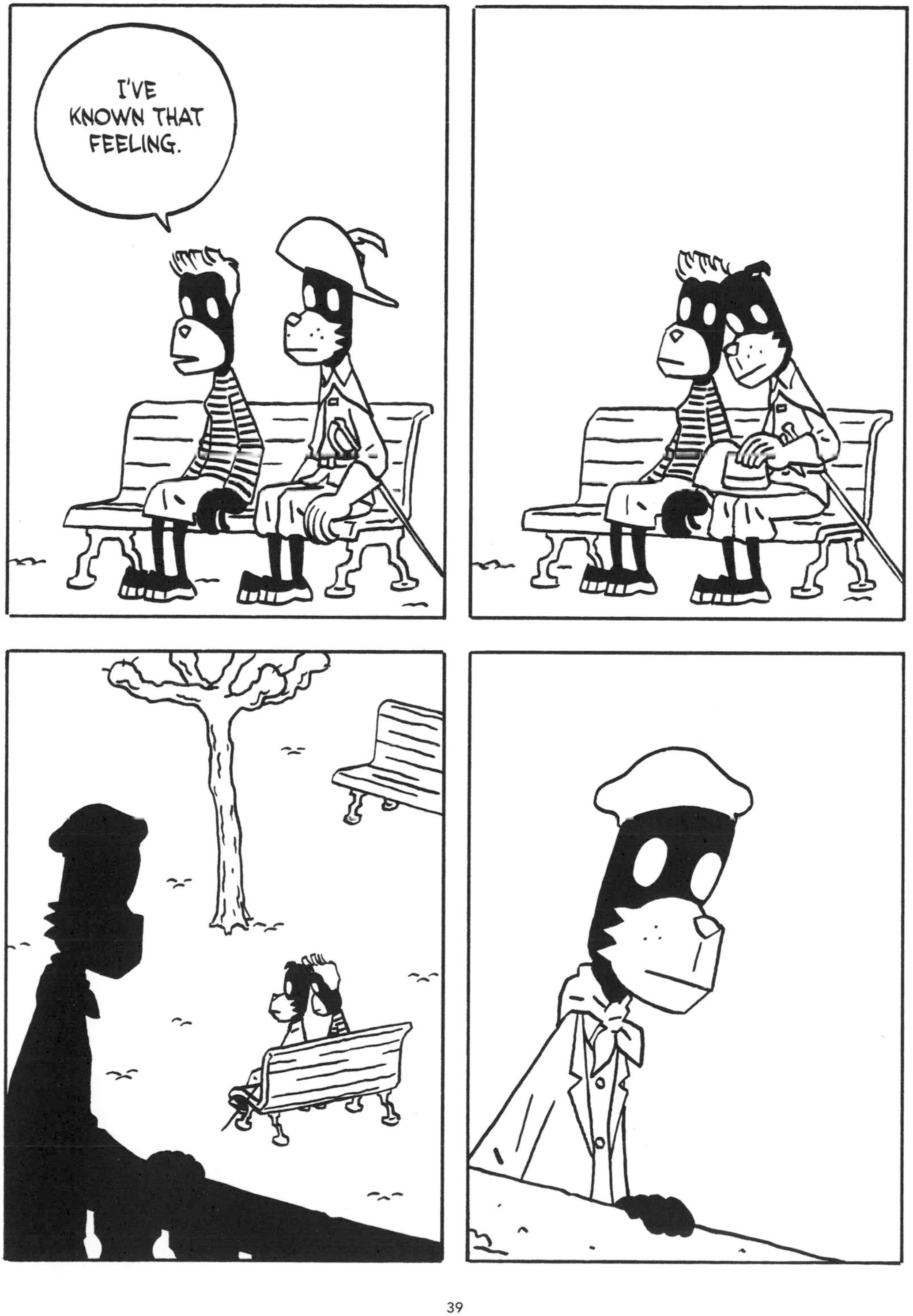
I'VE KNOWN THAT FEELING.

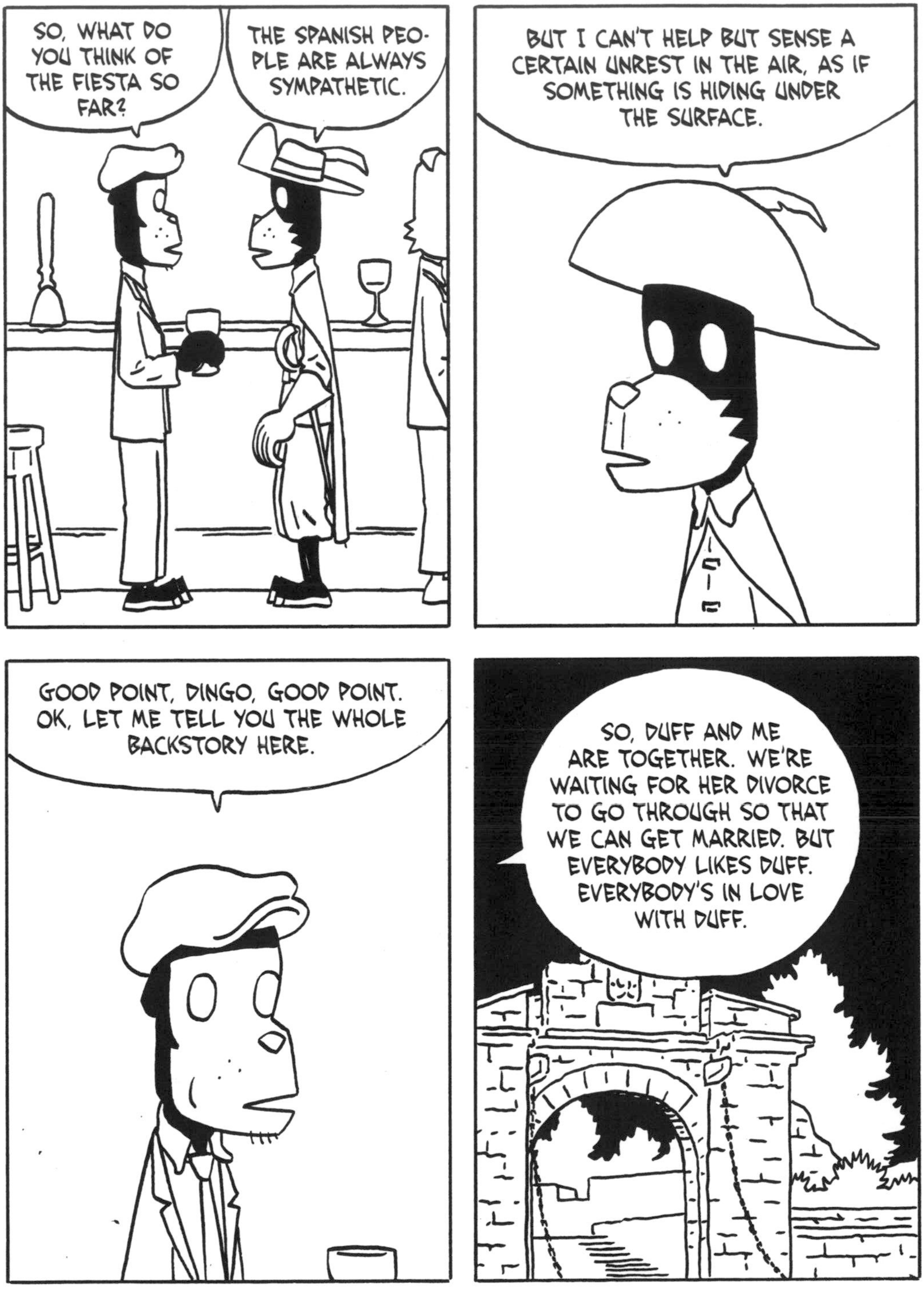
SO, WHAT DO YOU THINK OF THE FIESTA SO FAR?
THE SPANISH PEOPLE ARE ALWAYS SYMPATHETIC.
BUT I CAN'T HELP BUT SENSE A CERTAIN UNREST IN THE AIR, AS IF SOMETHING IS HIDING UNDER THE SURFACE.
GOOD POINT, DINGO, GOOD POINT. OK, LET ME TELL YOU THE WHOLE BACKSTORY HERE.
SO, DUFF AND ME ARE TOGETHER. WE'RE WAITING FOR HER DIVORCE TO GO THROUGH SO THAT WE CAN GET MARRIED. BUT EVERYBODY LIKES DUFF. EVERYBODY'S IN LOVE WITH DUFF.

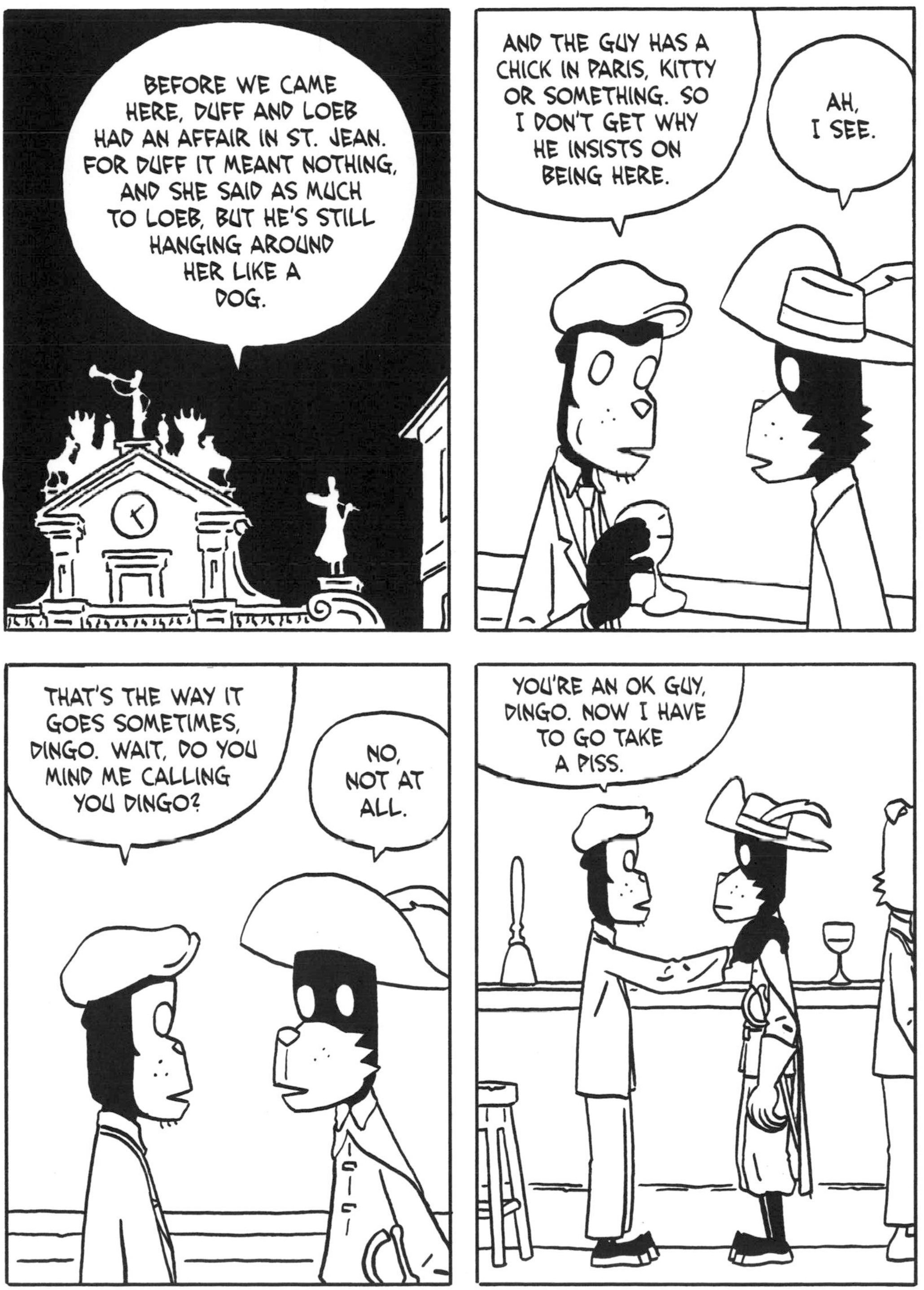
BEFORE WE CAME HERE, DUFF AND LOEB HAD AN AFFAIR IN ST. JEAN. FOR DUFF IT MEANT NOTHING, AND SHE SAID AS MUCH TO LOEB, BUT HE'S STILL HANGING AROUND HER LIKE A DOG.
AND THE GUY HAS A CHICK IN PARIS, KITTY OR SOMETHING. SO I DON'T GET WHY HE INSISTS ON BEING HERE.
AH, I SEE.
THAT'S THE WAY IT GOES SOMETIMES, DINGO. WAIT, DO YOU MIND ME CALLING YOU DINGO?
NO, NOT AT ALL.
YOU'RE AN OK GUY, DINGO. NOW I HAVE TO GO TAKE A PISS.

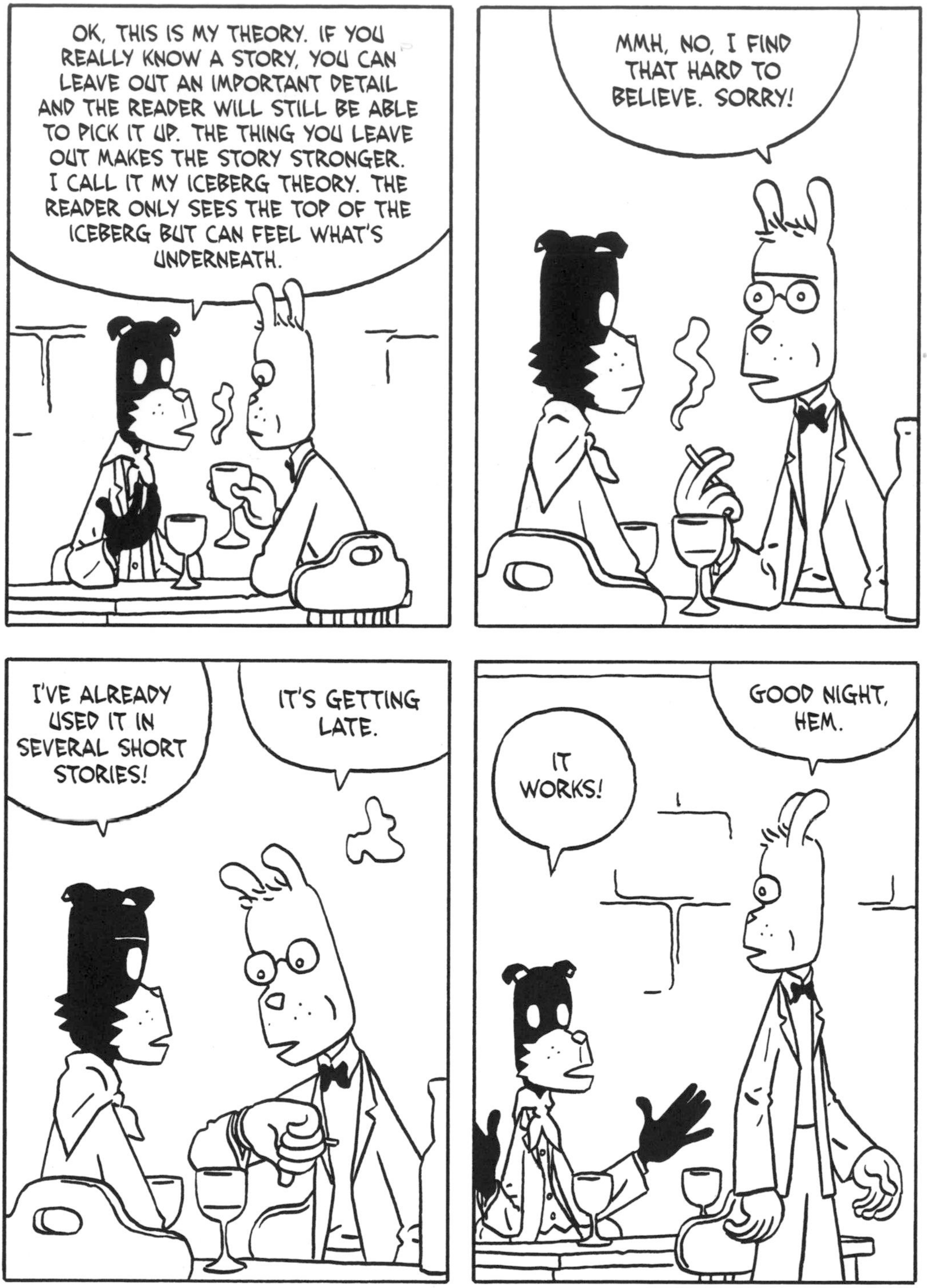
OK, THIS IS MY THEORY. IF YOU REALLY KNOW A STORY, YOU CAN LEAVE OUT AN IMPORTANT DETAIL AND THE READER WILL STILL BE ABLE TO PICK IT UP. THE THING YOU LEAVE OUT MAKES THE STORY STRONGER. I CALL IT MY ICEBERG THEORY. THE READER ONLY SEES THE TOP OF THE ICEBERG BUT CAN FEEL WHAT'S UNDERNEATH.
MMH, NO, I FIND THAT HARD TO BELIEVE. SORRY!
I'VE ALREADY USED IT IN SEVERAL SHORT STORIES!
IT'S GETTING LATE.
IT WORKS!
GOOD NIGHT, HEM.

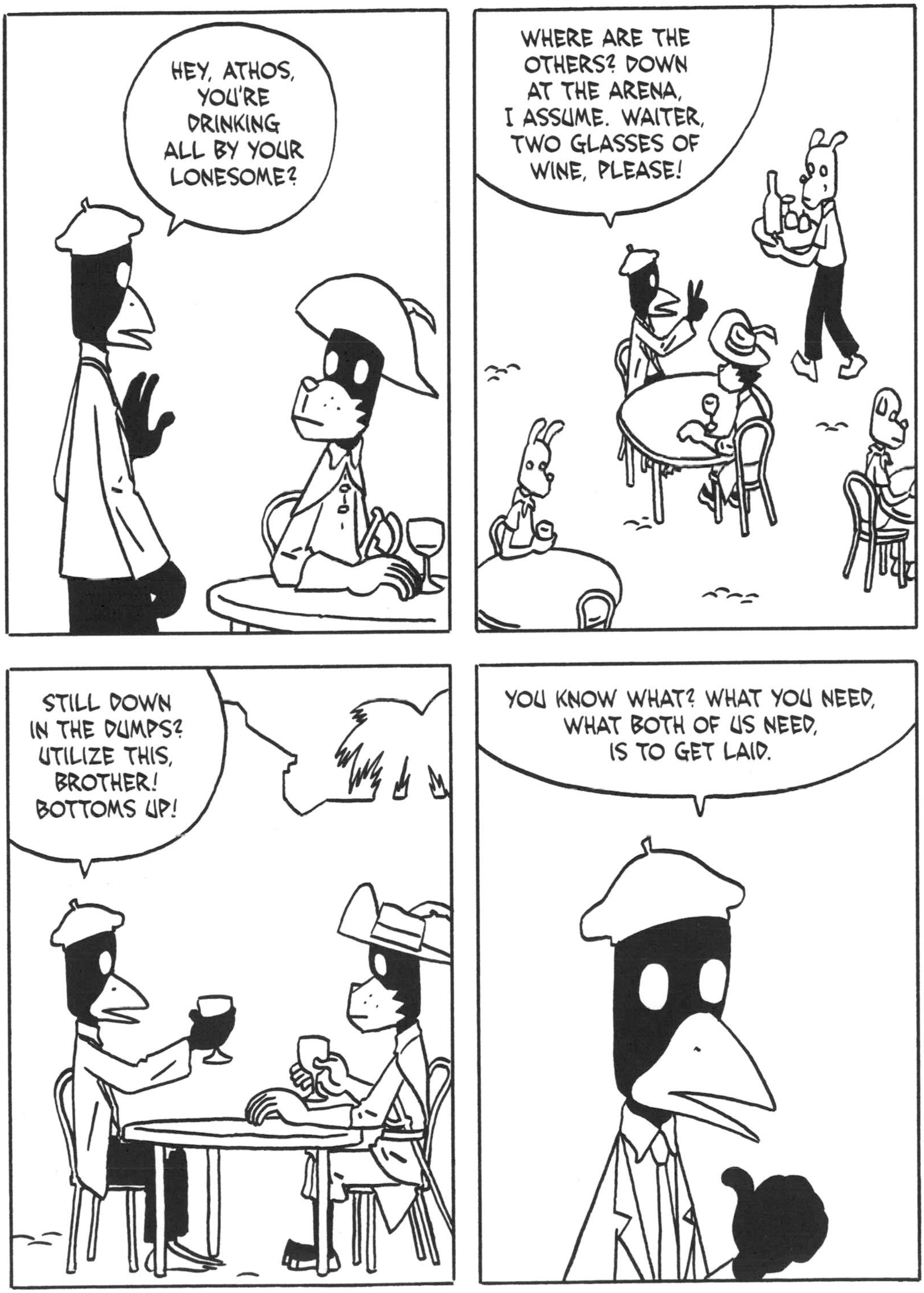
HEY, ATHOS, YOU'RE DRINKING ALL BY YOUR LONESOME?
WHERE ARE THE OTHERS? DOWN AT THE ARENA, I ASSUME. WAITER, TWO GLASSES OF WINE, PLEASE!
STILL DOWN IN THE DUMPS? UTILIZE THIS, BROTHER! BOTTOMS UP!
YOU KNOW WHAT? WHAT YOU NEED, WHAT BOTH OF US NEED, IS TO GET LAID.

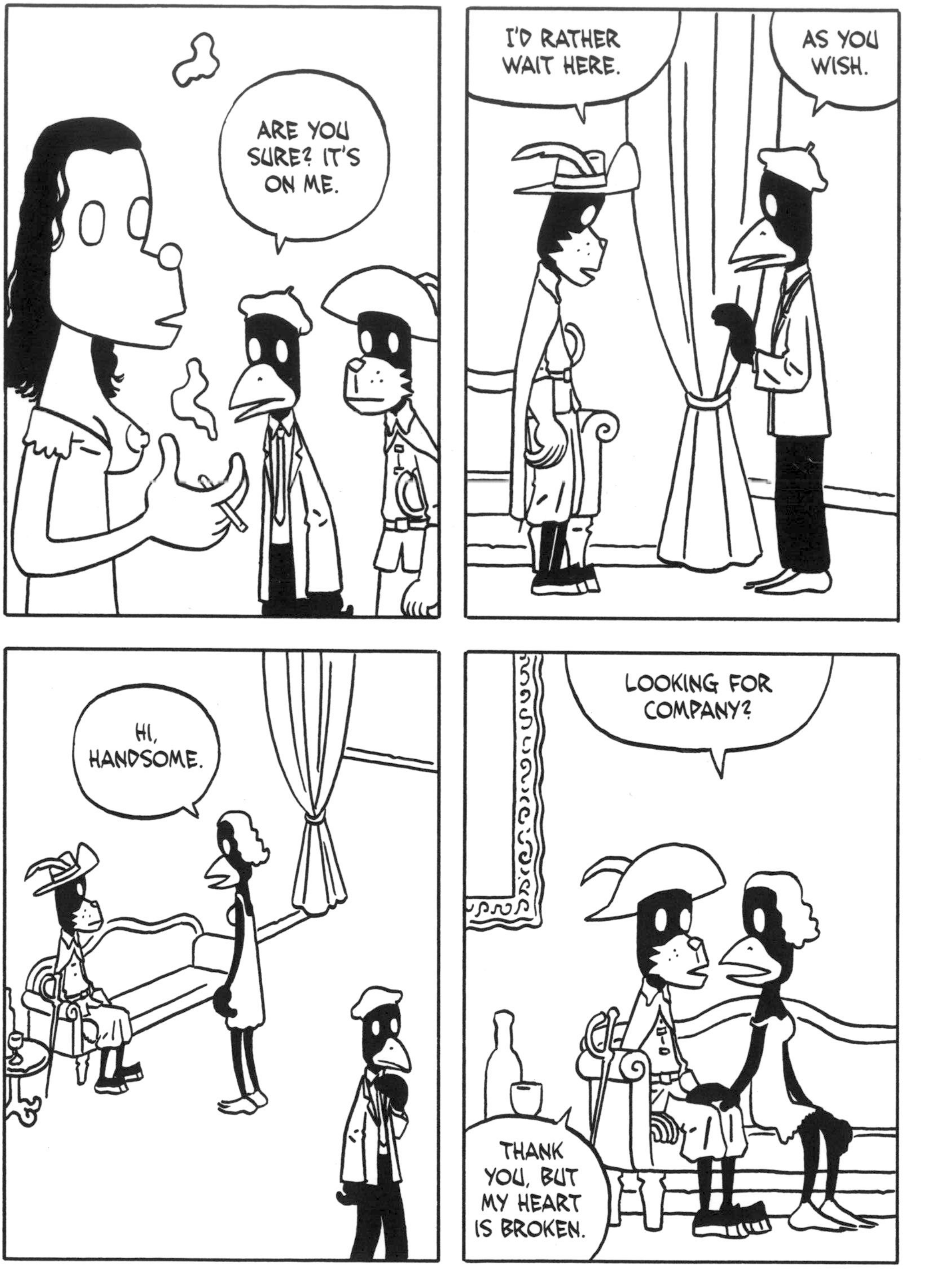
ARE YOU SURE? IT'S ON ME.
I'D RATHER WAIT HERE.
AS YOU WISH.
HI, HANDSOME.
LOOKING FOR COMPANY?
THANK YOU, BUT MY HEART IS BROKEN.

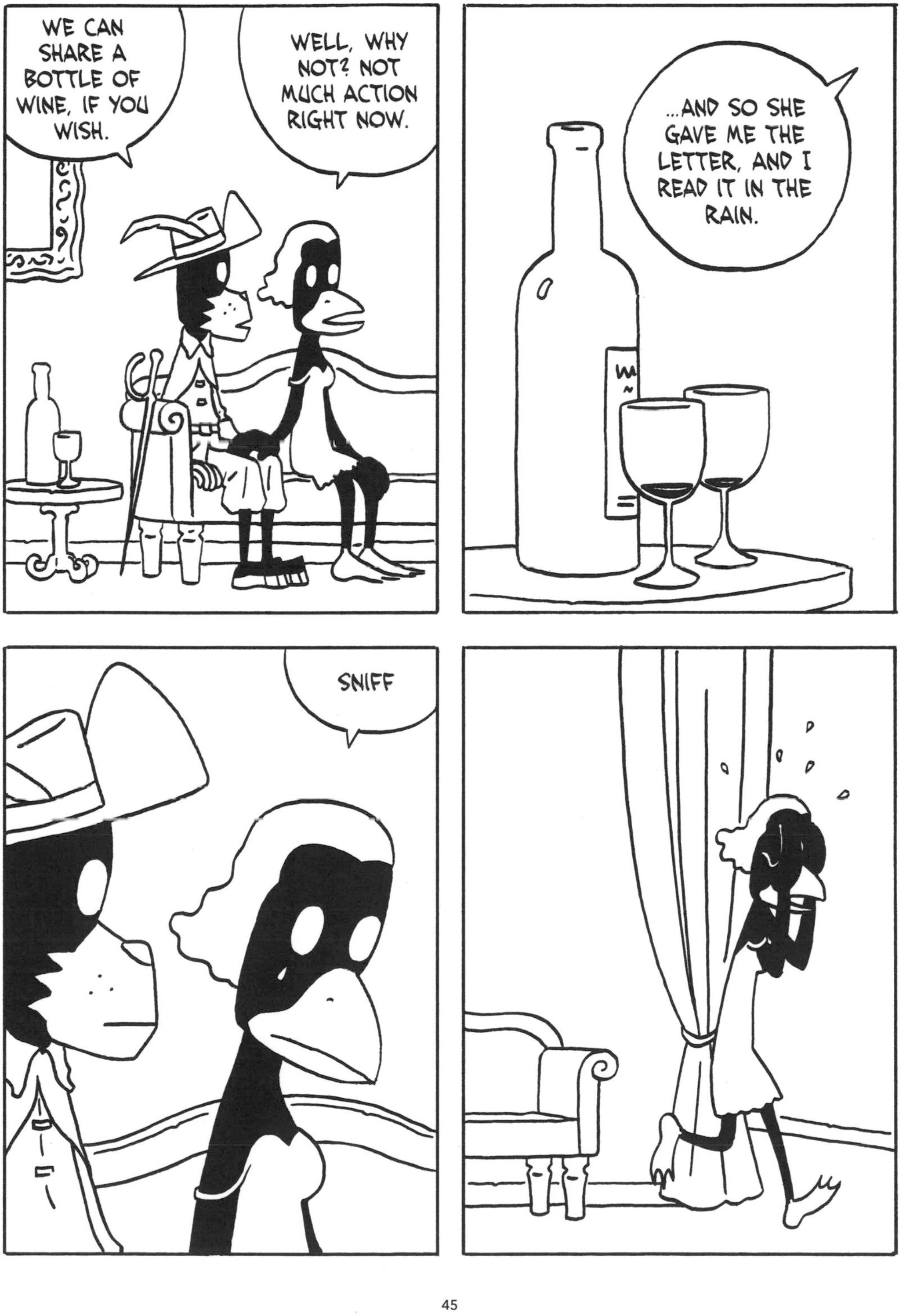
WE CAN SHARE A BOTTLE OF WINE, IF YOU WISH.
WELL, WHY NOT? NOT MUCH ACTION RIGHT NOW.
...AND SO SHE GAVE ME THE LETTER, AND I READ IT IN THE RAIN.
SNIFF

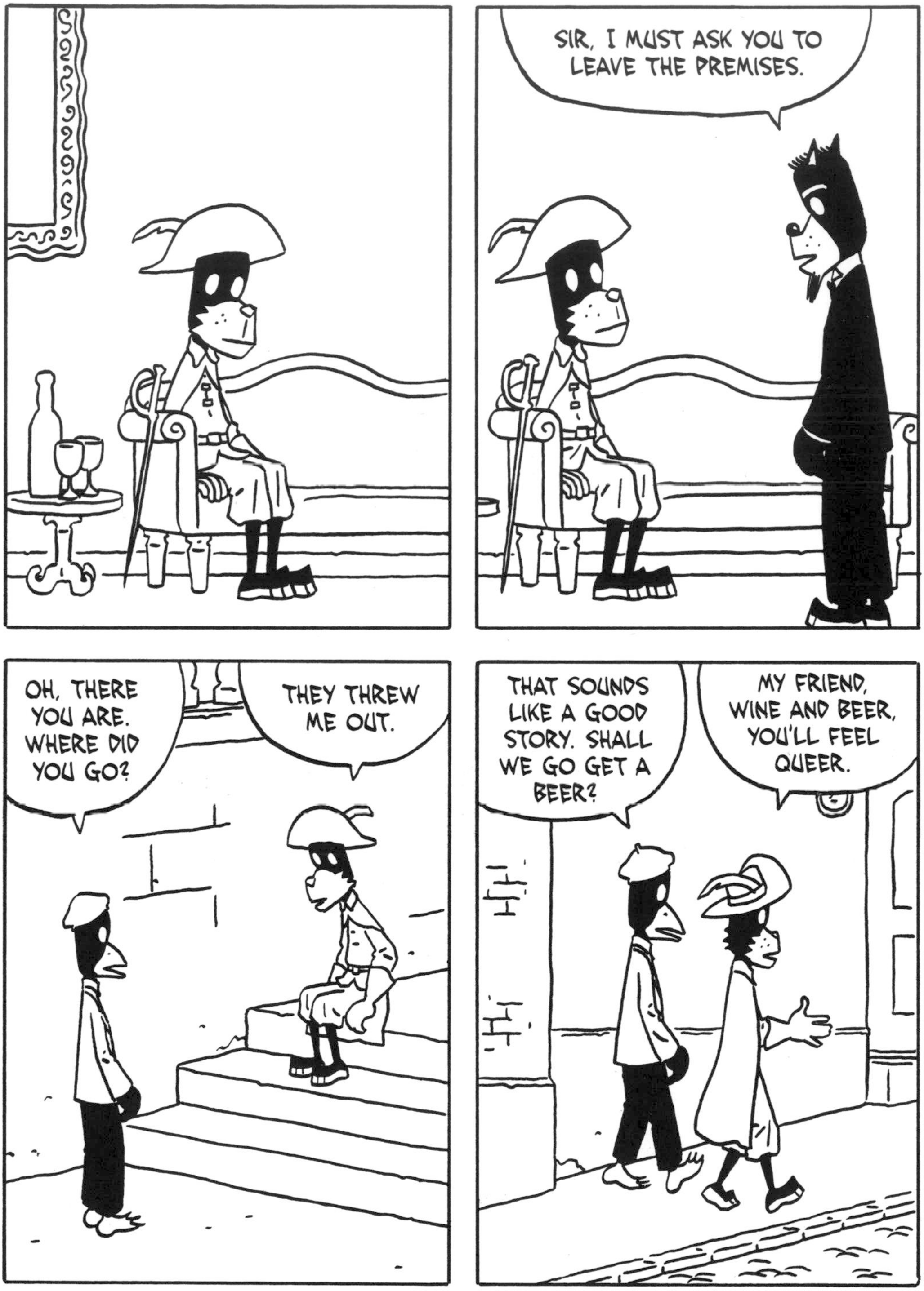
SIR, I MUST ASK YOU TO LEAVE THE PREMISES.
OH, THERE YOU ARE. WHERE DID YOU GO?
THEY THREW ME OUT.
THAT SOUNDS LIKE A GOOD STORY. SHALL WE GO GET A BEER?
MY FRIEND, WINE AND BEER, YOU'LL FEEL QUEER.

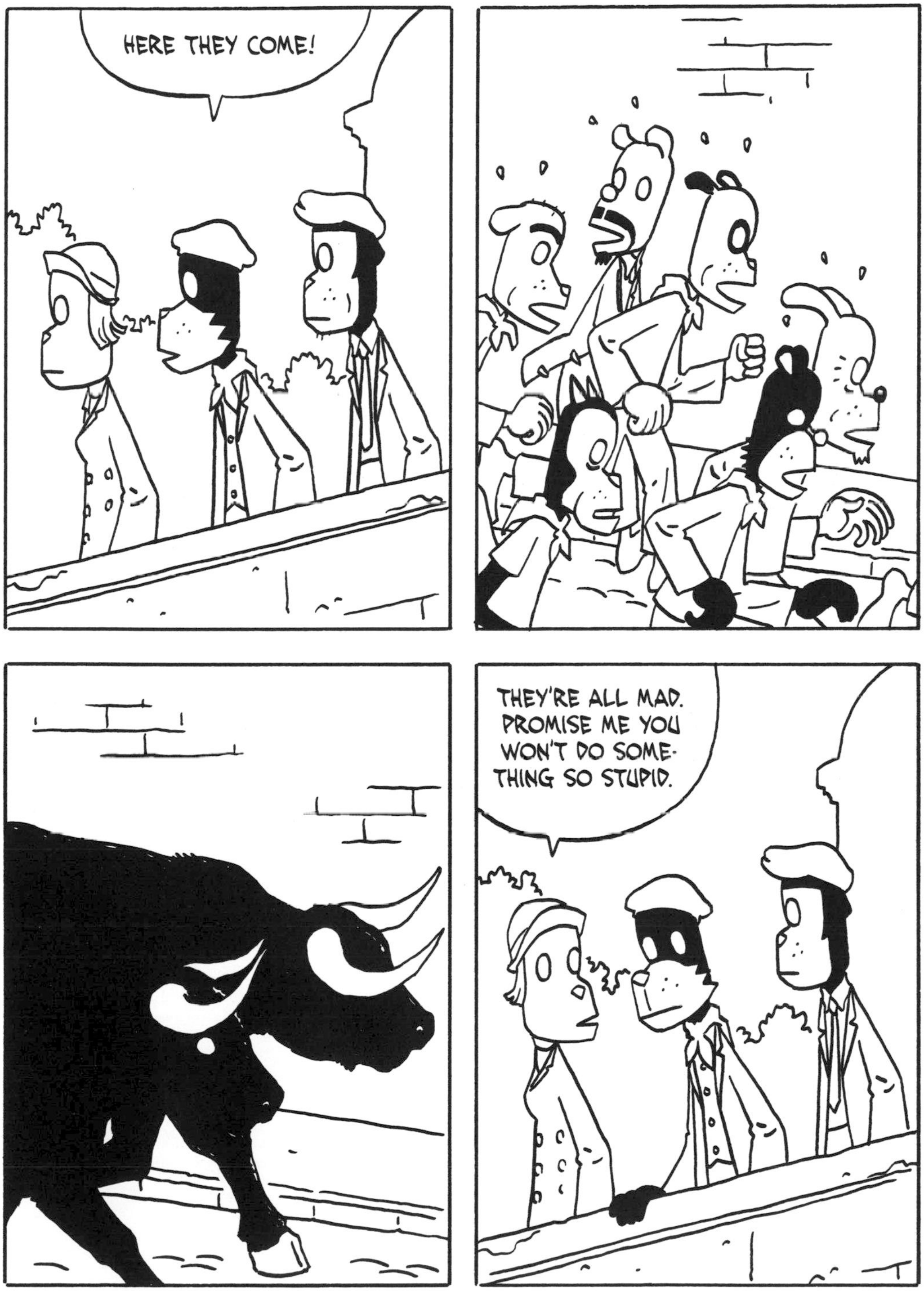
HERE THEY COME!
THEY'RE ALL MAD. PROMISE ME YOU WON'T DO SOME-THING SO STUPID.

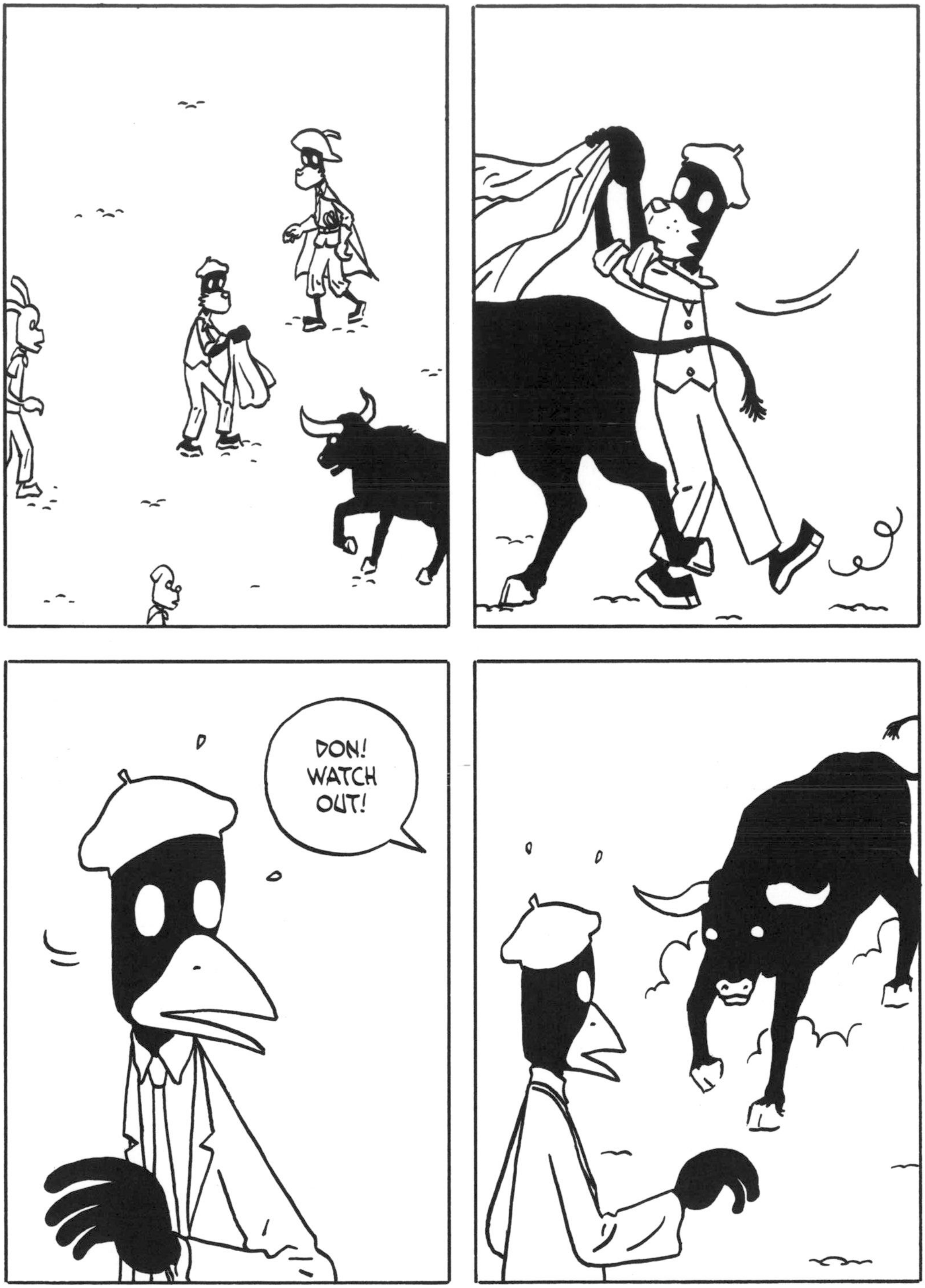
DON! WATCH OUT!

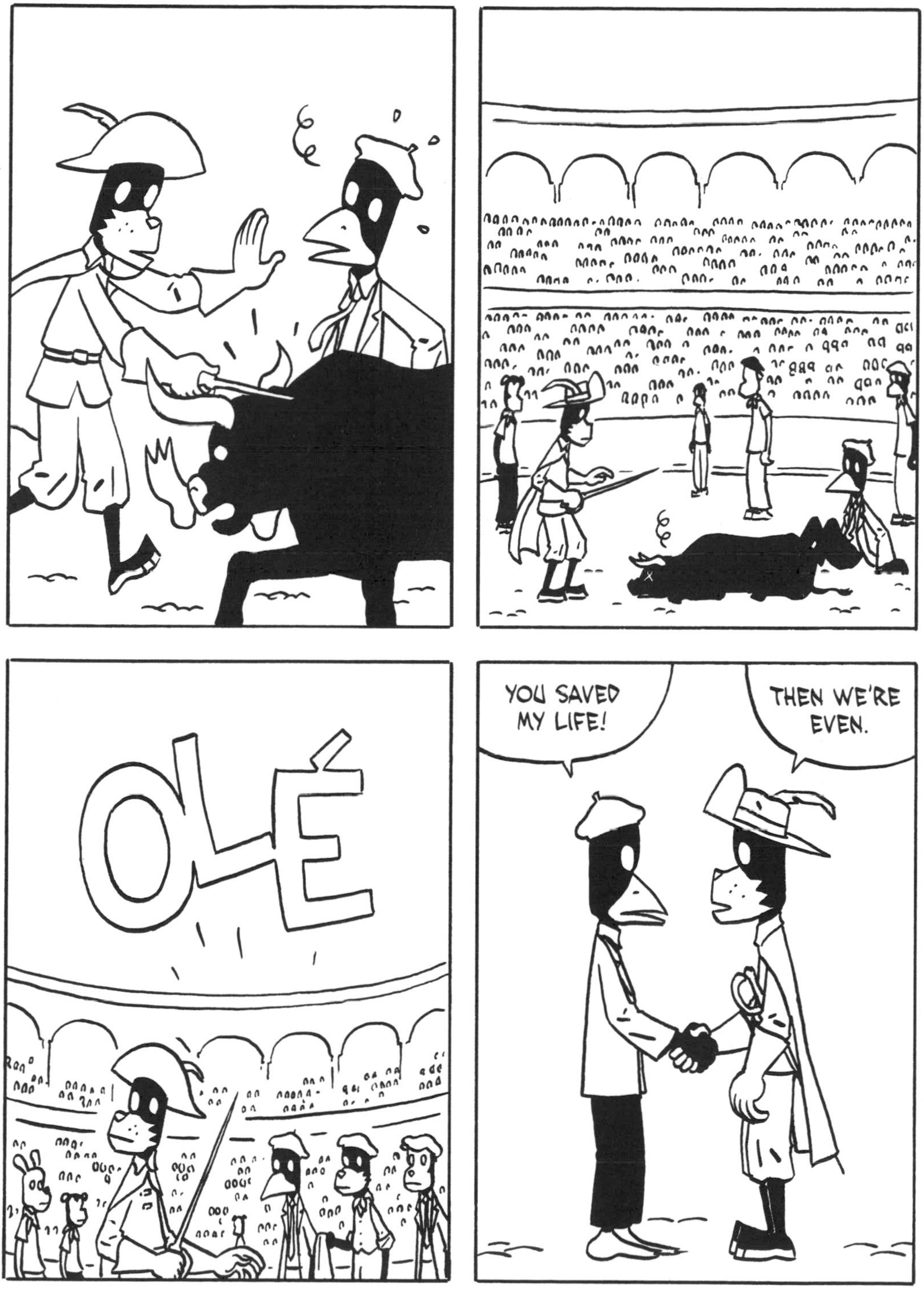
OLÉ
YOU SAVED MY LIFE!
THEN WE'RE EVEN.

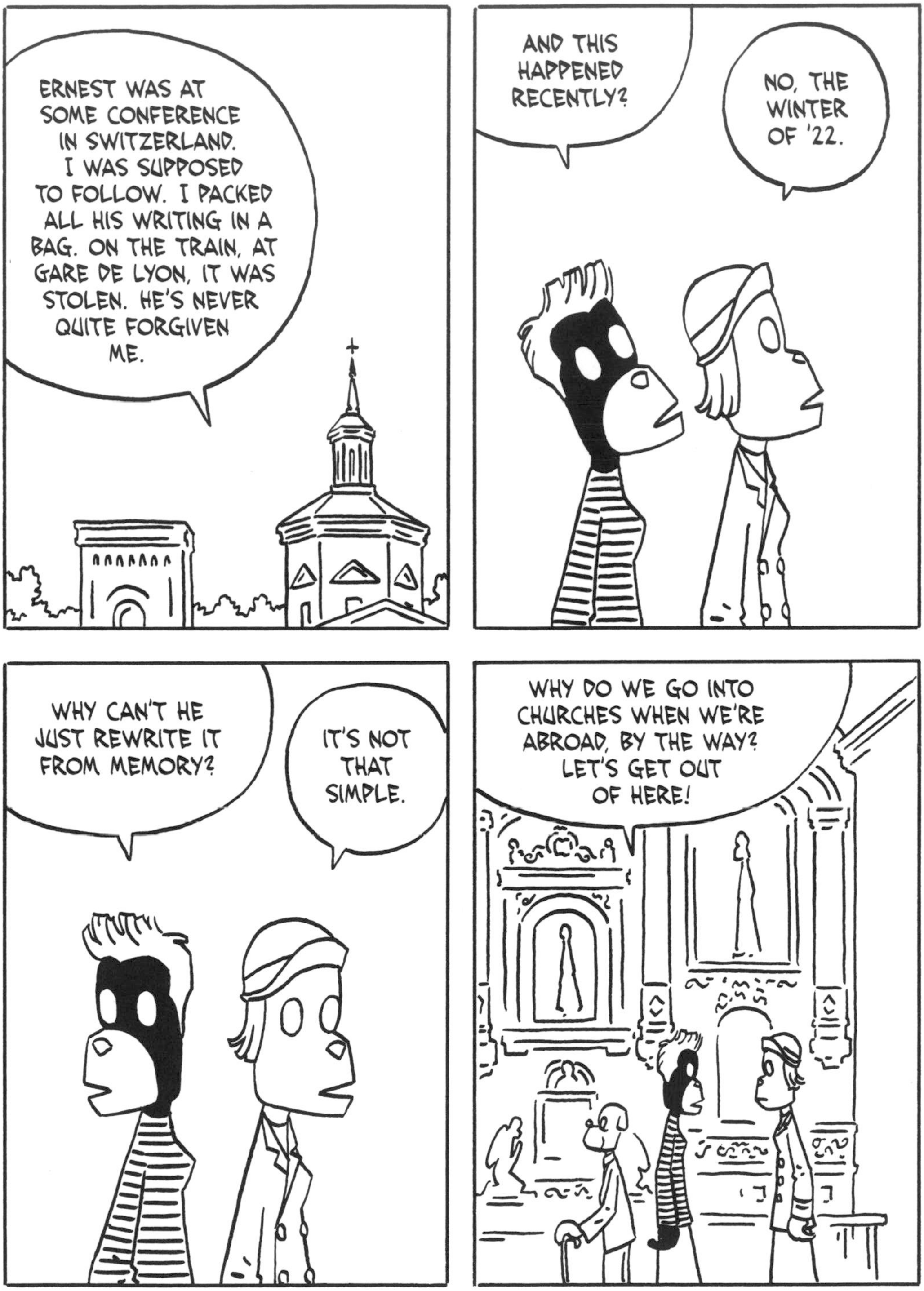
ERNEST WAS AT SOME CONFERENCE IN SWITZERLAND. I WAS SUPPOSED TO FOLLOW. I PACKED ALL HIS WRITING IN A BAG. ON THE TRAIN, AT GARE DE LYON, IT WAS STOLEN. HE'S NEVER QUITE FORGIVEN ME.
AND THIS HAPPENED RECENTLY?
NO, THE WINTER OF '22.
WHY CAN'T HE JUST REWRITE IT FROM MEMORY?
IT'S NOT THAT SIMPLE.
WHY DO WE GO INTO CHURCHES WHEN WE'RE ABROAD, BY THE WAY? LET'S GET OUT OF HERE!

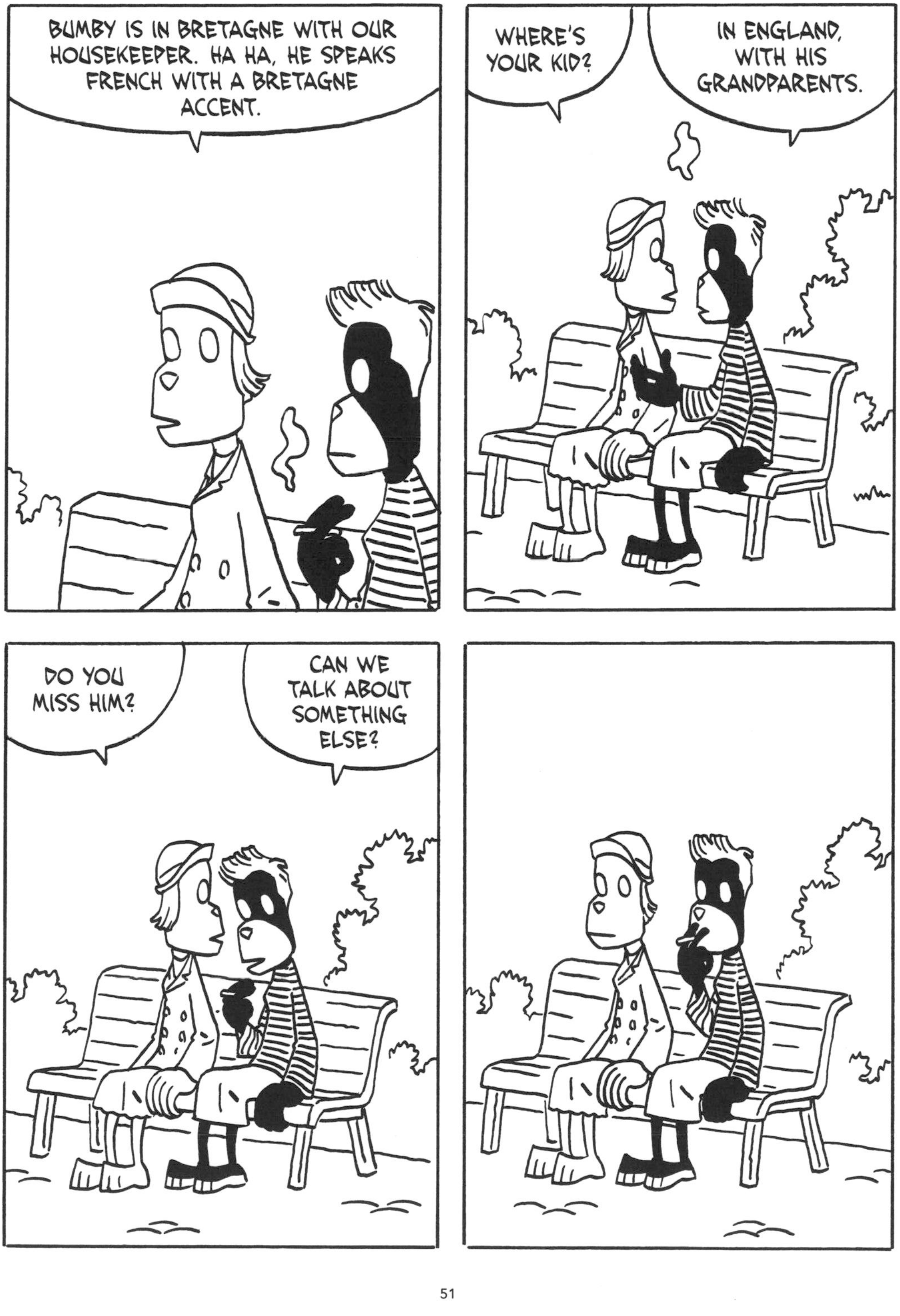
BUMBY IS IN BRETAGNE WITH OUR HOUSEKEEPER. HA HA, HE SPEAKS FRENCH WITH A BRETAGNE ACCENT.
WHERE'S YOUR KID?
IN ENGLAND, WITH HIS GRANDPARENTS.
DO YOU MISS HIM?
CAN WE TALK ABOUT SOMETHING ELSE?

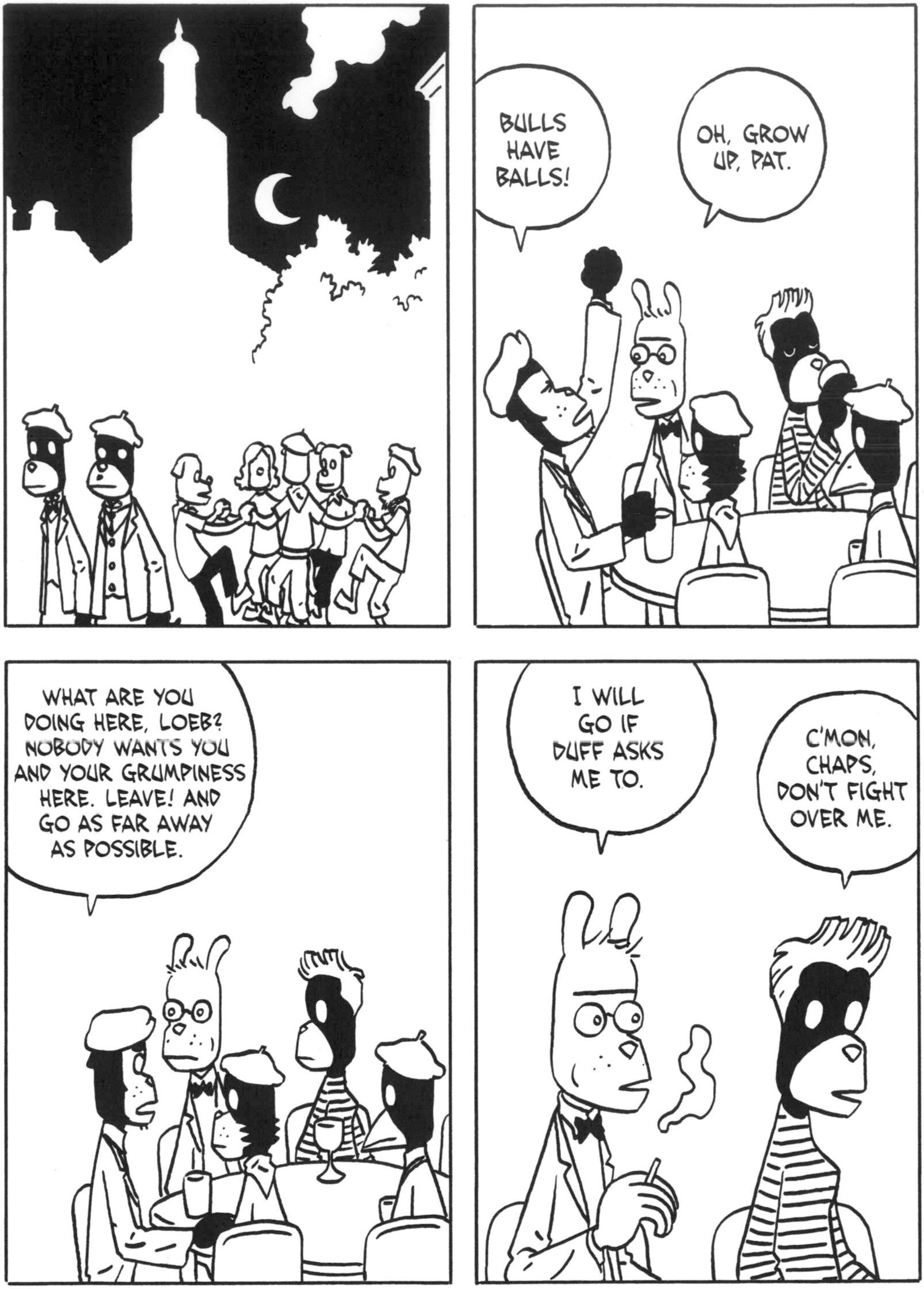
BULLS HAVE BALLS!
OH, GROW UP, PAT.
WHAT ARE YOU DOING HERE, LOEB? NOBODY WANTS YOU AND YOUR GRUMPINESS HERE. LEAVE! AND GO AS FAR AWAY AS POSSIBLE.
I WILL GO IF DUFF ASKS ME TO.
C'MON, CHAPS, DON'T FIGHT OVER ME.

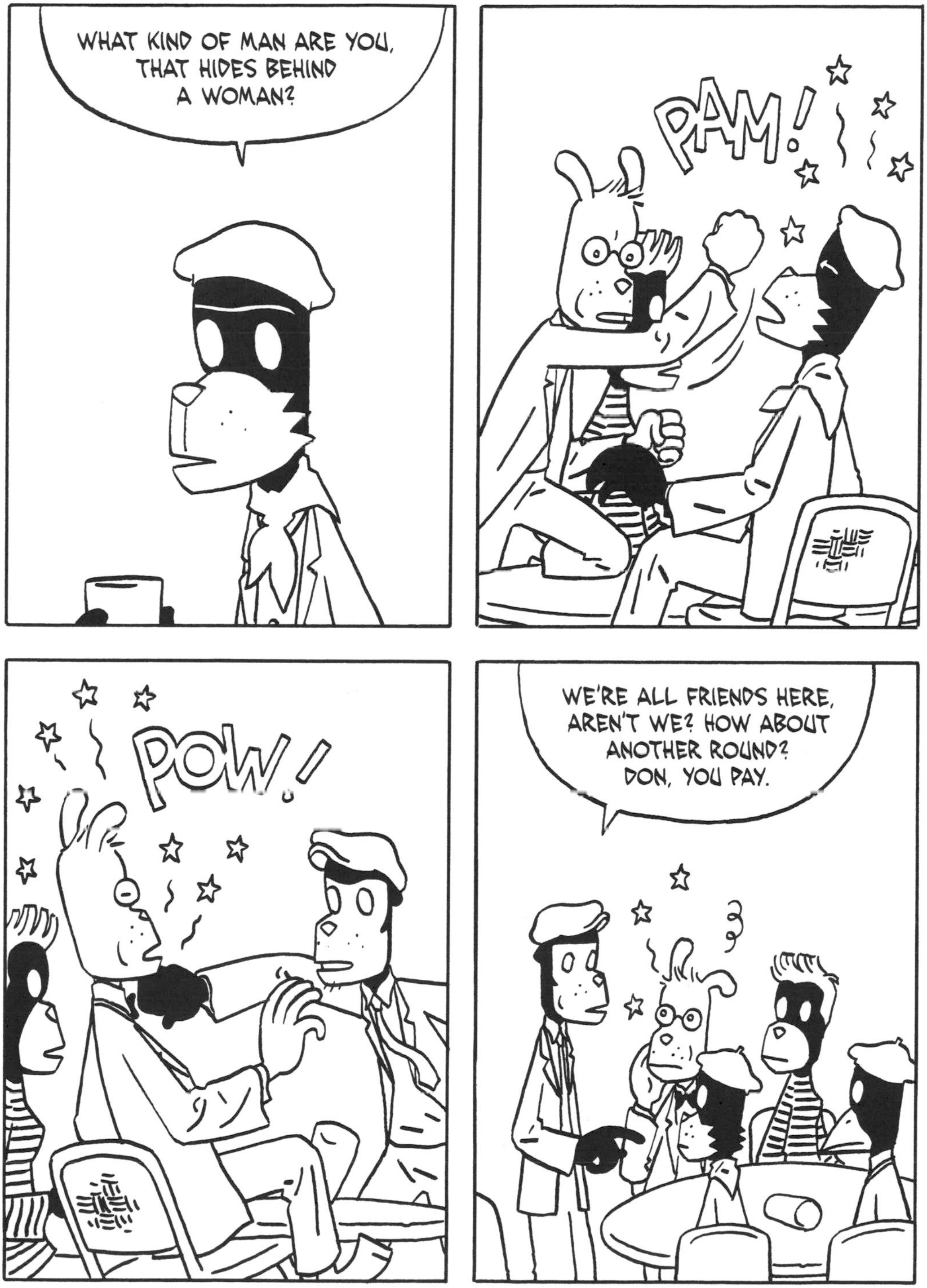
WHAT KIND OF MAN ARE YOU, THAT HIDES BEHIND A WOMAN?
PAM!
POW!
WE'RE ALL FRIENDS HERE, AREN'T WE? HOW ABOUT ANOTHER ROUND? DON, YOU PAY.

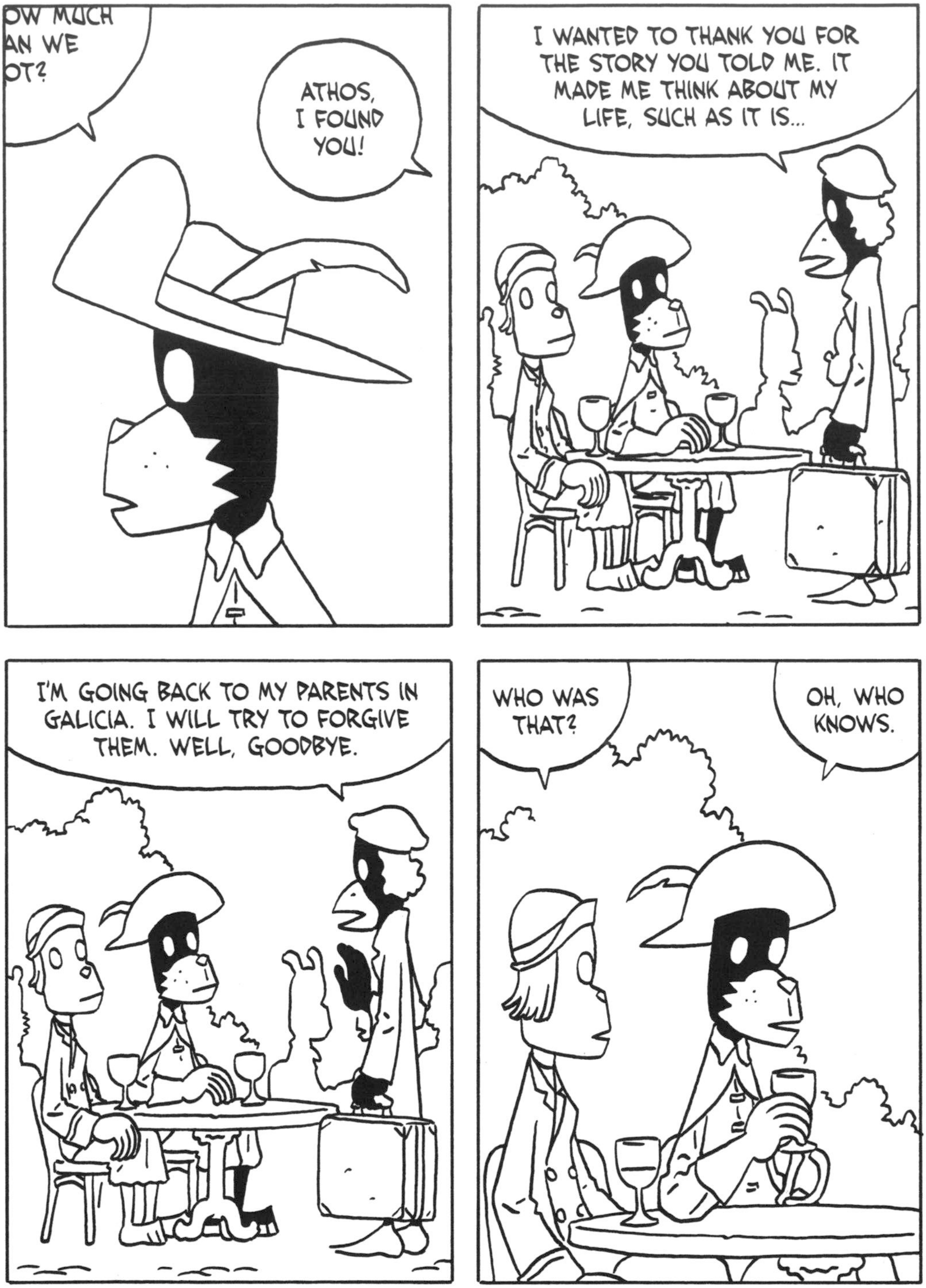
OW MUCH
AN WE
OT?
ATHOS, I FOUND YOU!
I WANTED TO THANK YOU FOR THE STORY YOU TOLD ME. IT MADE ME THINK ABOUT MY LIFE, SUCH AS IT IS...
I'M GOING BACK TO MY PARENTS IN GALICIA. I WILL TRY TO FORGIVE THEM. WELL, GOODBYE.
WHO WAS THAT?
OH, WHO KNOWS.

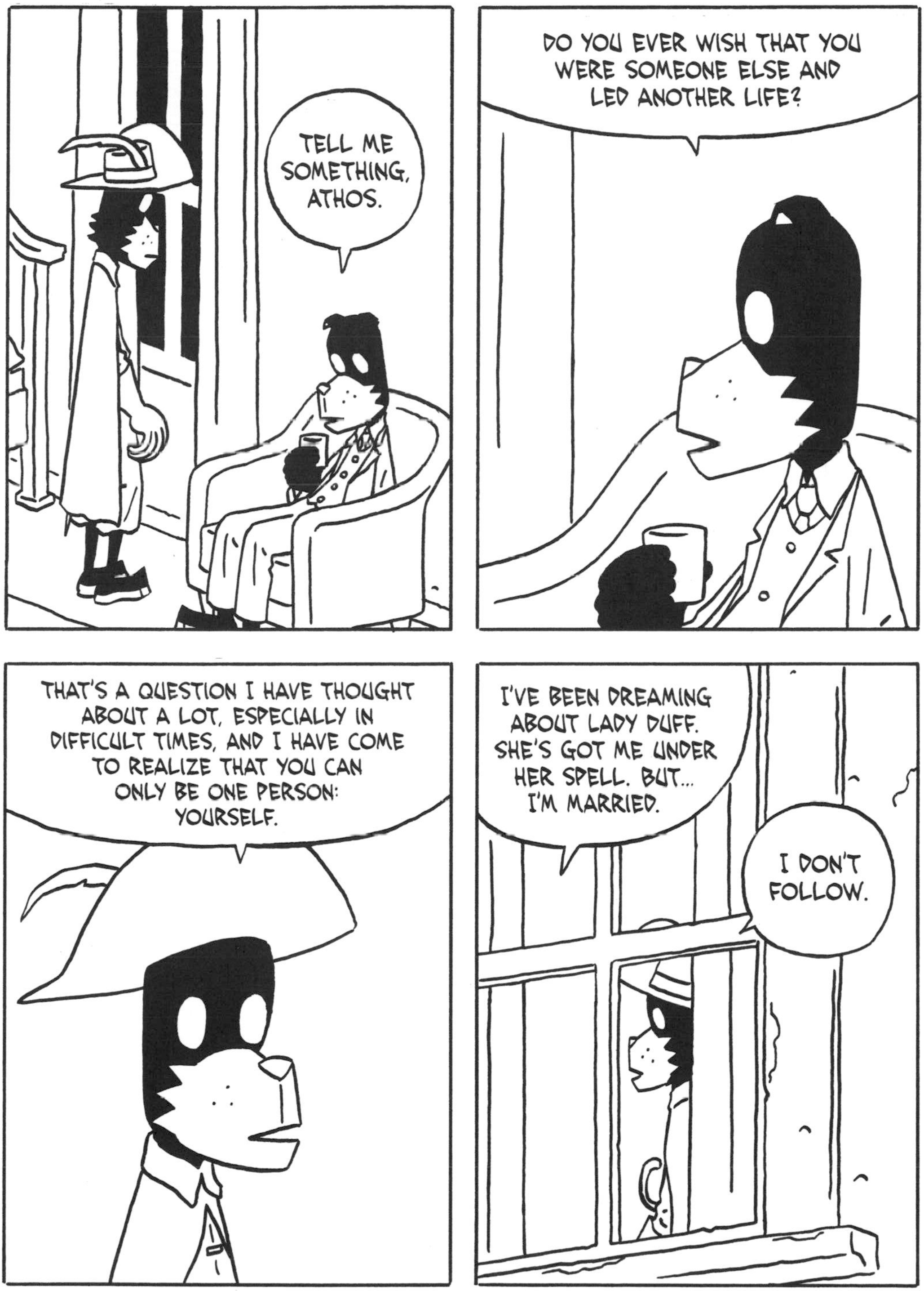
TELL ME SOMETHING, ATHOS.
DO YOU EVER WISH THAT YOU WERE SOMEONE ELSE AND LED ANOTHER LIFE?
THAT'S A QUESTION I HAVE THOUGHT ABOUT A LOT, ESPECIALLY IN DIFFICULT TIMES, AND I HAVE COME TO REALIZE THAT YOU CAN ONLY BE ONE PERSON: YOURSELF.
I'VE BEEN DREAMING ABOUT LADY DUFF. SHE'S GOT ME UNDER HER SPELL. BUT... I'M MARRIED.
I DON'T FOLLOW.

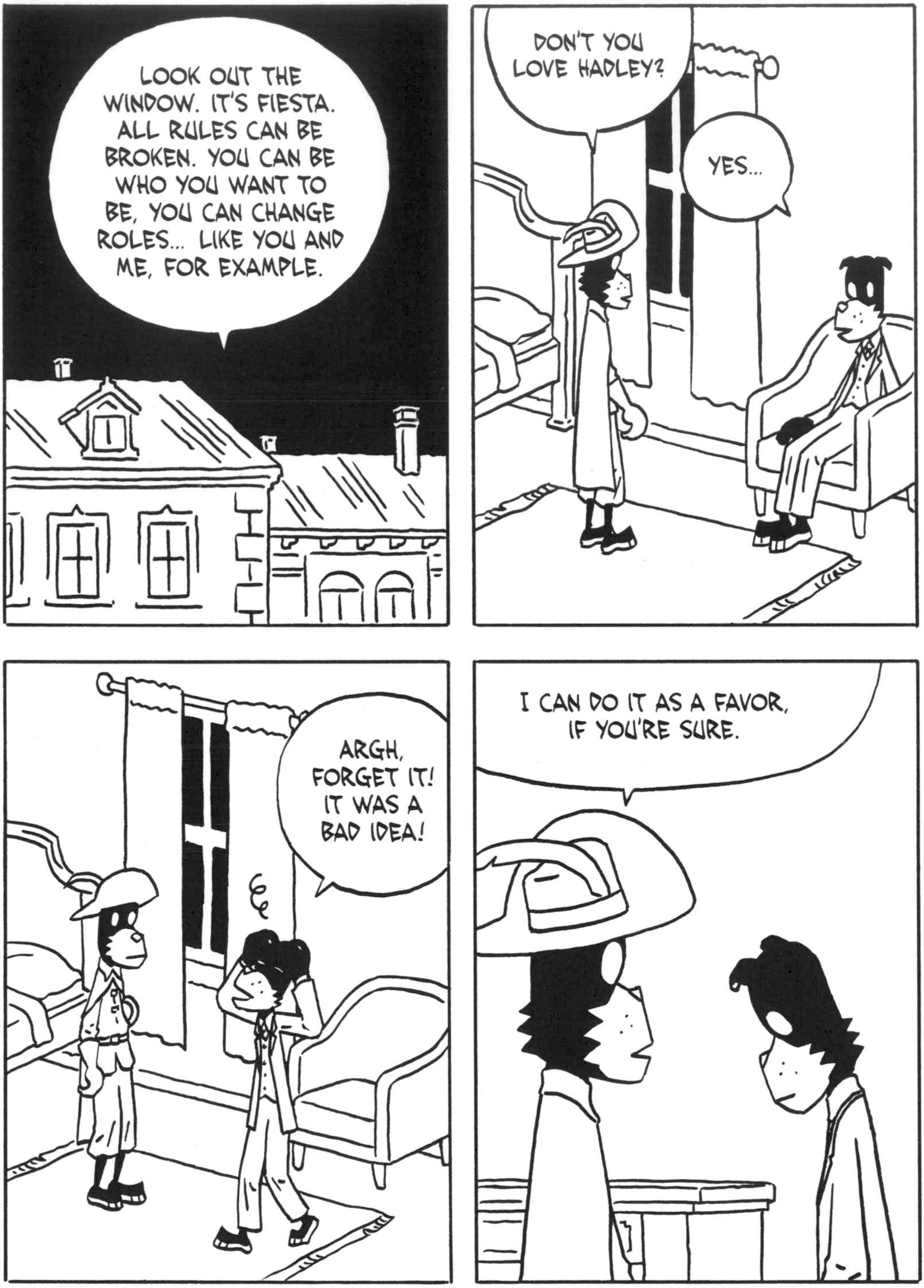
LOOK OUT THE WINDOW. IT'S FIESTA. ALL RULES CAN BE BROKEN. YOU CAN BE WHO YOU WANT TO BE, YOU CAN CHANGE ROLES... LIKE YOU AND ME, FOR EXAMPLE.
DON'T YOU LOVE HADLEY?
YES...
ARGH, FORGET IT! IT WAS A BAD IDEA!
I CAN DO IT AS A FAVOR, IF YOU'RE SURE.

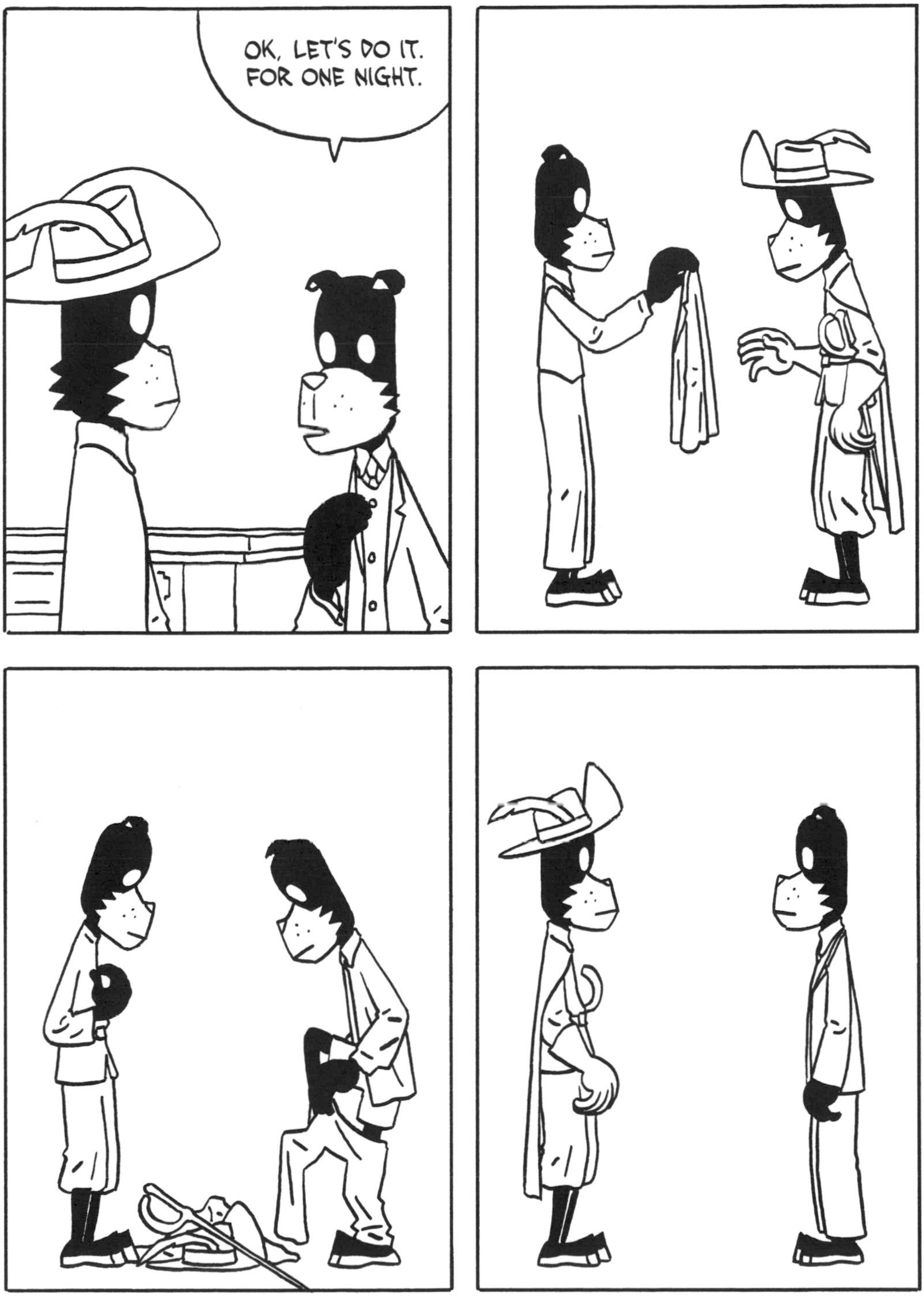
OK, LET'S DO IT. FOR ONE NIGHT.

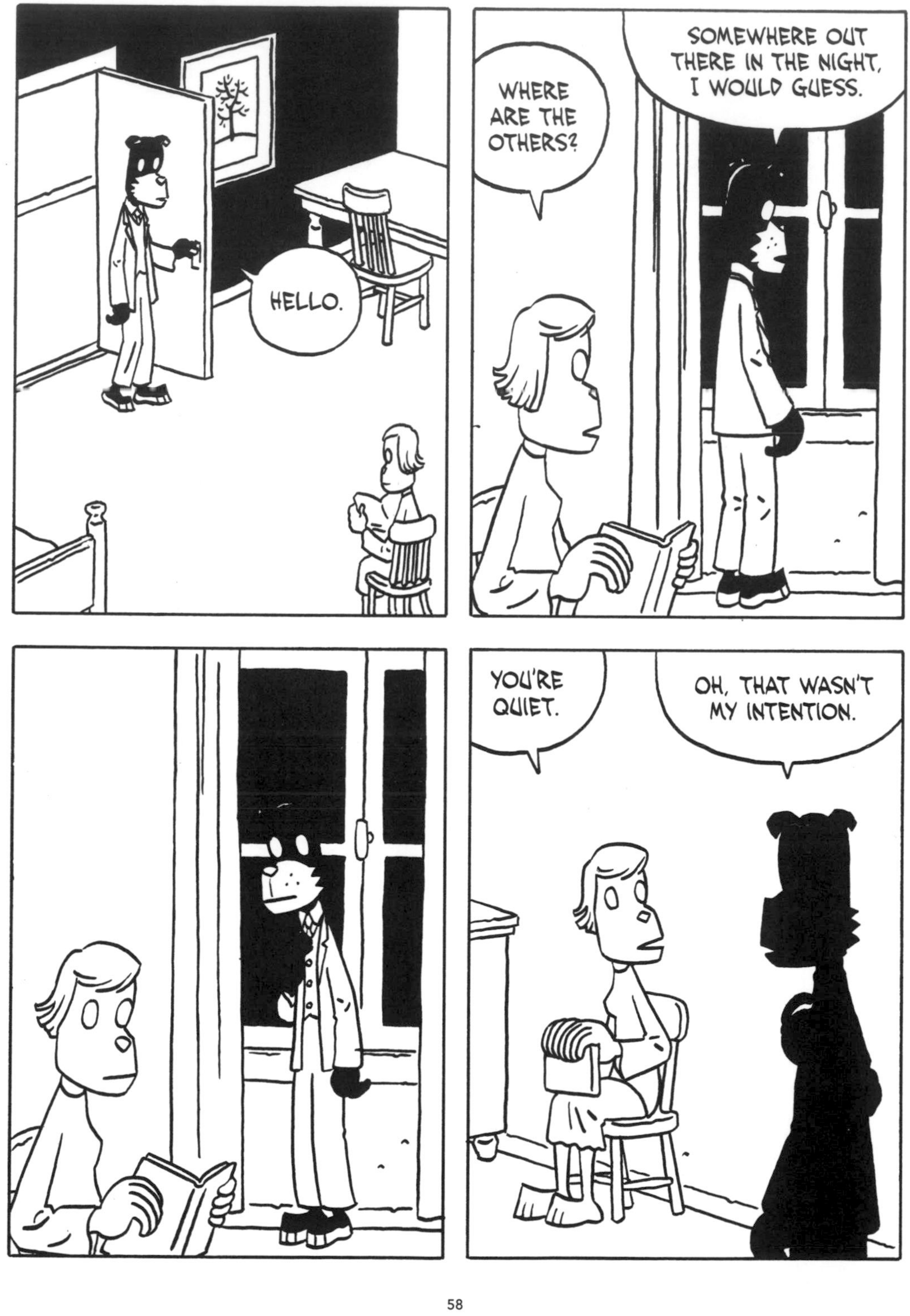
HELLO.
WHERE ARE THE OTHERS?
SOMEWHERE OUT THERE IN THE NIGHT, I WOULD GUESS.
YOU'RE QUIET.
OH, THAT WASN'T MY INTENTION.

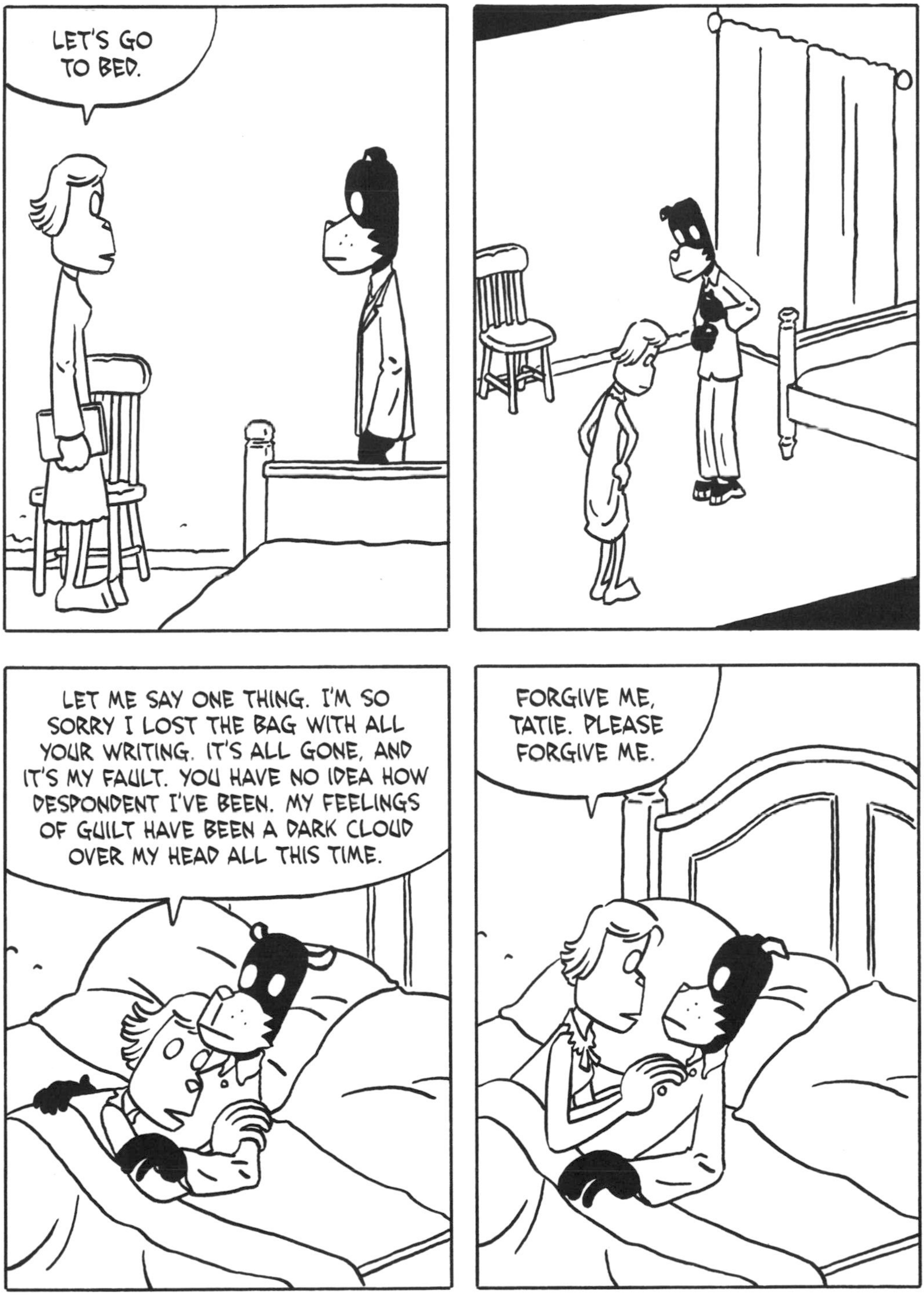
LET'S GO TO BED.
LET ME SAY ONE THING. I'M SO SORRY I LOST THE BAG WITH ALL YOUR WRITING. IT'S ALL GONE, AND IT'S MY FAULT. YOU HAVE NO IDEA HOW DESPONDENT I'VE BEEN. MY FEELINGS OF GUILT HAVE BEEN A DARK CLOUD OVER MY HEAD ALL THIS TIME.
FORGIVE ME, TATIE. PLEASE FORGIVE ME.

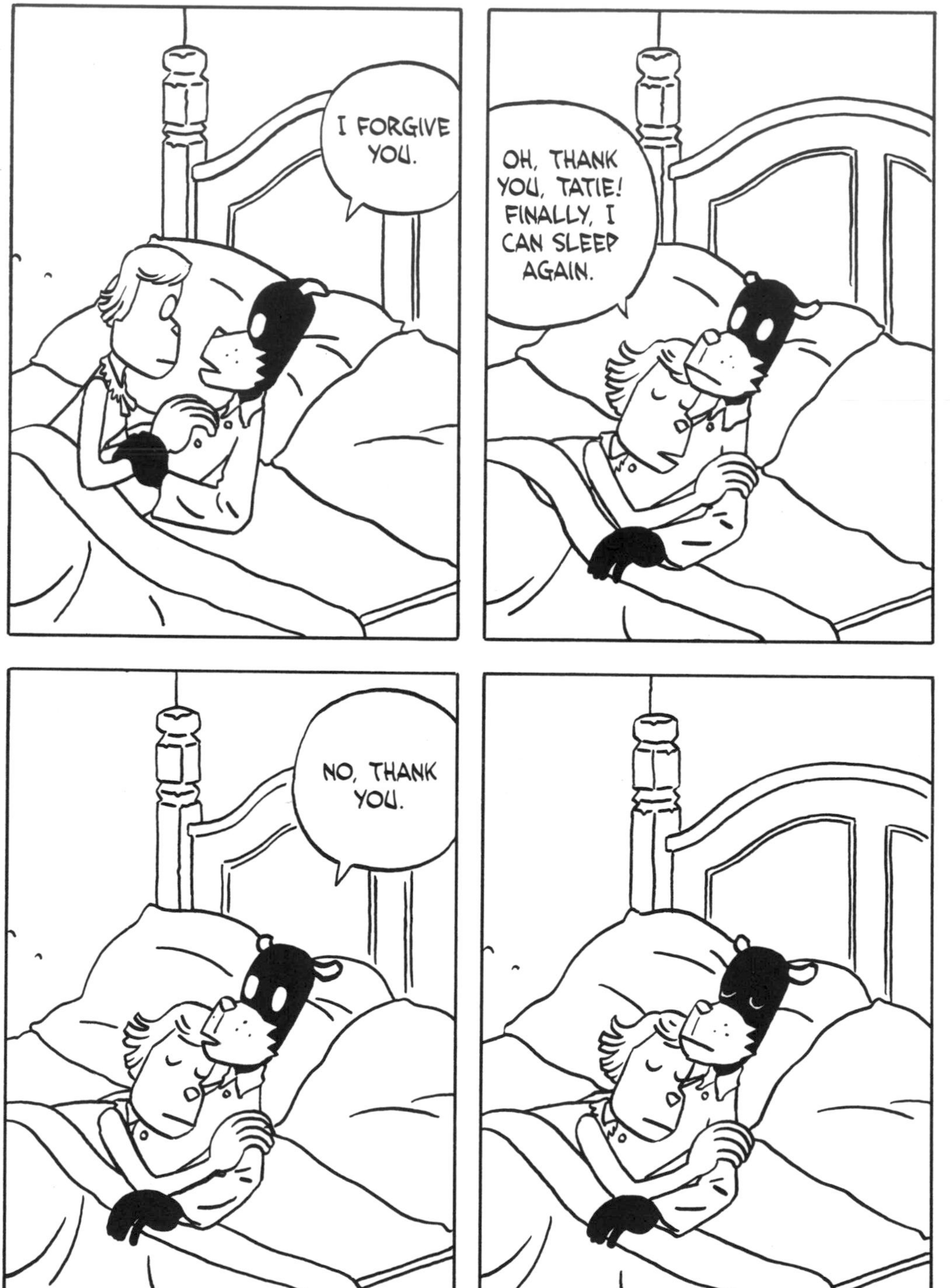
I FORGIVE YOU.
OH, THANK YOU, TATIE! FINALLY, I CAN SLEEP AGAIN.
NO, THANK YOU.

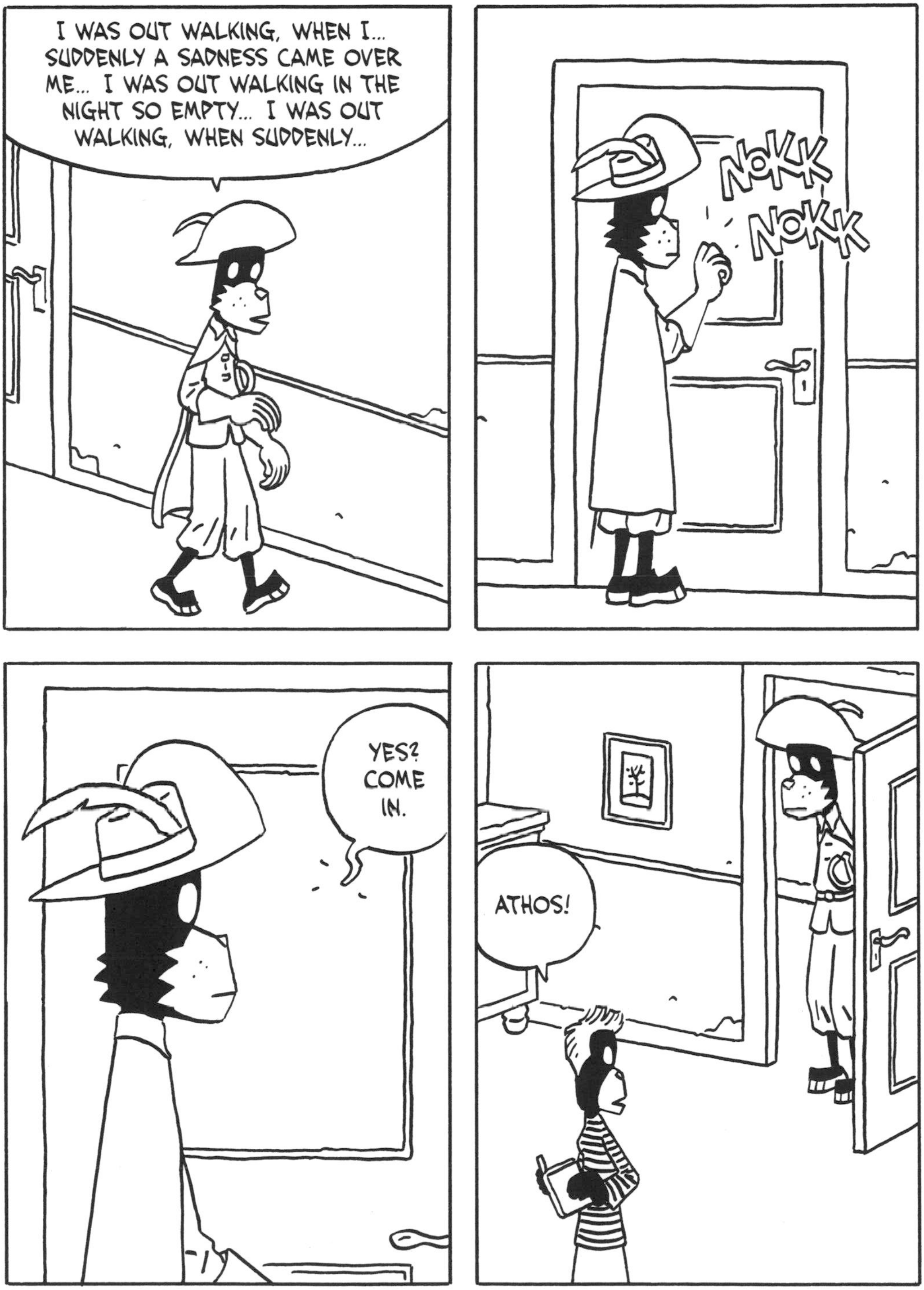
I WAS OUT WALKING, WHEN I... SUDDENLY A SADNESS CAME OVER ME... I WAS OUT WALKING IN THE NIGHT SO EMPTY... I WAS OUT WALKING, WHEN SUDDENLY...
NOKK
NOKK
YES? COME IN.
ATHOS!

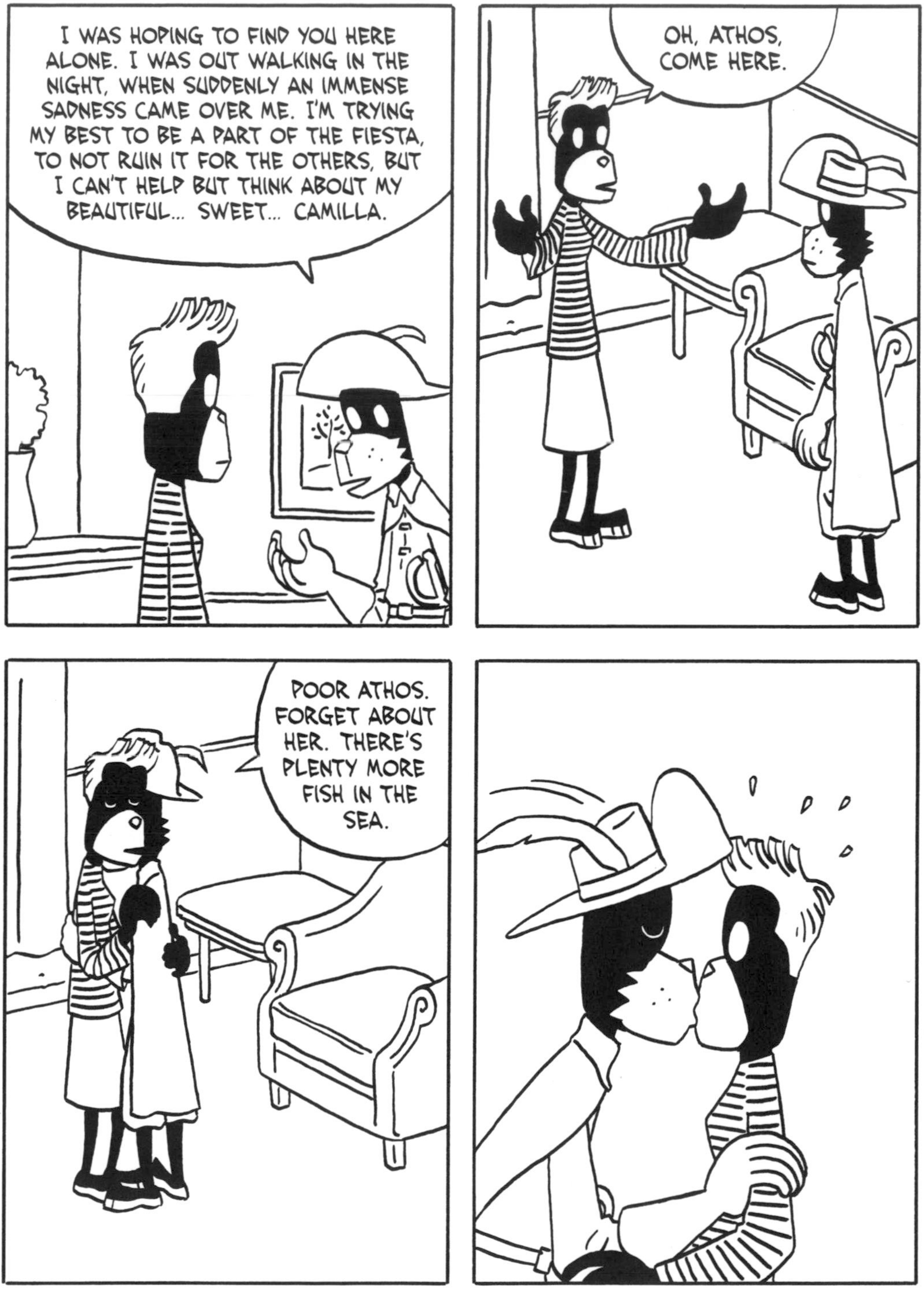
I WAS HOPING TO FIND YOU HERE ALONE. I WAS OUT WALKING IN THE NIGHT, WHEN SUDDENLY AN IMMENSE SADNESS CAME OVER ME. I'M TRYING MY BEST TO BE A PART OF THE FIESTA, TO NOT RUIN IT FOR THE OTHERS, BUT I CAN'T HELP BUT THINK ABOUT MY BEAUTIFUL... SWEET... CAMILLA.
OH, ATHOS, COME HERE.
POOR ATHOS. FORGET ABOUT HER. THERE'S PLENTY MORE FISH IN THE SEA.

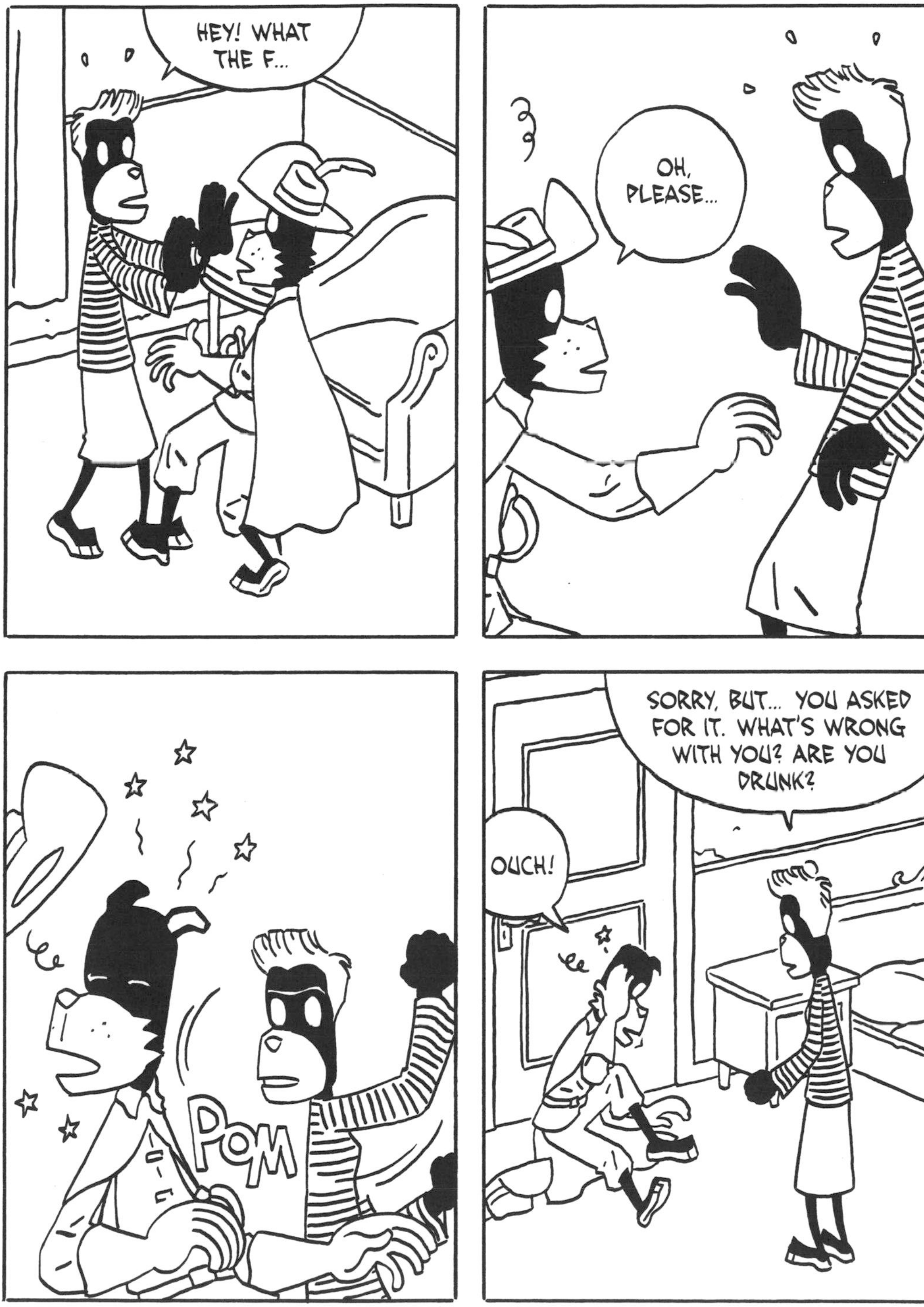
HEY! WHAT THE F...
OH, PLEASE...
POM
SORRY, BUT... YOU ASKED FOR IT. WHAT'S WRONG WITH YOU? ARE YOU DRUNK?
OUCH!

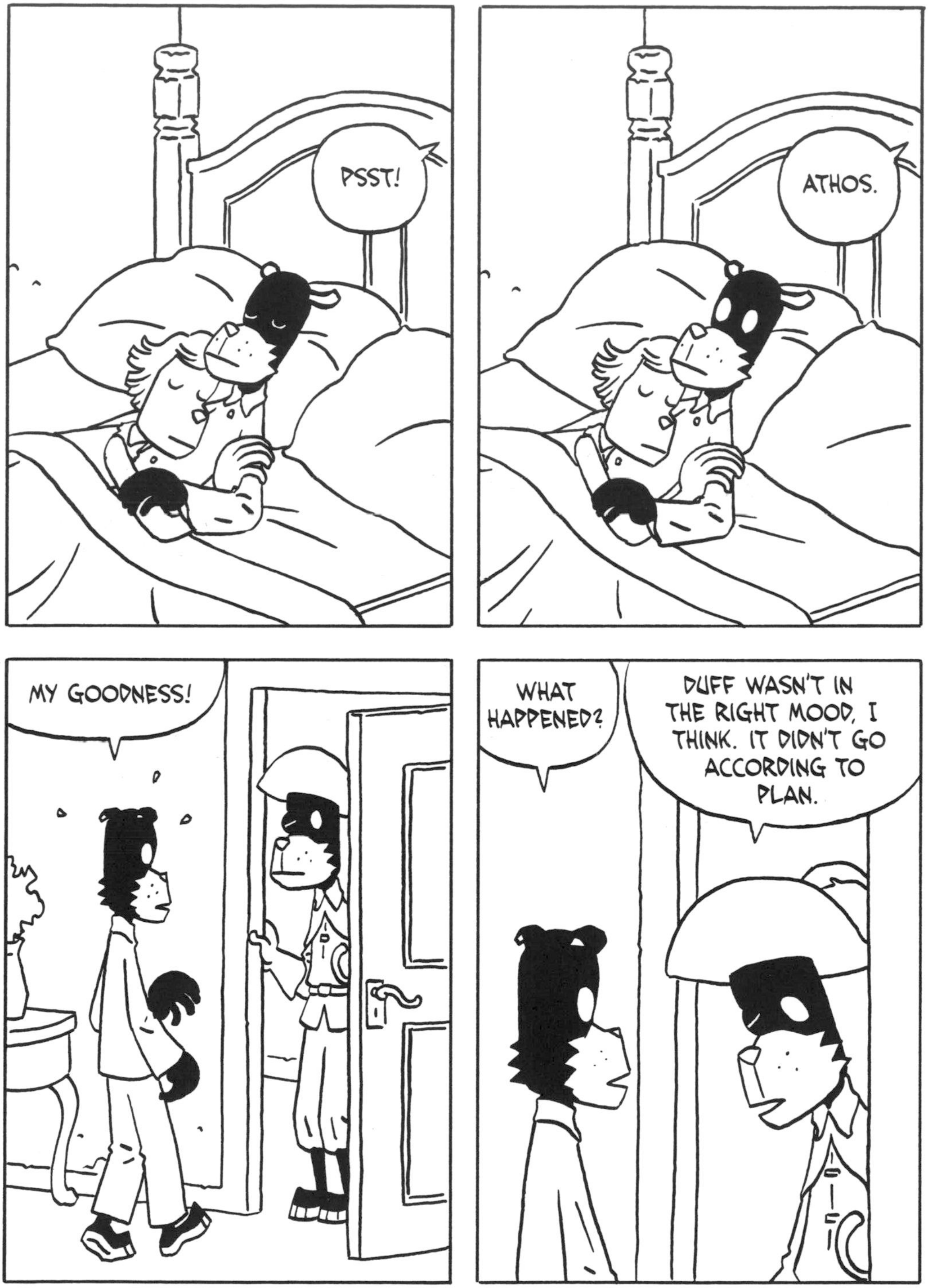
PSST!
ATHOS.
MY GOODNESS!
WHAT HAPPENED?
DUFF WASN'T IN THE RIGHT MOOD, I THINK. IT DIDN'T GO ACCORDING TO PLAN.

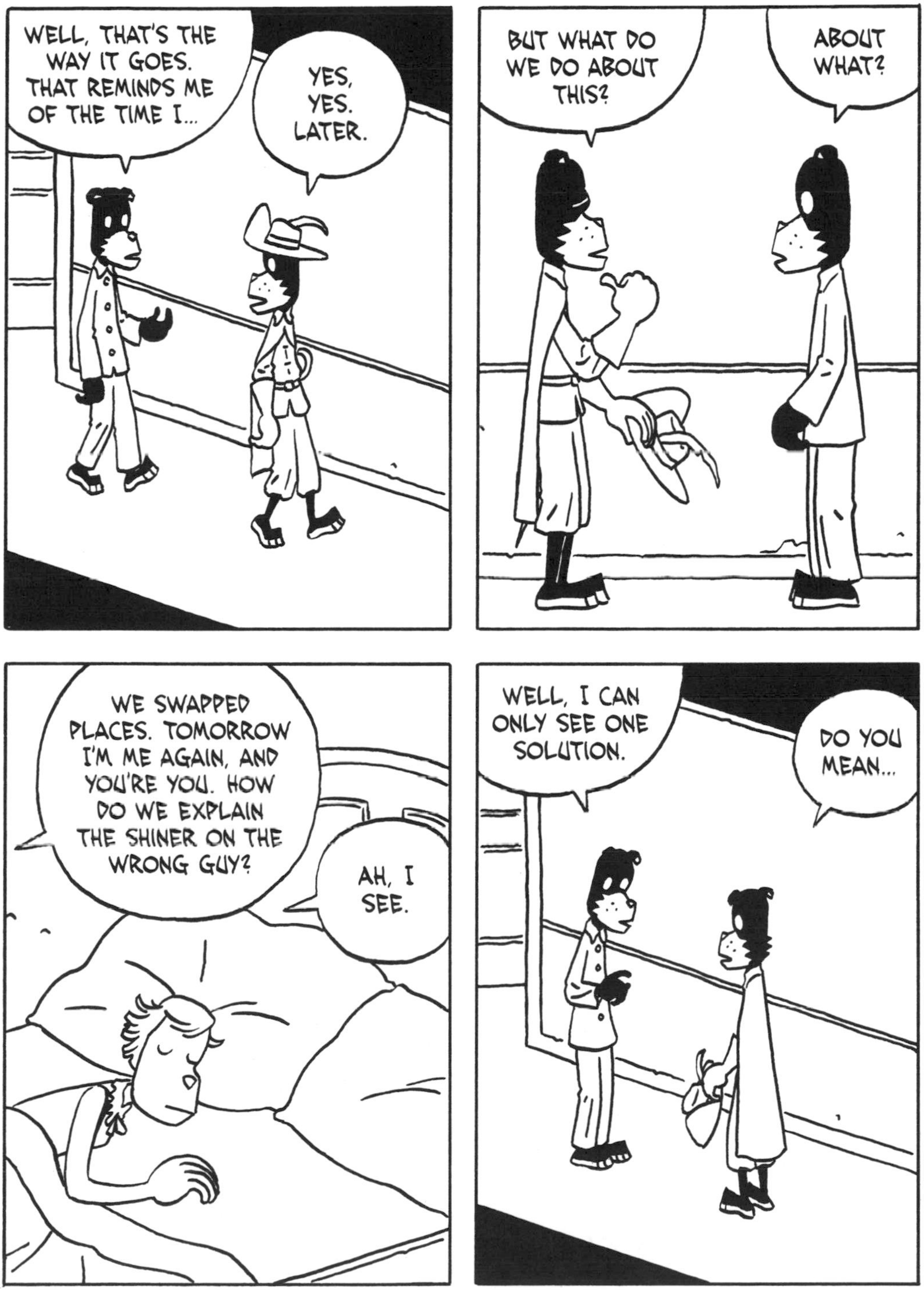
WELL, THAT'S THE WAY IT GOES. THAT REMINDS ME OF THE TIME I...
YES, YES. LATER.
BUT WHAT DO WE DO ABOUT THIS?
ABOUT WHAT?
WE SWAPPED PLACES. TOMORROW I'M ME AGAIN, AND YOU'RE YOU. HOW DO WE EXPLAIN THE SHINER ON THE WRONG GUY?
AH, I SEE.
WELL, I CAN ONLY SEE ONE SOLUTION.
DO YOU MEAN...

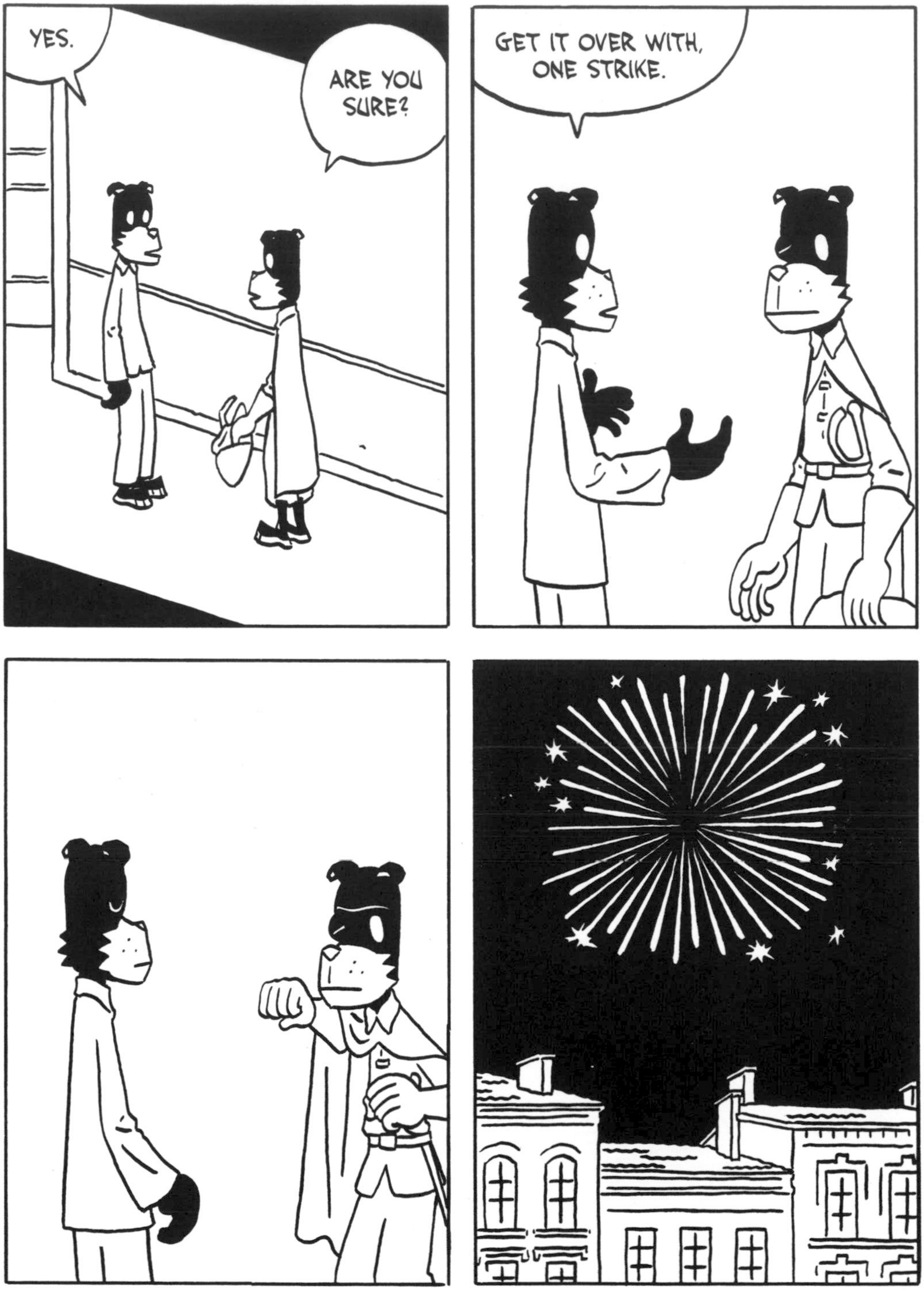
YES.
ARE YOU SURE?
GET IT OVER WITH, ONE STRIKE.

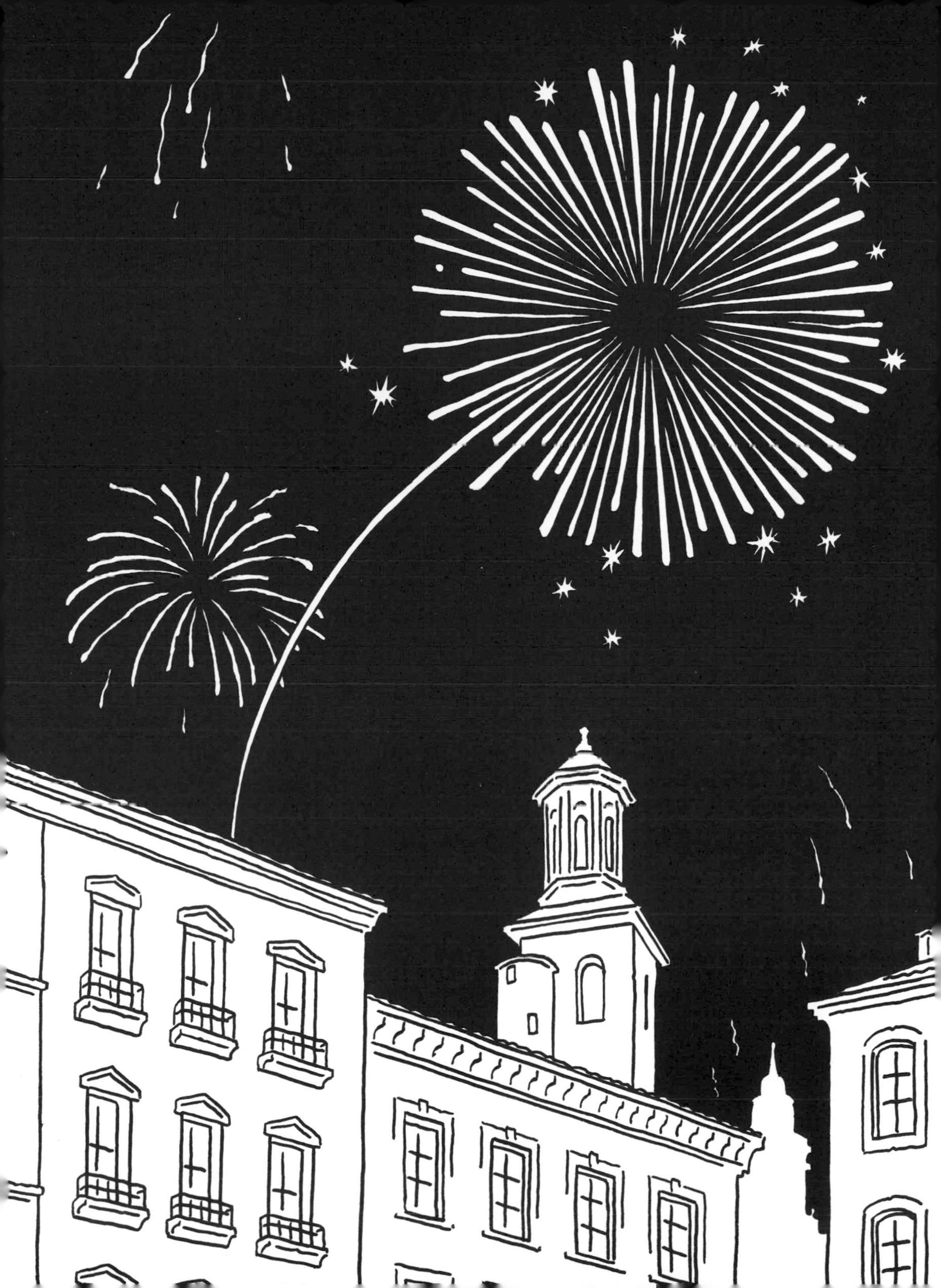

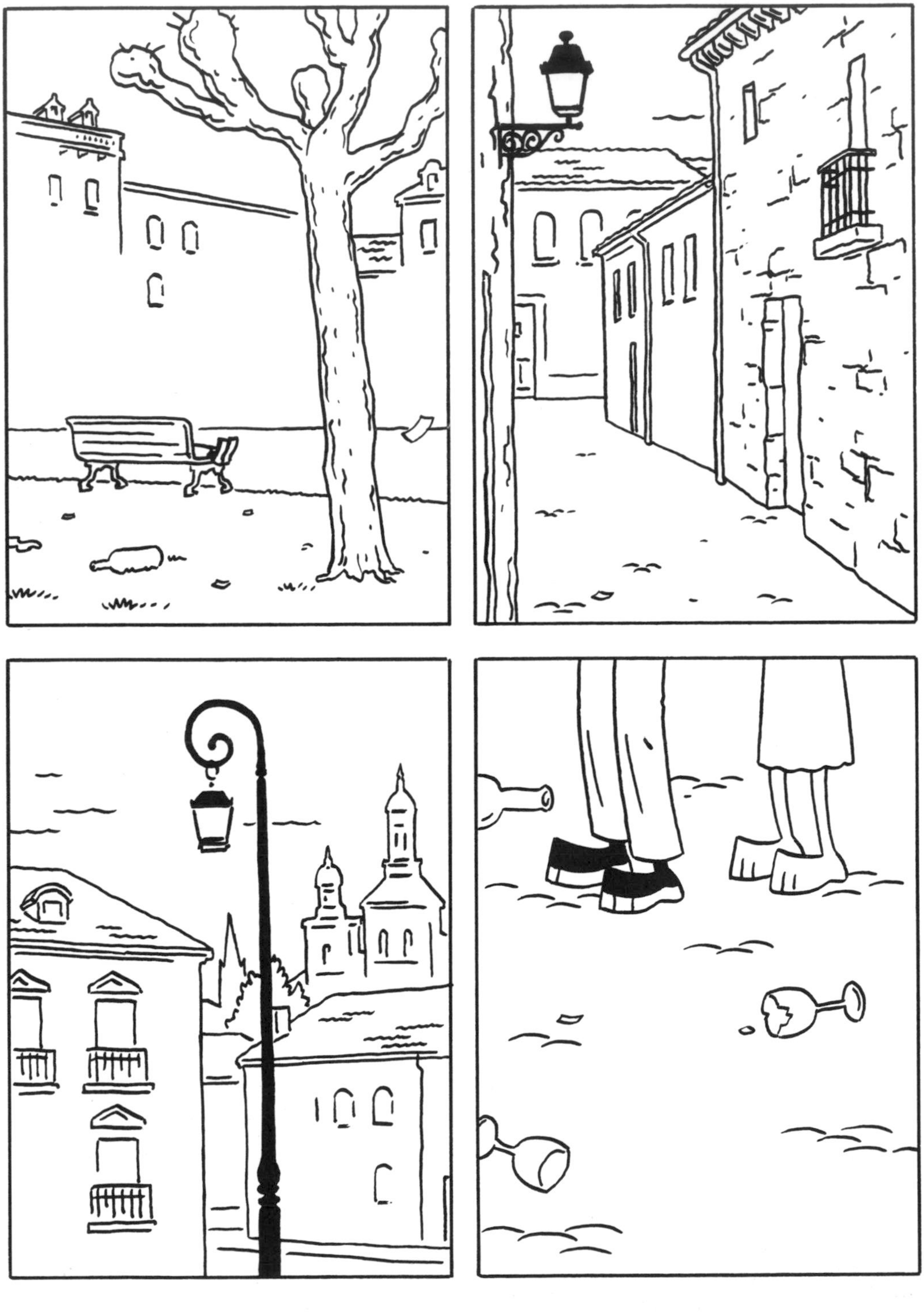

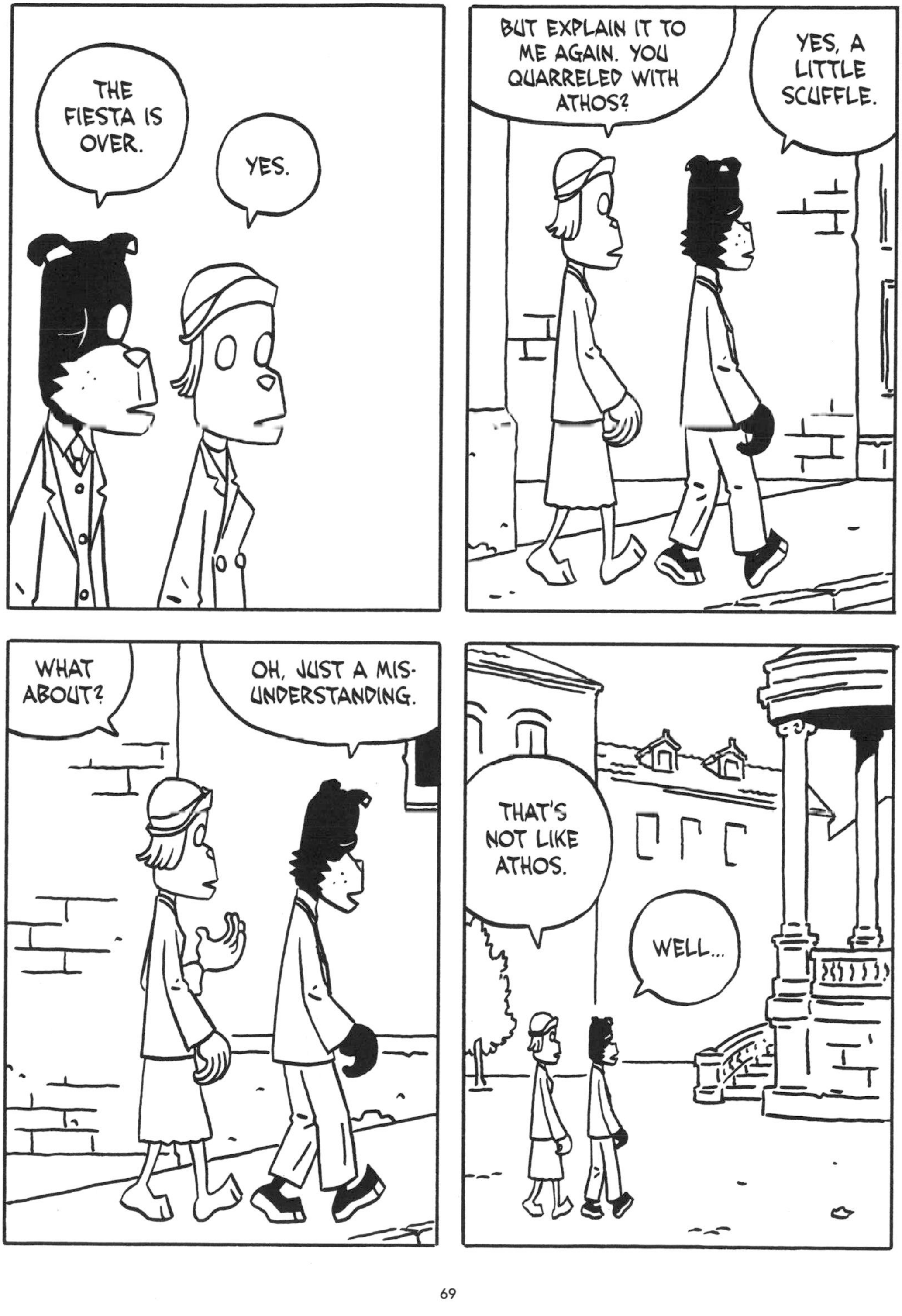
THE FIESTA IS OVER.
YES.
BUT EXPLAIN IT TO ME AGAIN. YOU QUARRELED WITH ATHOS?
YES, A LITTLE SCUFFLE.
WHAT ABOUT?
OH, JUST A MIS-UNDERSTANDING.
THAT'S NOT LIKE ATHOS.
WELL...

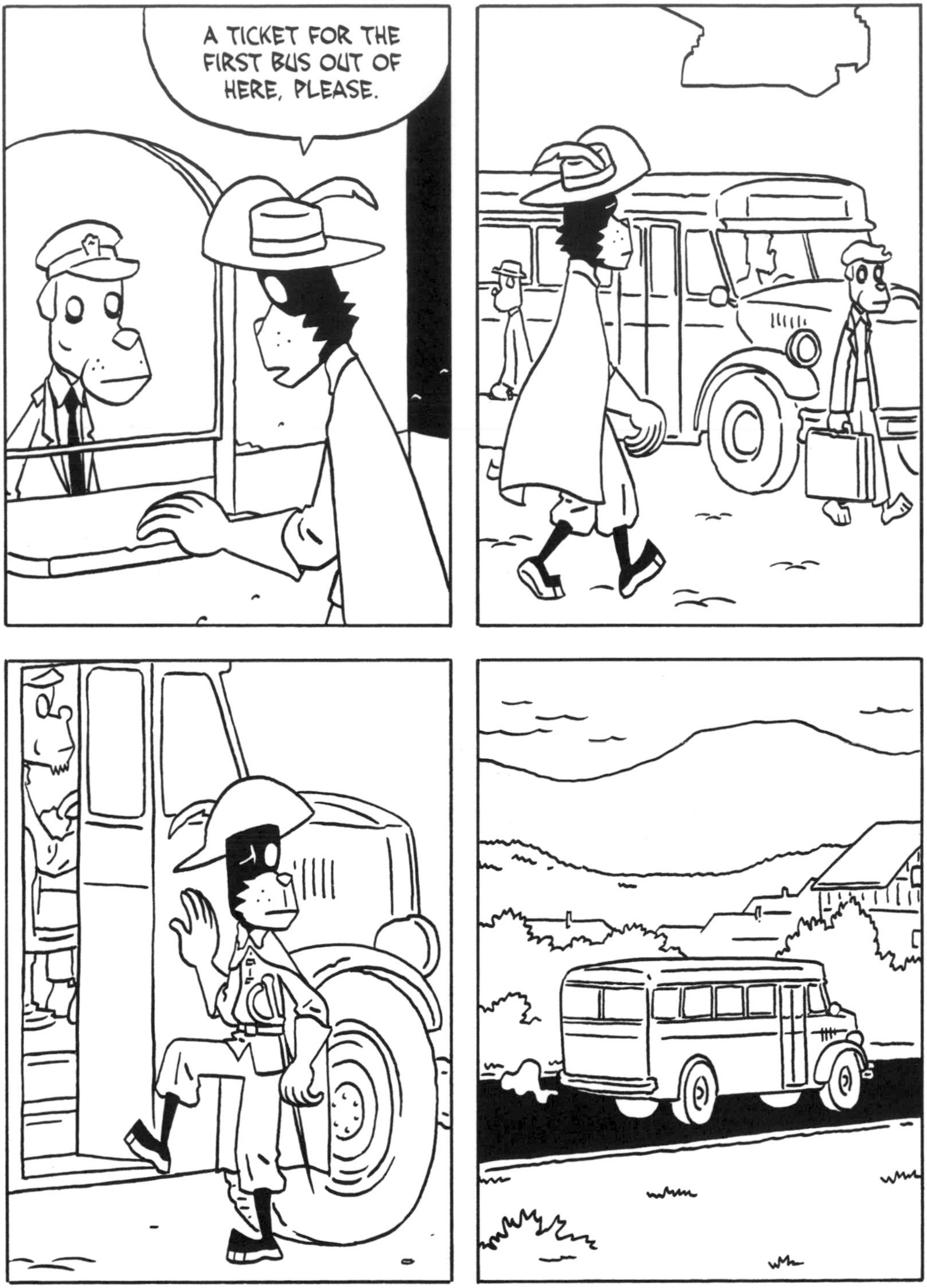
A TICKET FOR THE FIRST BUS OUT OF HERE, PLEASE.

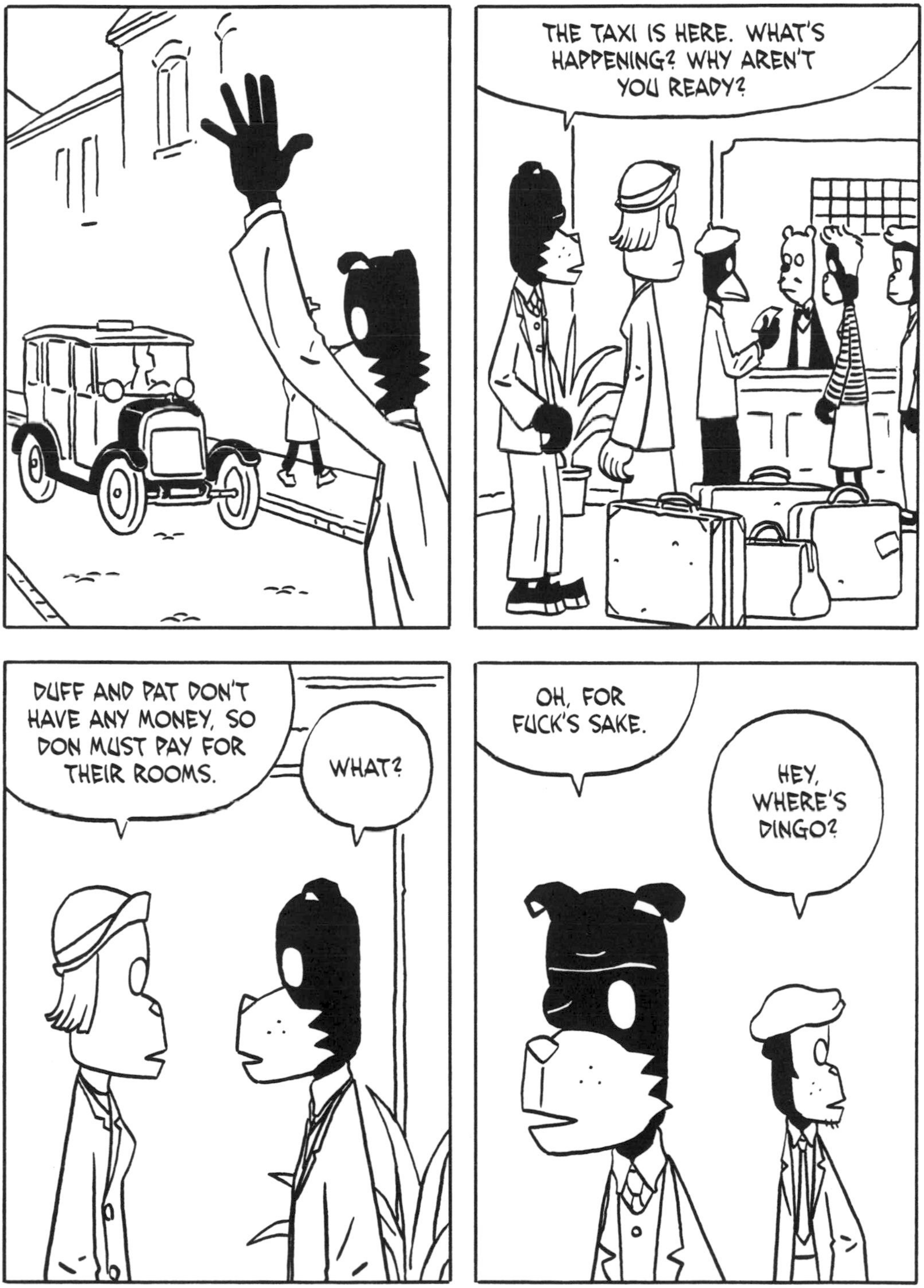
THE TAXI IS HERE. WHAT'S HAPPENING? WHY AREN'T YOU READY?
DUFF AND PAT DON'T HAVE ANY MONEY, SO DON MUST PAY FOR THEIR ROOMS.
WHAT?
OH, FOR FUCK'S SAKE.
HEY, WHERE'S DINGO?

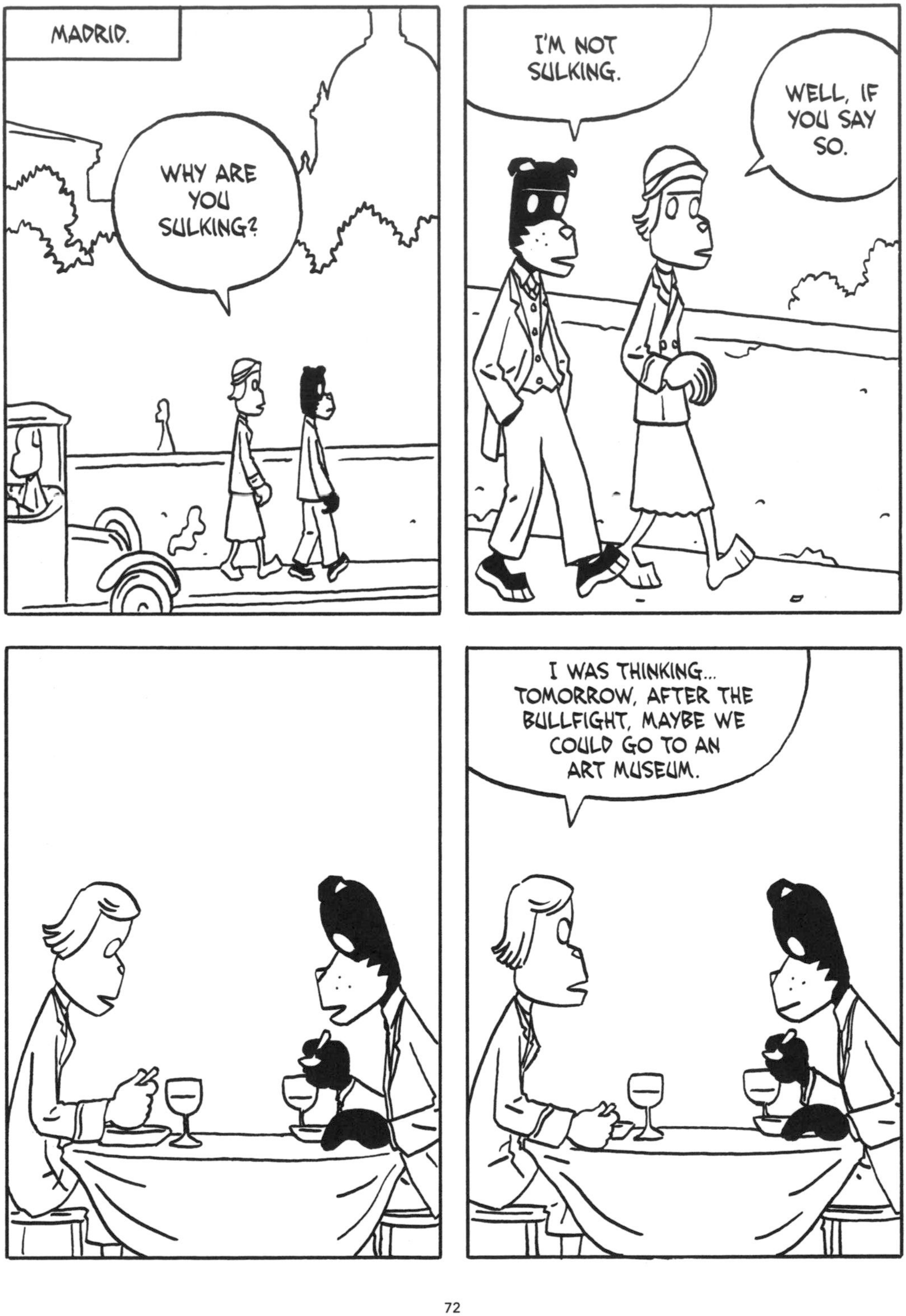
MADRID.
WHY ARE YOU SULKING?
I'M NOT SULKING.
WELL, IF YOU SAY SO.
I WAS THINKING... TOMORROW, AFTER THE BULLFIGHT, MAYBE WE COULD GO TO AN ART MUSEUM.

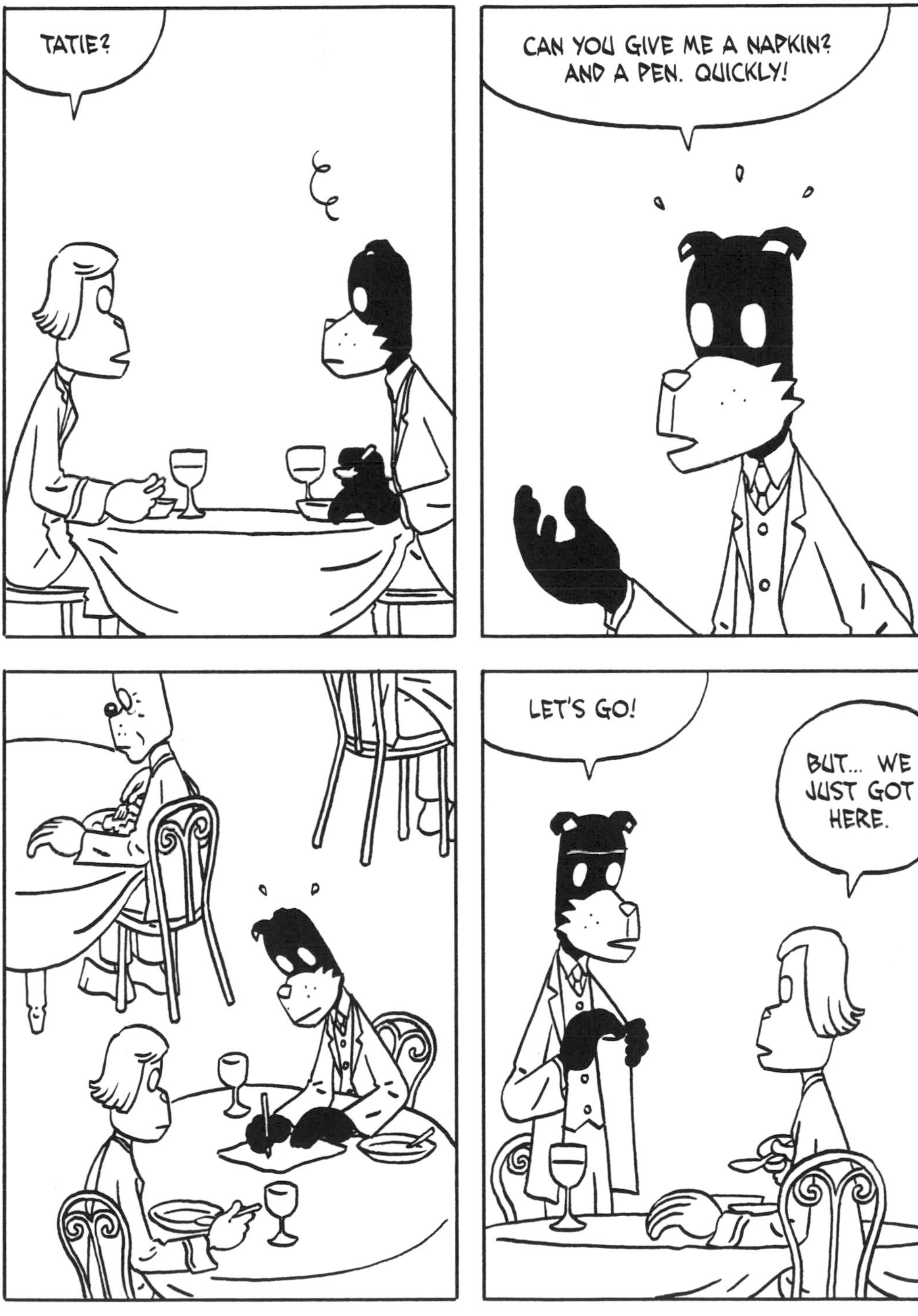
TATIE?
CAN YOU GIVE ME A NAPKIN? AND A PEN. QUICKLY!
LET'S GO!
BUT... WE JUST GOT HERE.

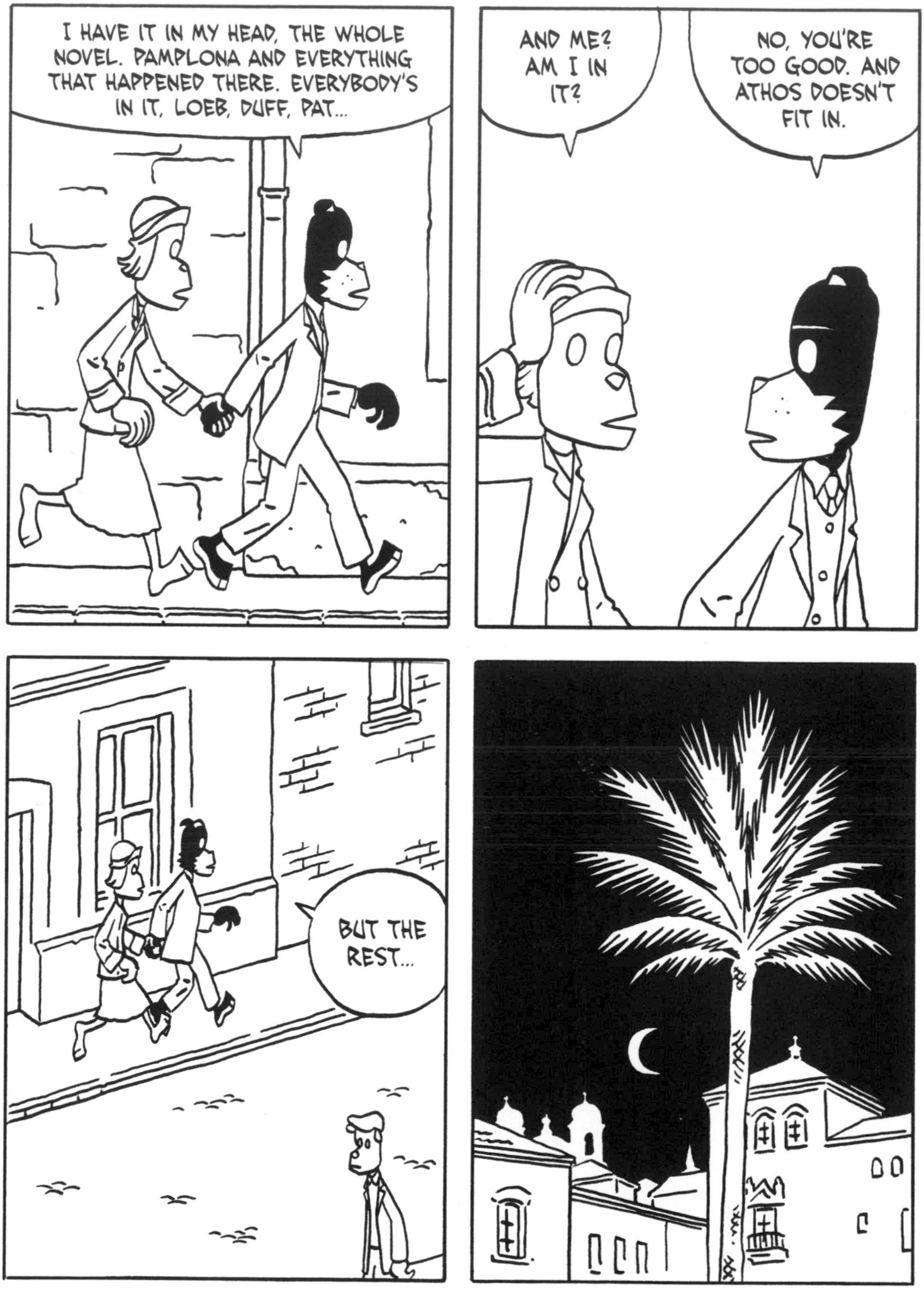
I HAVE IT IN MY HEAD, THE WHOLE NOVEL. PAMPLONA AND EVERYTHING THAT HAPPENED THERE. EVERYBODY'S IN IT, LOEB, DUFF, PAT...
AND ME? AM I IN IT?
NO, YOU'RE TOO GOOD. AND ATHOS DOESN'T FIT IN.
BUT THE REST...

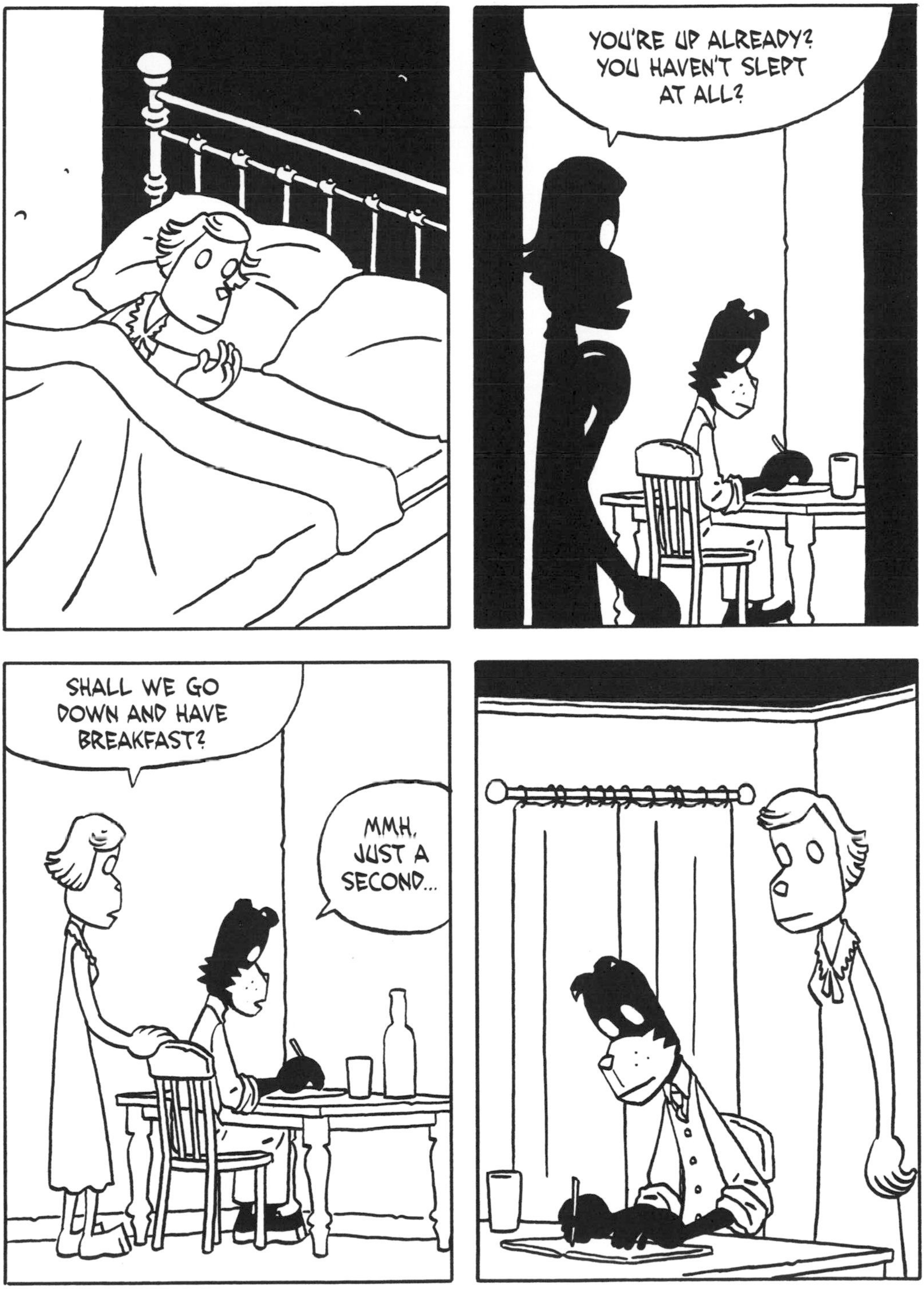
YOU'RE UP ALREADY? YOU HAVEN'T SLEPT AT ALL?
SHALL WE GO DOWN AND HAVE BREAKFAST?
MMH, JUST A SECOND...

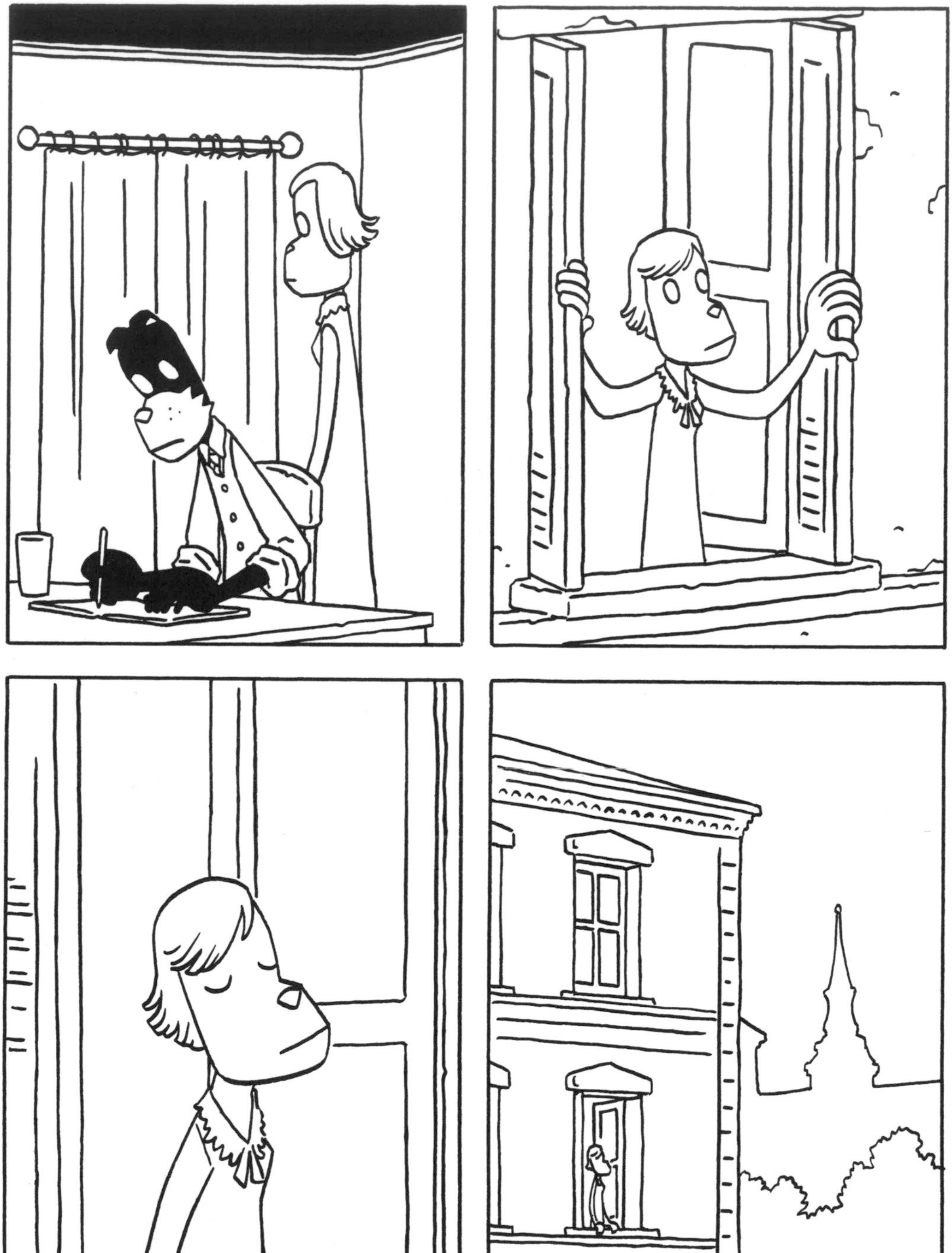
jason · 20

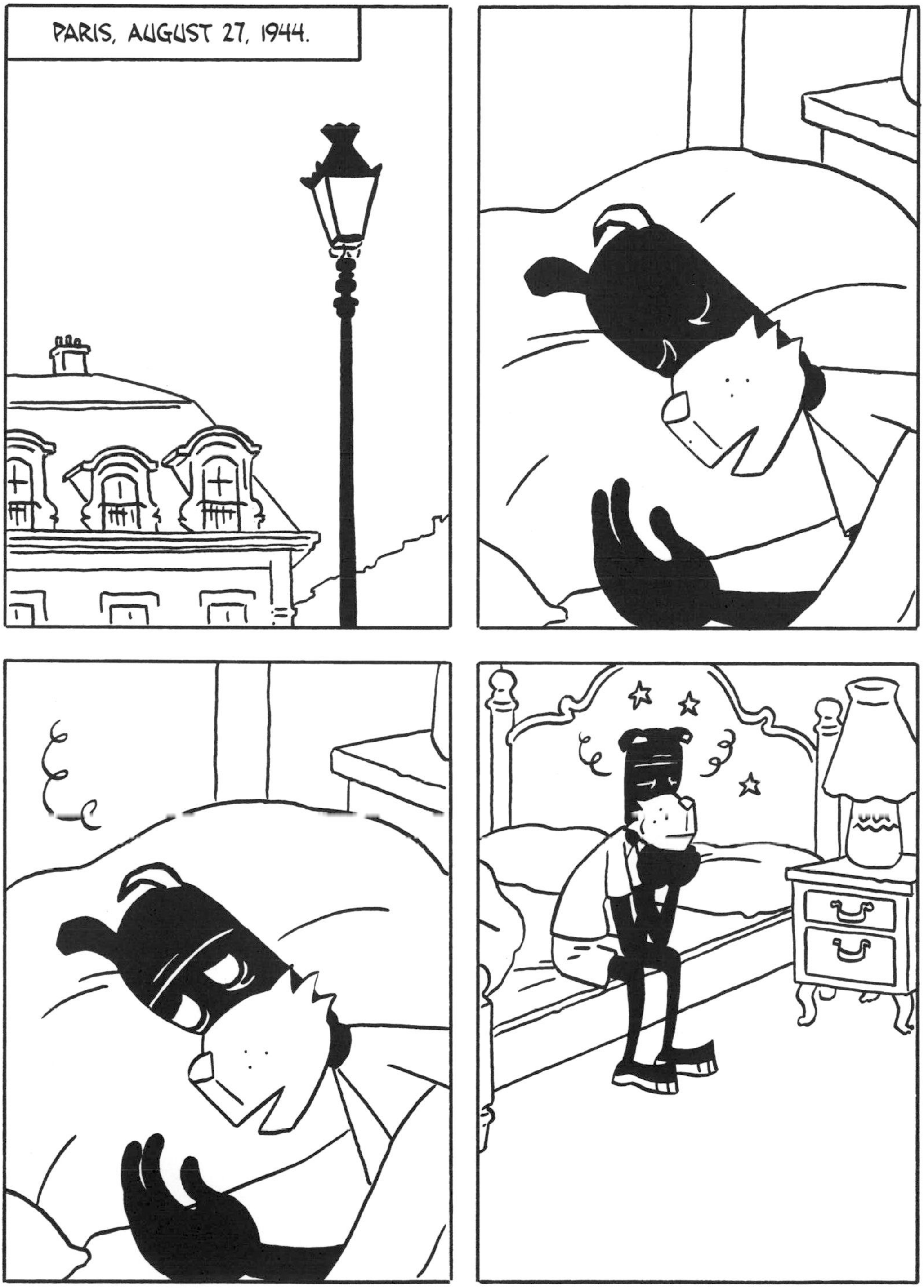
PARIS, AUGUST 27, 1944.

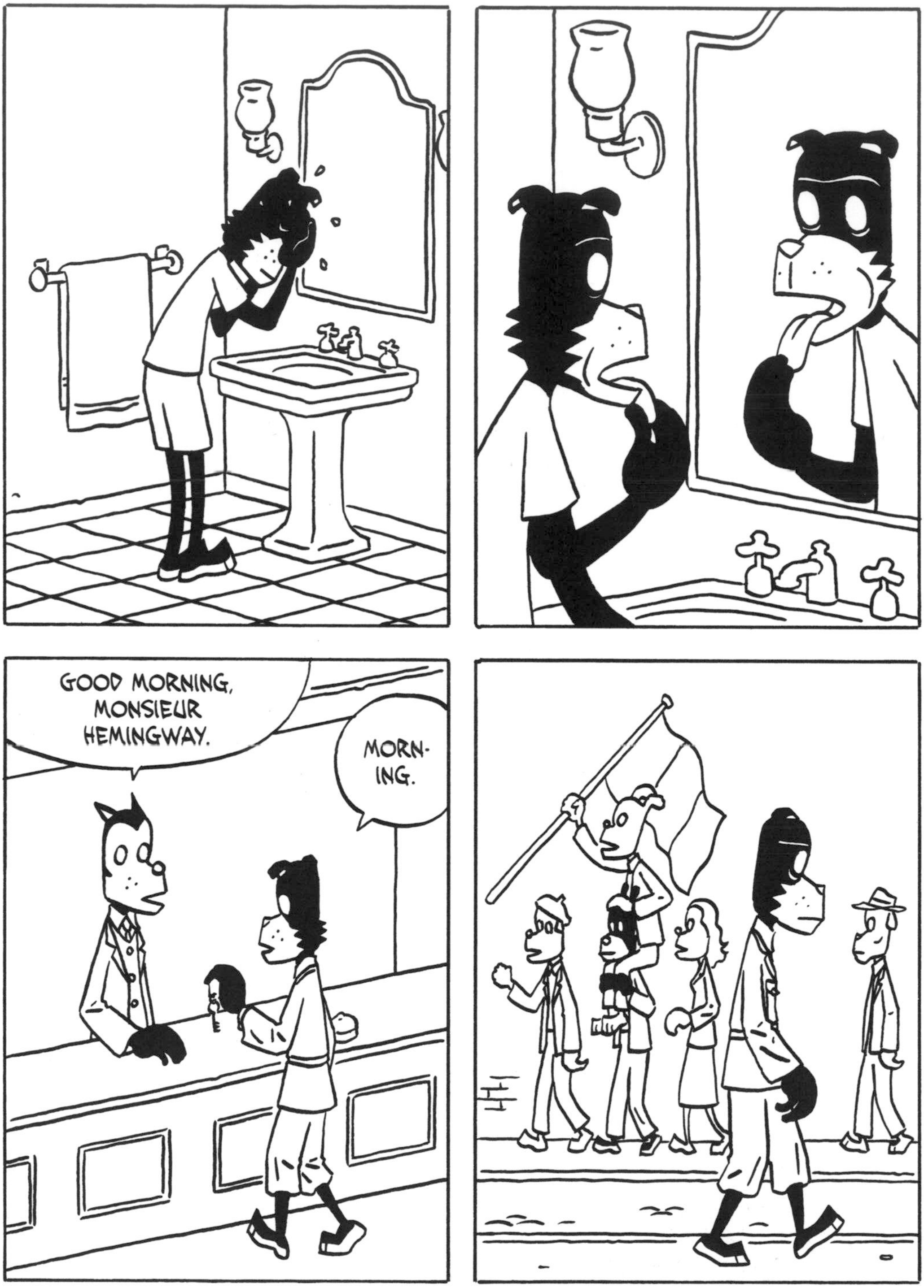
GOOD MORNING, MONSIEUR HEMINGWAY.
MORN-ING.

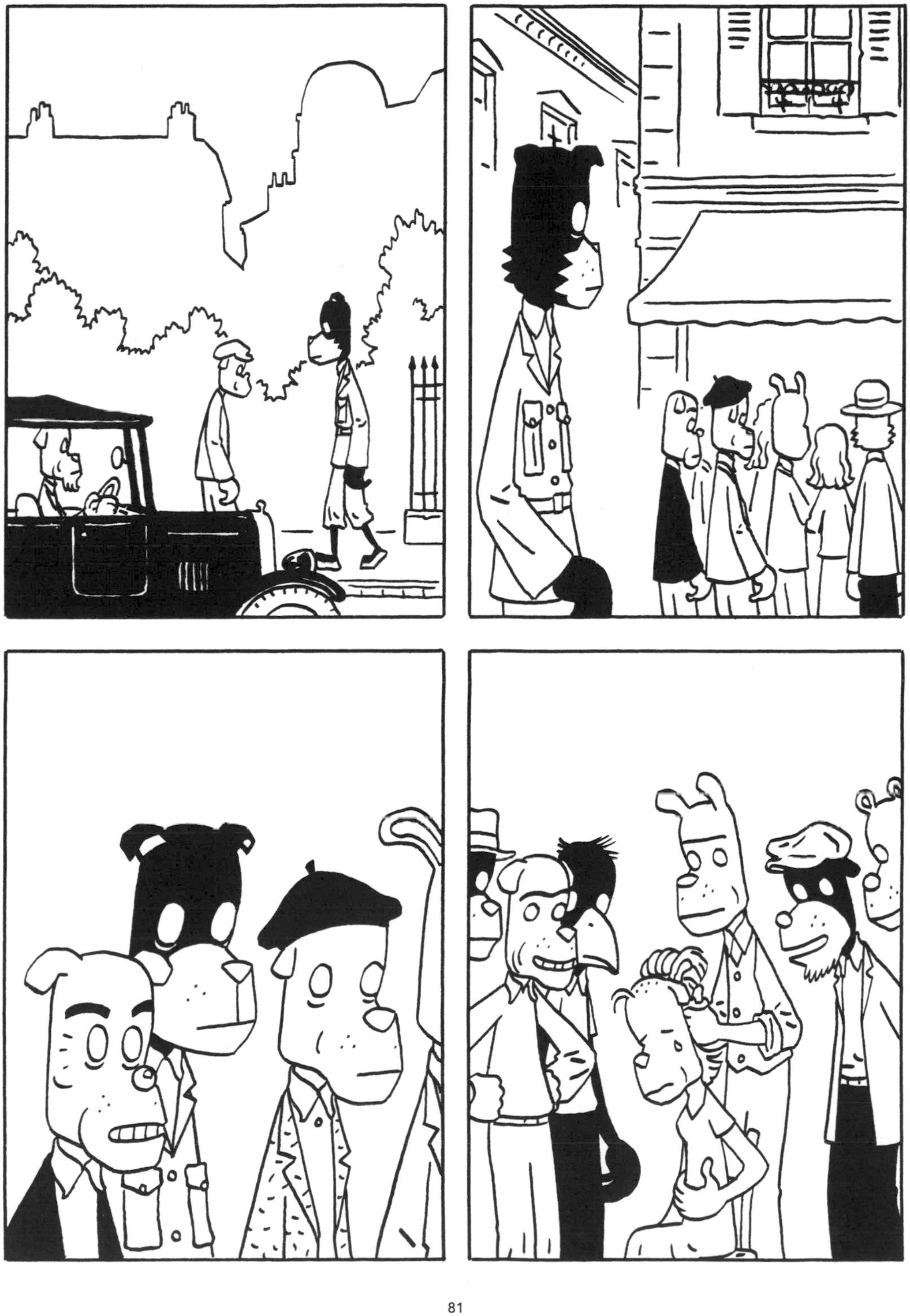

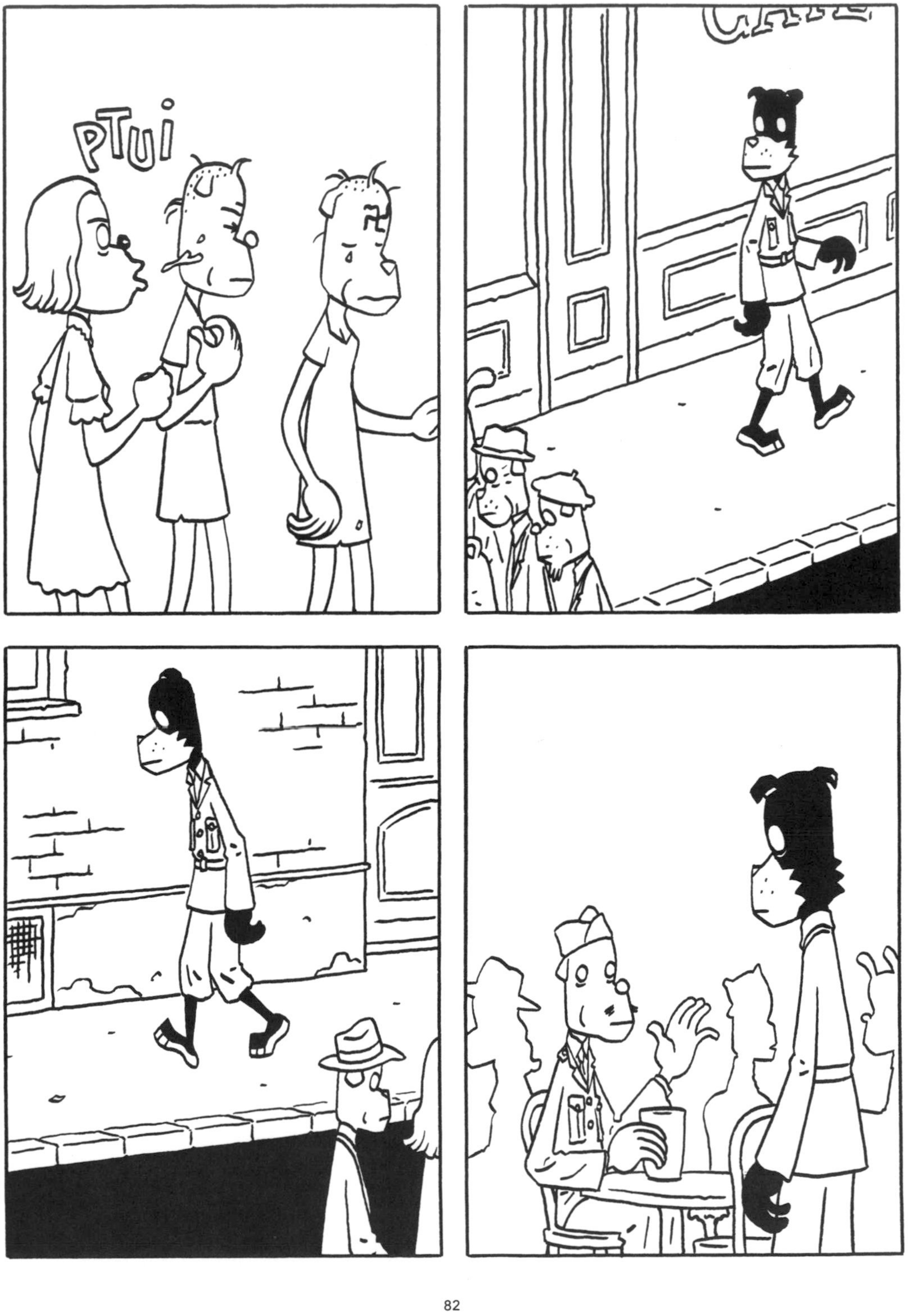
PTUi

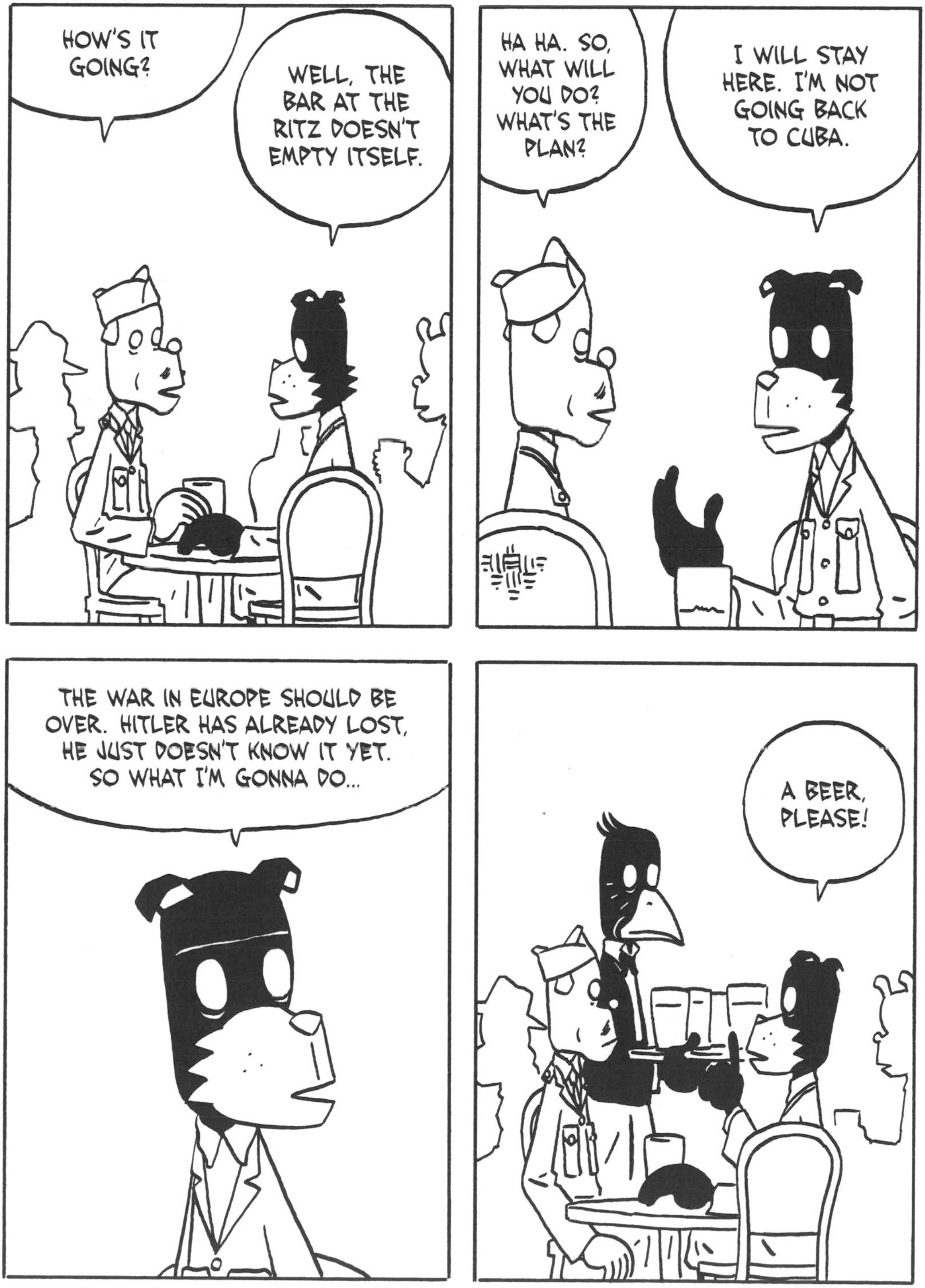
HOW'S IT GOING?
WELL, THE BAR AT THE RITZ DOESN'T EMPTY ITSELF.
HA HA. SO, WHAT WILL YOU DO? WHAT'S THE PLAN?
I WILL STAY HERE. I'M NOT GOING BACK TO CUBA.
THE WAR IN EUROPE SHOULD BE OVER. HITLER HAS ALREADY LOST, HE JUST DOESN'T KNOW IT YET. SO WHAT I'M GONNA DO...
A BEER, PLEASE!

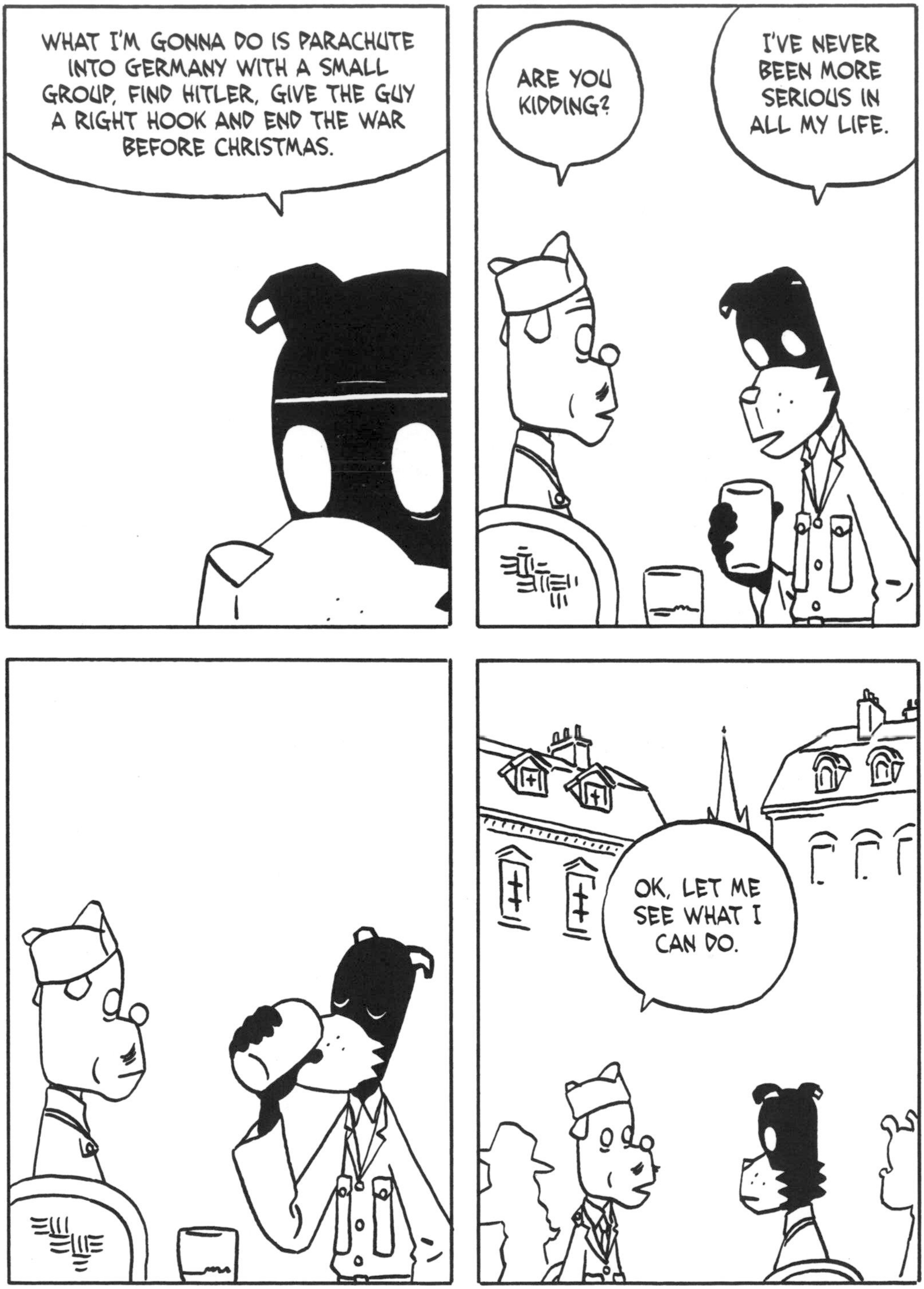
WHAT I'M GONNA DO IS PARACHUTE INTO GERMANY WITH A SMALL GROUP, FIND HITLER, GIVE THE GUY A RIGHT HOOK AND END THE WAR BEFORE CHRISTMAS.
ARE YOU KIDDING?
I'VE NEVER BEEN MORE SERIOUS IN ALL MY LIFE.
OK, LET ME SEE WHAT I CAN DO.

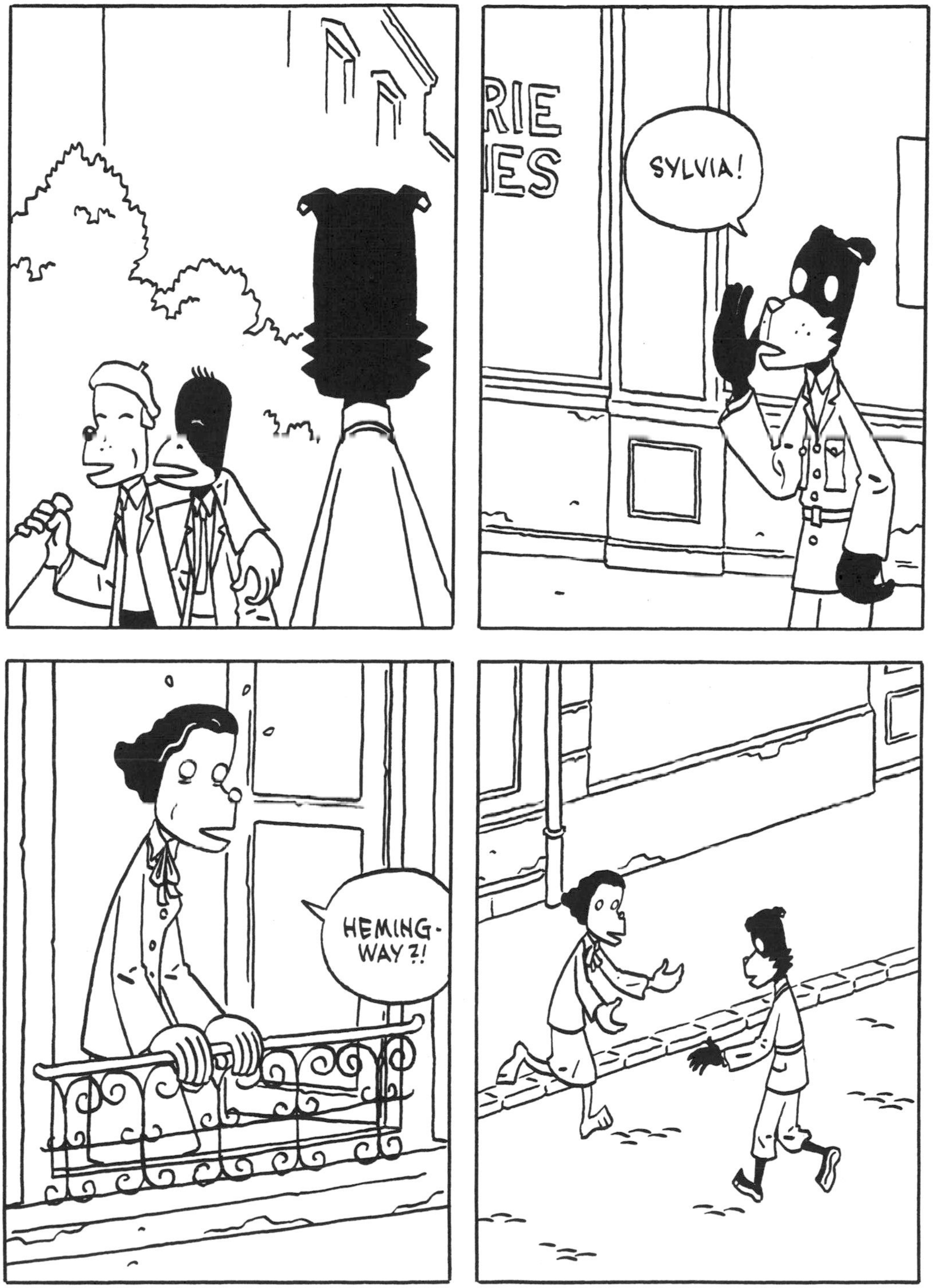
RIE
IES
SYLVIA!
HEMING-
WAY?!

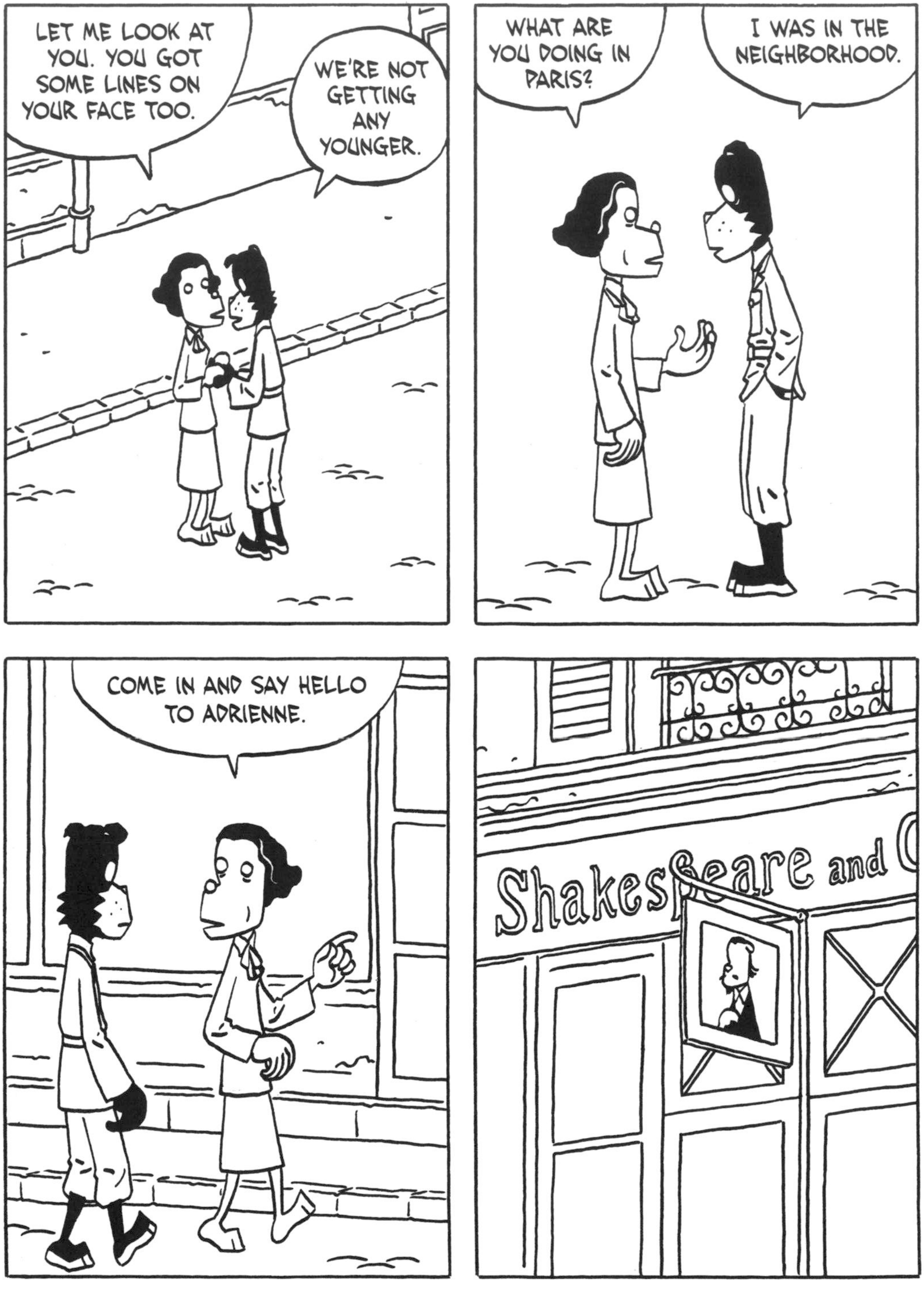
LET ME LOOK AT YOU. YOU GOT SOME LINES ON YOUR FACE TOO.
WE'RE NOT GETTING ANY YOUNGER.
WHAT ARE YOU DOING IN PARIS?
I WAS IN THE NEIGHBORHOOD.
COME IN AND SAY HELLO TO ADRIENNE.
Shakespeare and C

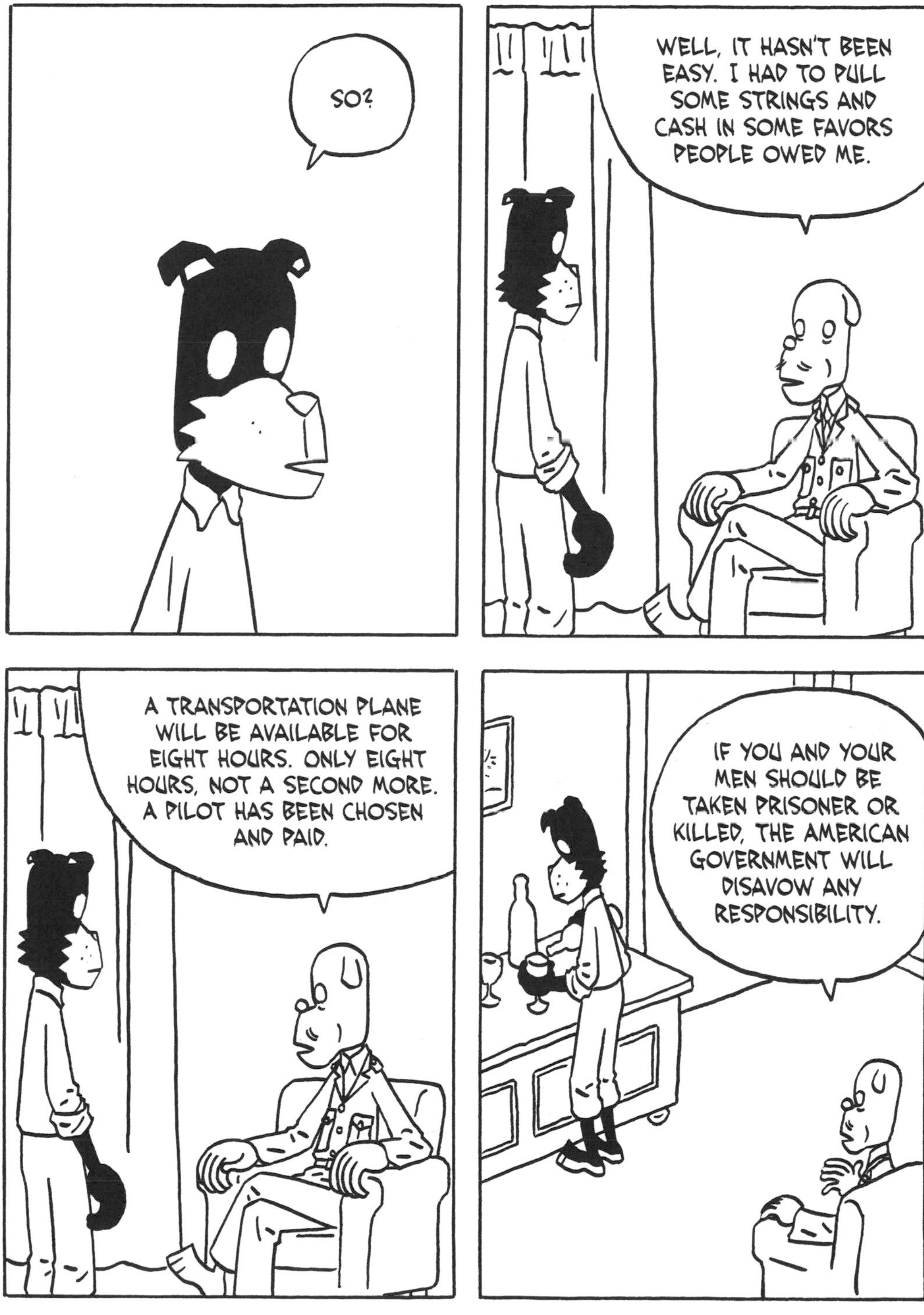
SO?
WELL, IT HASN'T BEEN EASY. I HAD TO PULL SOME STRINGS AND CASH IN SOME FAVORS PEOPLE OWED ME.
A TRANSPORTATION PLANE WILL BE AVAILABLE FOR EIGHT HOURS. ONLY EIGHT HOURS, NOT A SECOND MORE. A PILOT HAS BEEN CHOSEN AND PAID.
IF YOU AND YOUR MEN SHOULD BE TAKEN PRISONER OR KILLED, THE AMERICAN GOVERNMENT WILL DISAVOW ANY RESPONSIBILITY.

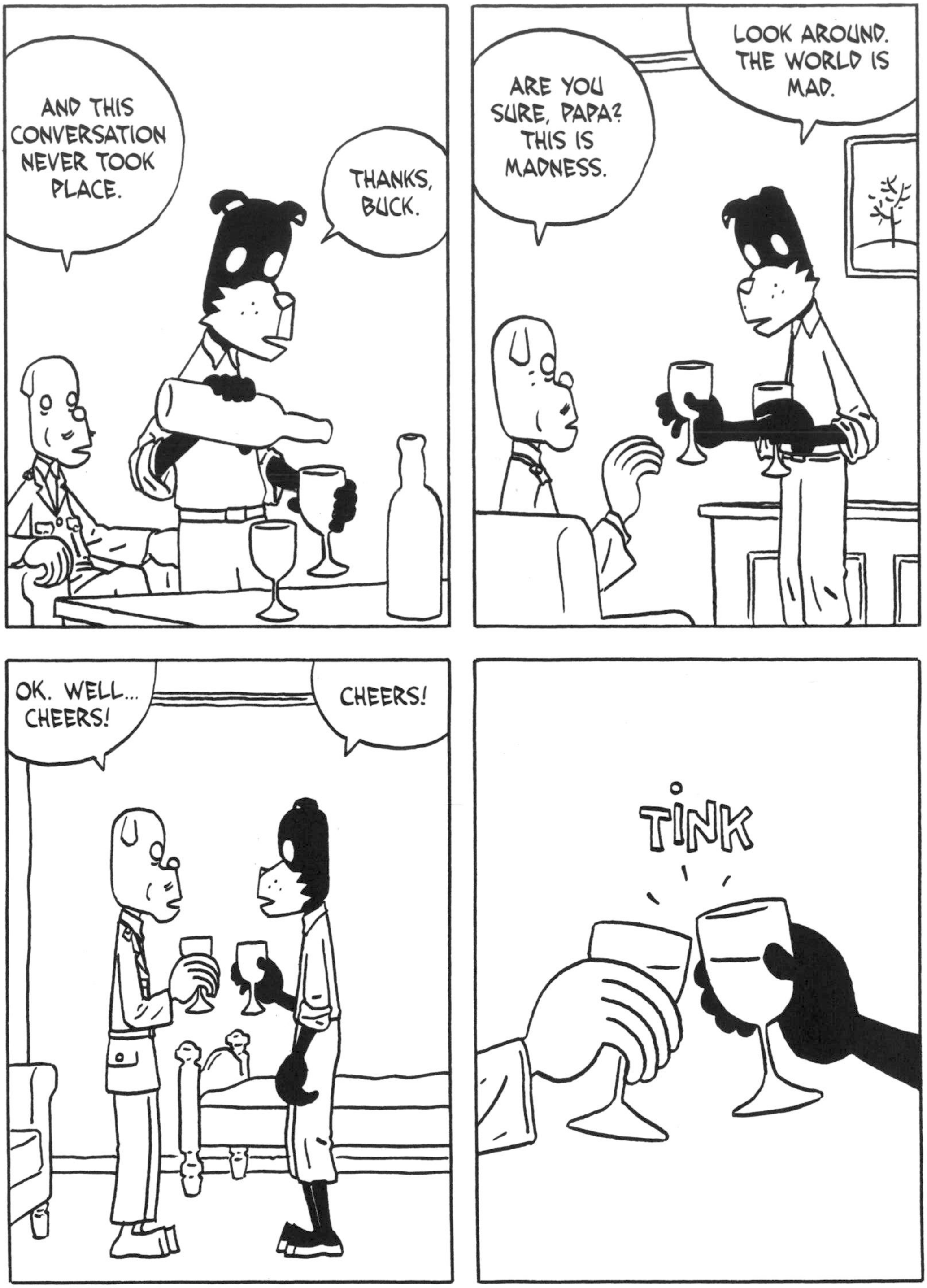
AND THIS CONVERSATION NEVER TOOK PLACE.
THANKS, BUCK.
ARE YOU SURE, PAPA? THIS IS MADNESS.
LOOK AROUND. THE WORLD IS MAD.
OK. WELL... CHEERS!
CHEERS!
TINK

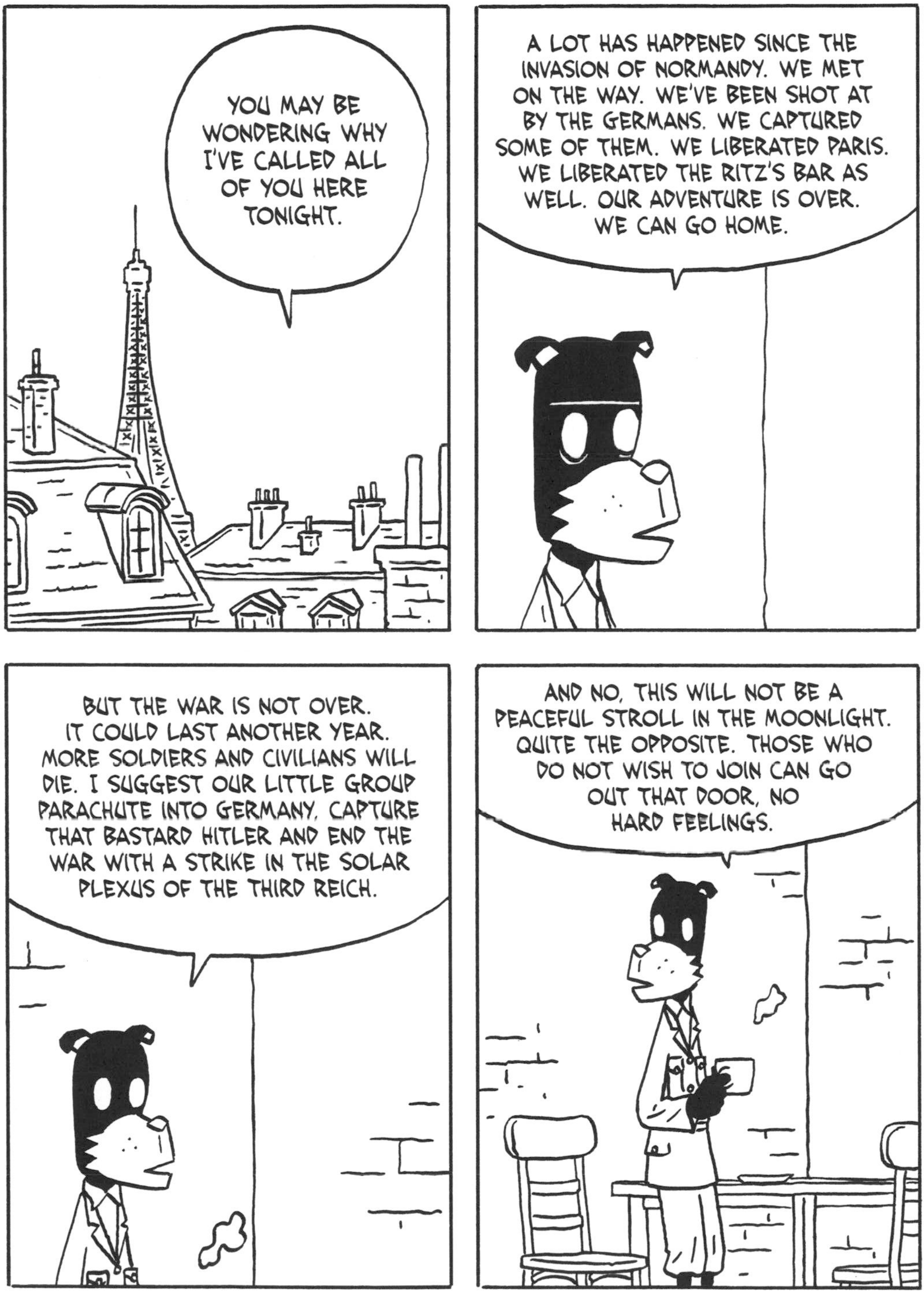
YOU MAY BE WONDERING WHY I'VE CALLED ALL OF YOU HERE TONIGHT.
A LOT HAS HAPPENED SINCE THE INVASION OF NORMANDY. WE MET ON THE WAY. WE'VE BEEN SHOT AT BY THE GERMANS. WE CAPTURED SOME OF THEM. WE LIBERATED PARIS. WE LIBERATED THE RITZ'S BAR AS WELL. OUR ADVENTURE IS OVER. WE CAN GO HOME.
BUT THE WAR IS NOT OVER. IT COULD LAST ANOTHER YEAR. MORE SOLDIERS AND CIVILIANS WILL DIE. I SUGGEST OUR LITTLE GROUP PARACHUTE INTO GERMANY, CAPTURE THAT BASTARD HITLER AND END THE WAR WITH A STRIKE IN THE SOLAR PLEXUS OF THE THIRD REICH.
AND NO, THIS WILL NOT BE A PEACEFUL STROLL IN THE MOONLIGHT. QUITE THE OPPOSITE. THOSE WHO DO NOT WISH TO JOIN CAN GO OUT THAT DOOR, NO HARD FEELINGS.

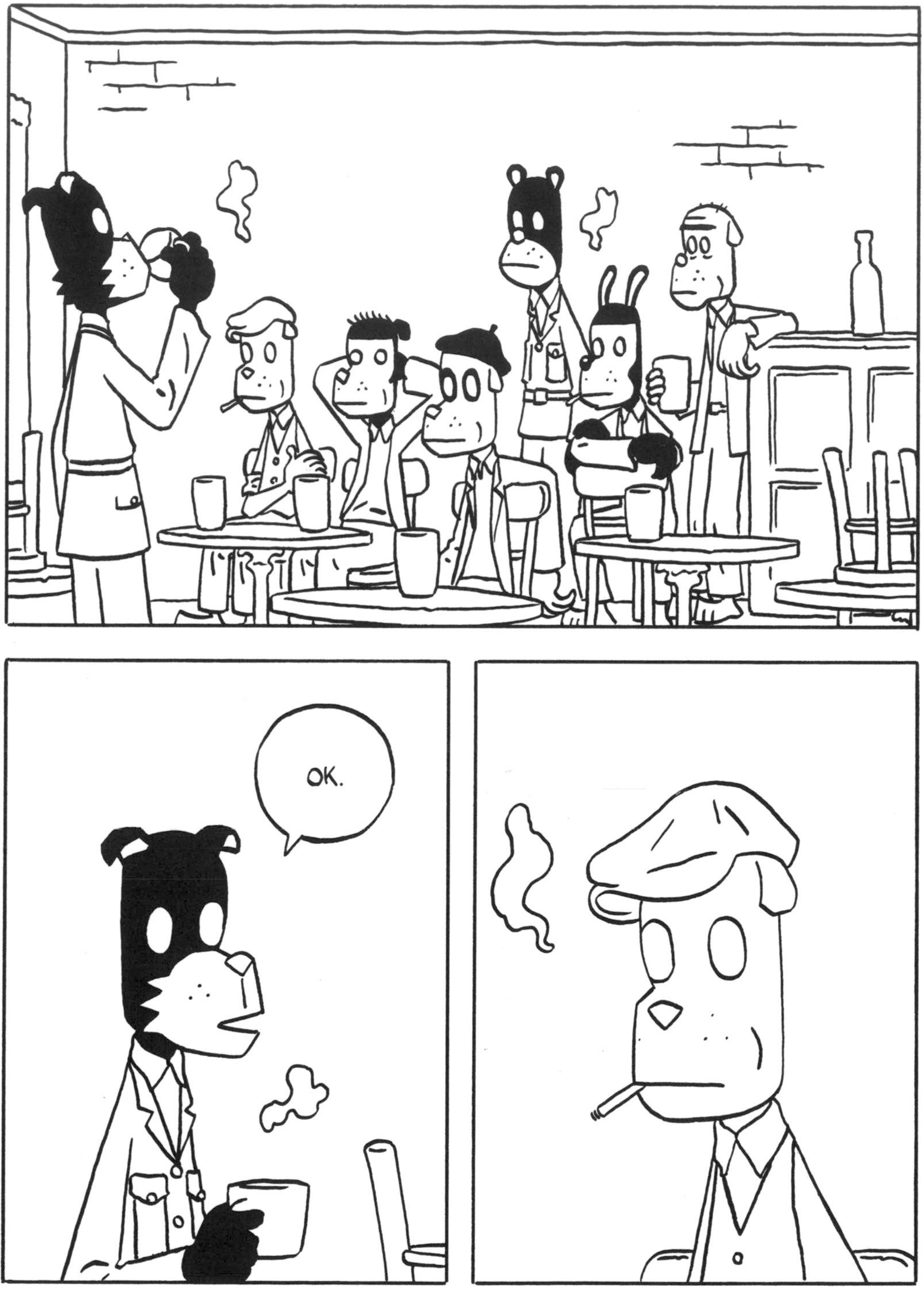
OK.

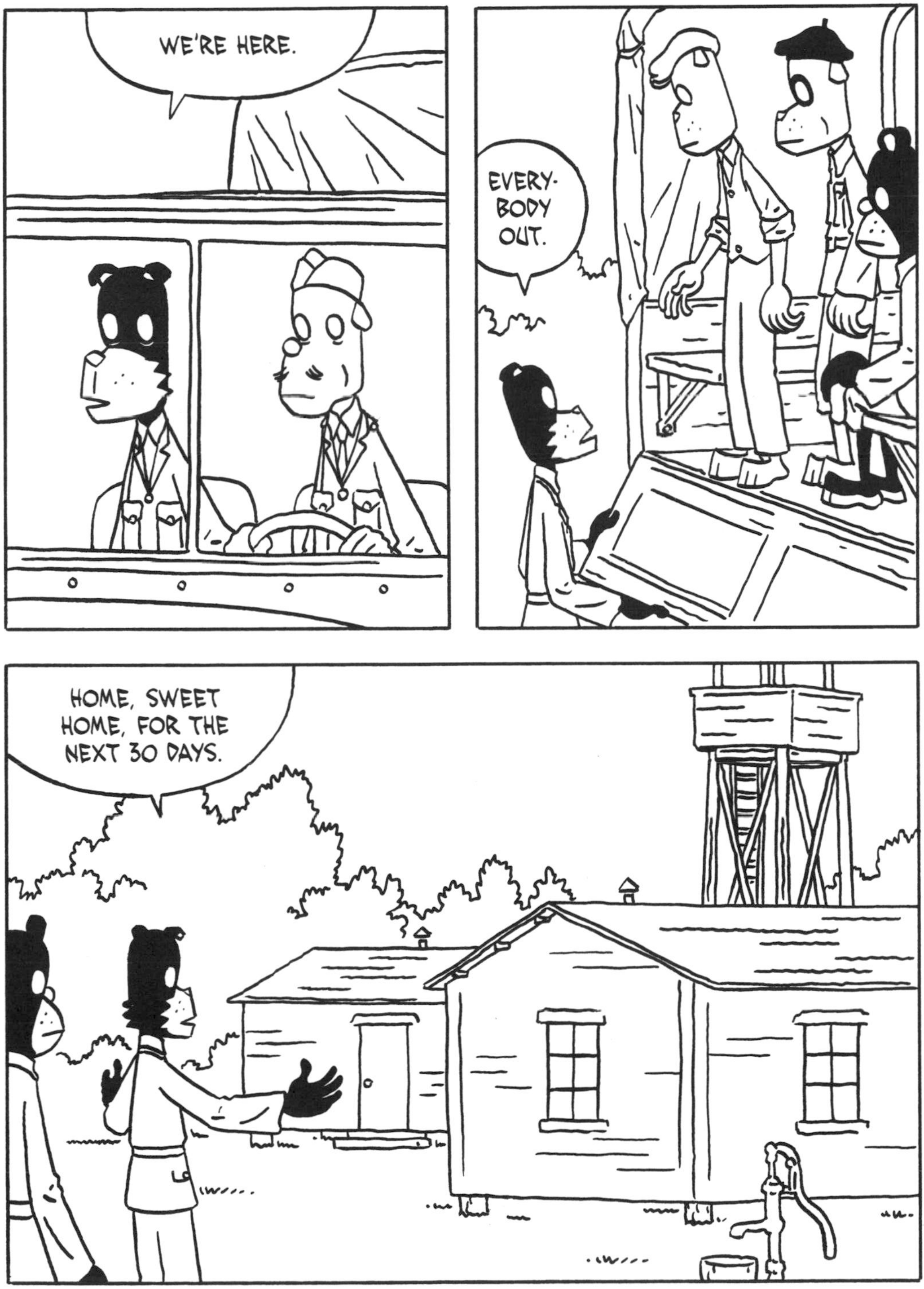
WE'RE HERE.
EVERY-BODY OUT.
HOME, SWEET HOME, FOR THE NEXT 30 DAYS.

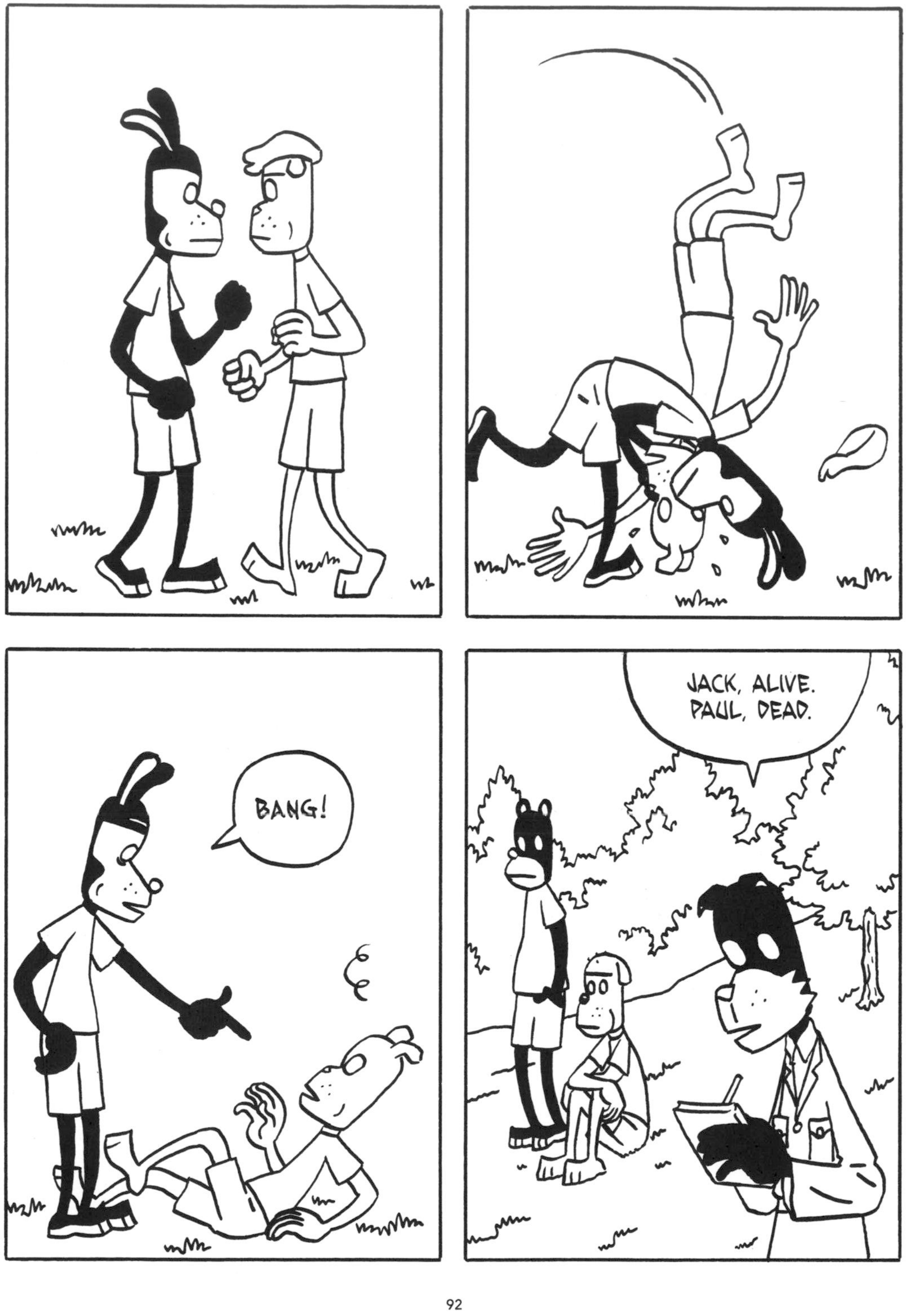
BANG!
JACK, ALIVE.
PAUL, DEAD.

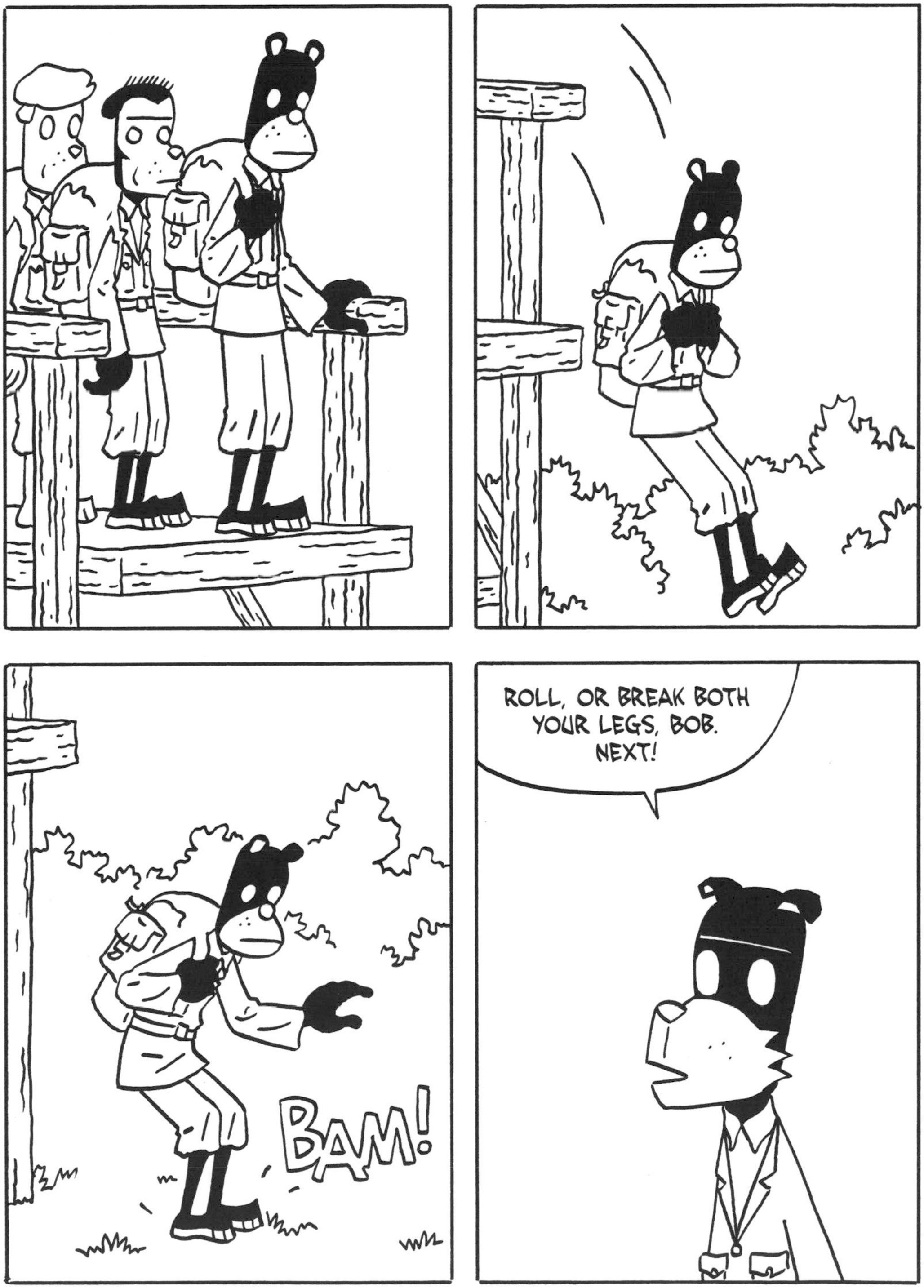

BAM!
ROLL, OR BREAK BOTH YOUR LEGS, BOB. NEXT!

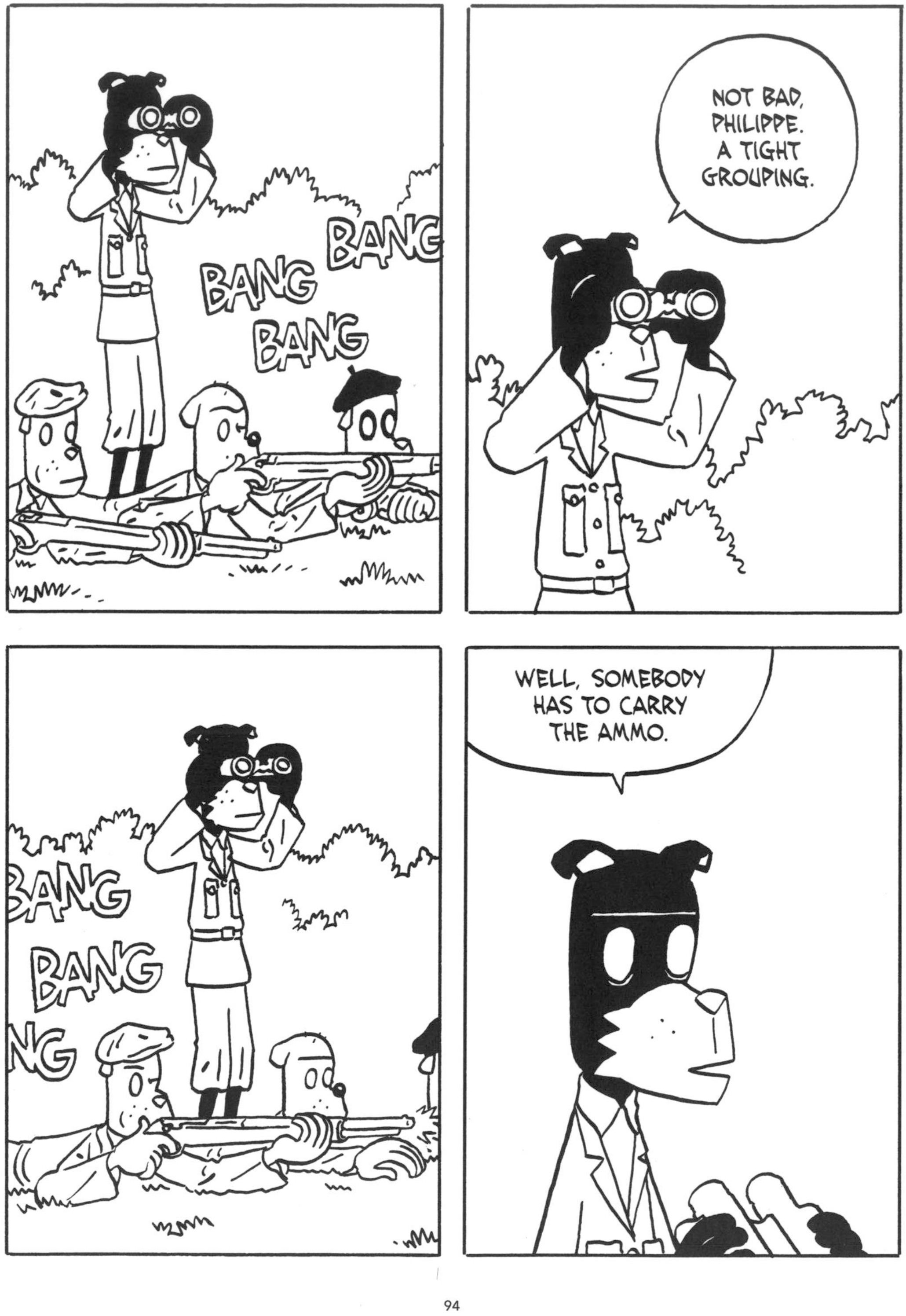
BANG
BANG
BANG
NOT BAD, PHILIPPE. A TIGHT GROUPING.
BANG
WELL, SOMEBODY HAS TO CARRY THE AMMO.

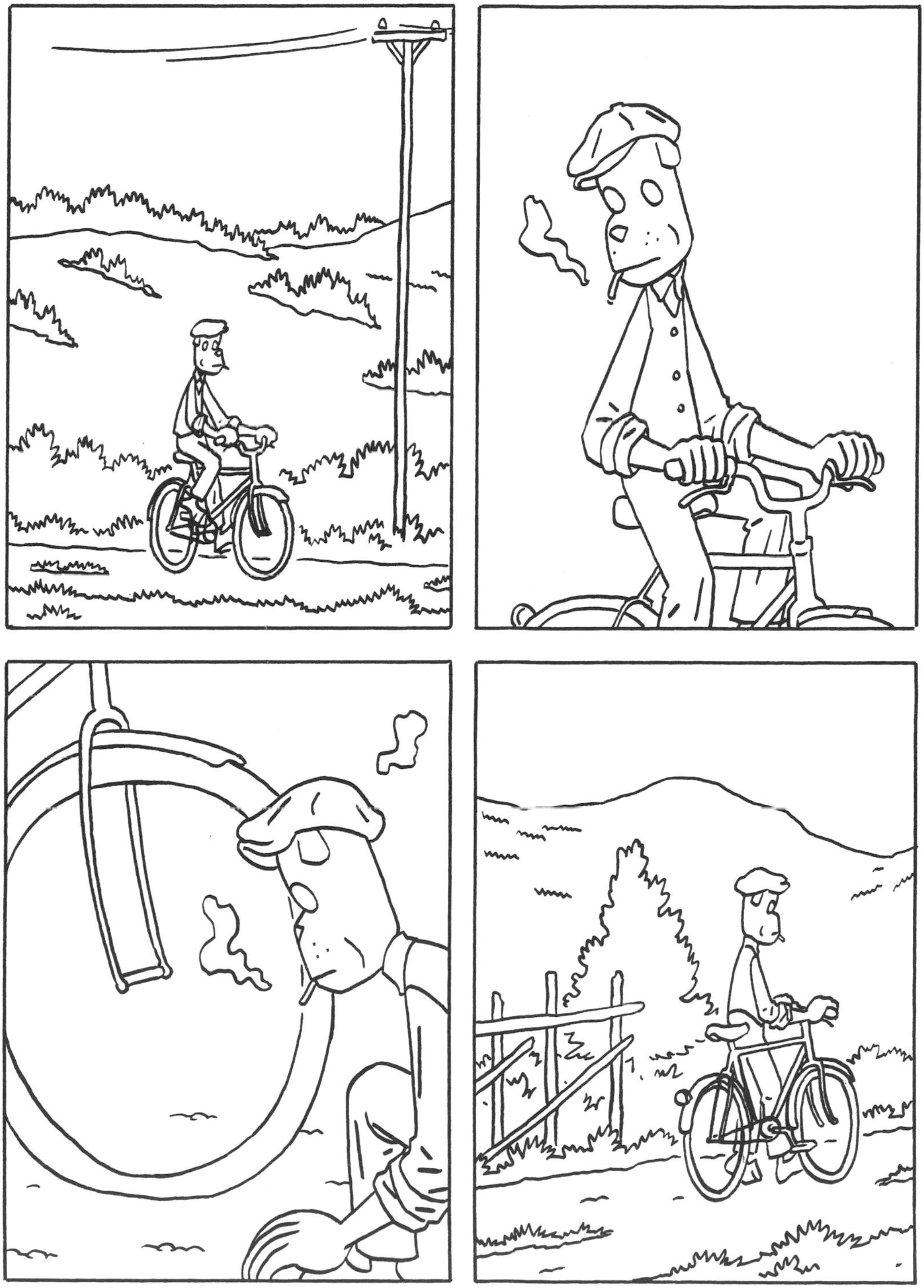

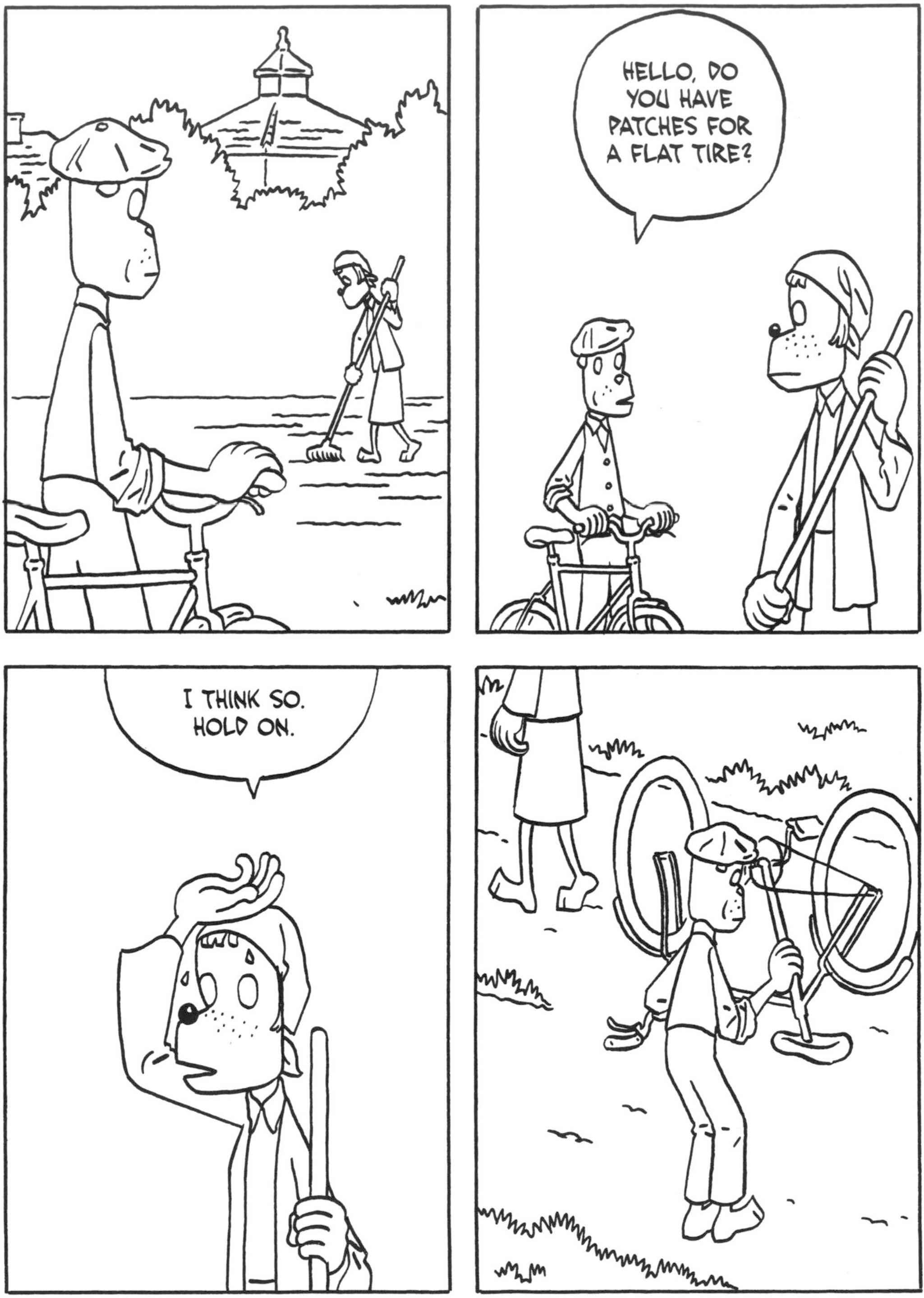
HELLO, DO YOU HAVE PATCHES FOR A FLAT TIRE?
I THINK SO. HOLD ON.

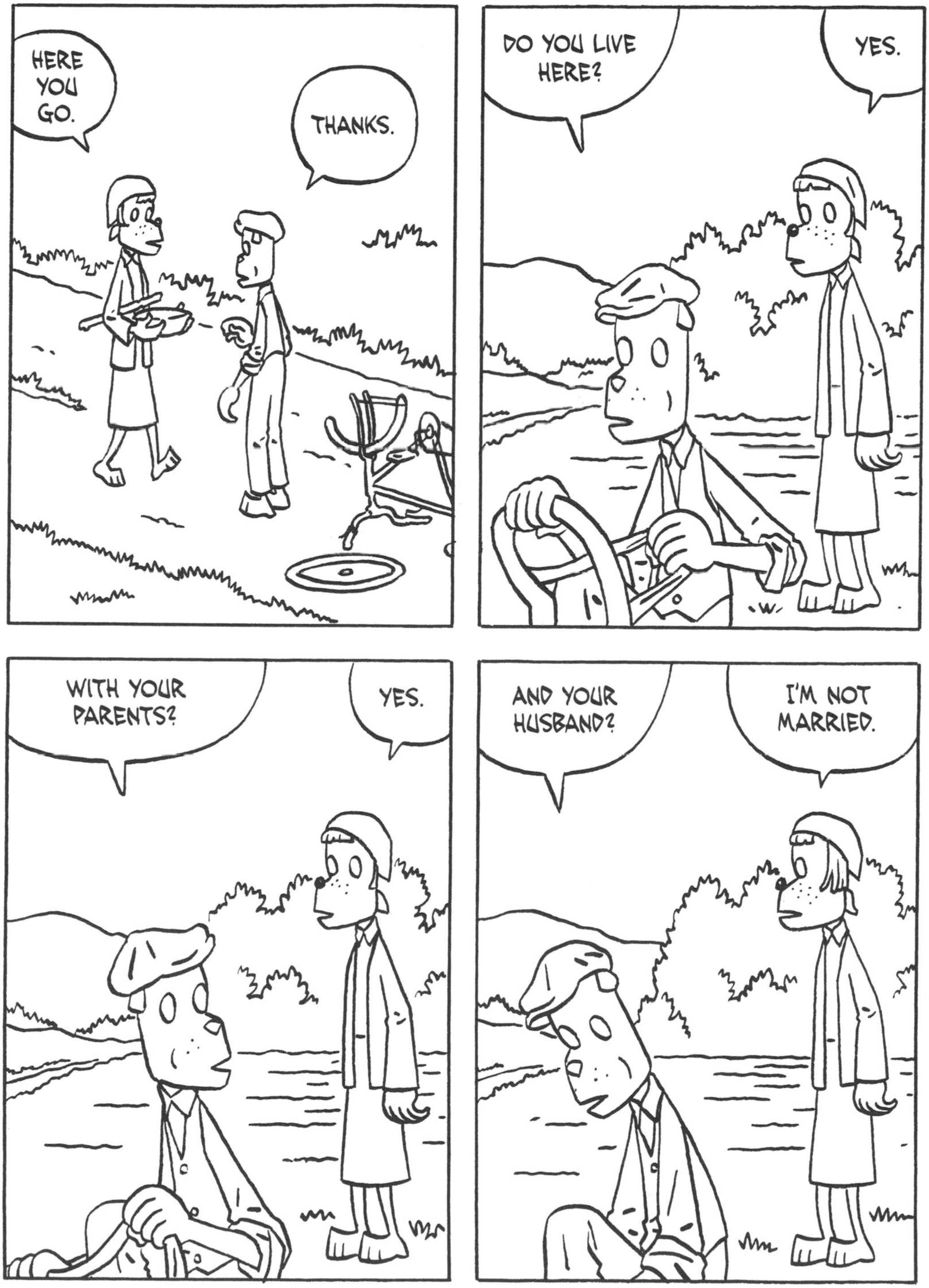
HERE YOU GO.
THANKS.
DO YOU LIVE HERE?
YES.
WITH YOUR PARENTS?
YES.
AND YOUR HUSBAND?
I'M NOT MARRIED.

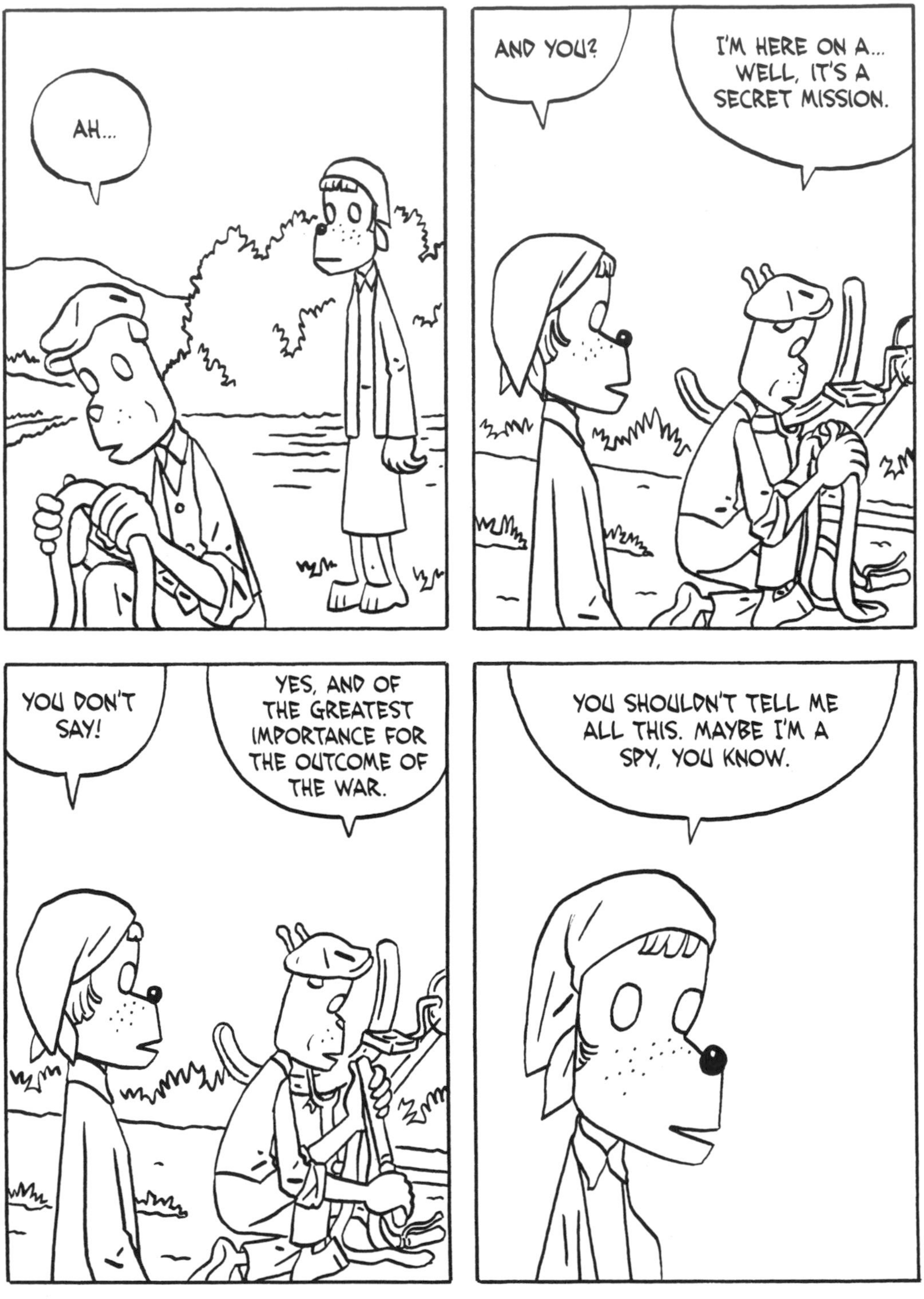
AH...
AND YOU?
I'M HERE ON A... WELL, IT'S A SECRET MISSION.
YOU DON'T SAY!
YES, AND OF THE GREATEST IMPORTANCE FOR THE OUTCOME OF THE WAR.
YOU SHOULDN'T TELL ME ALL THIS. MAYBE I'M A SPY, YOU KNOW.

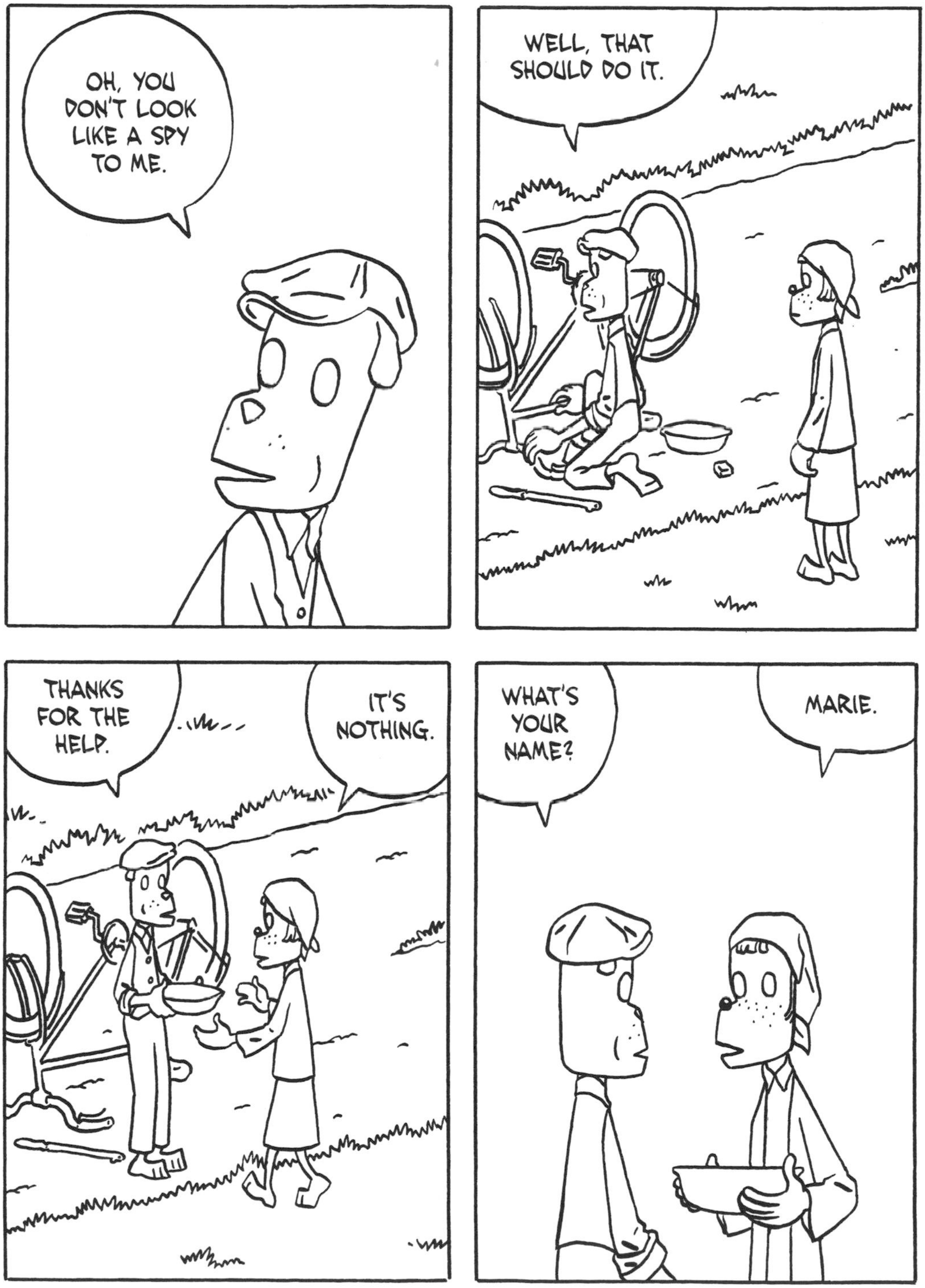
OH, YOU DON'T LOOK LIKE A SPY TO ME.
WELL, THAT SHOULD DO IT.
THANKS FOR THE HELP.
IT'S NOTHING.
WHAT'S YOUR NAME?
MARIE.

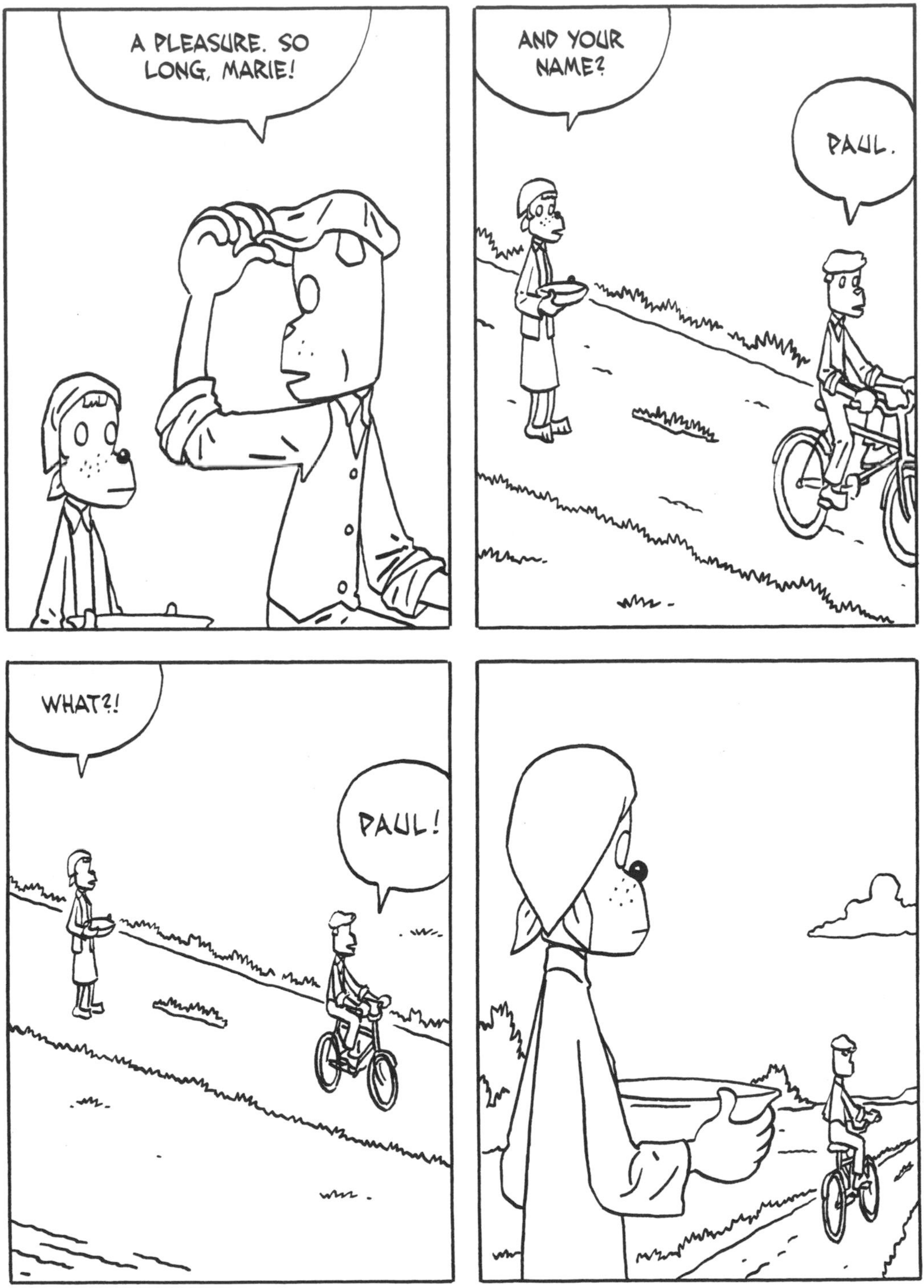
A PLEASURE. SO LONG, MARIE!
AND YOUR NAME?
PAUL.
WHAT?!
PAUL!

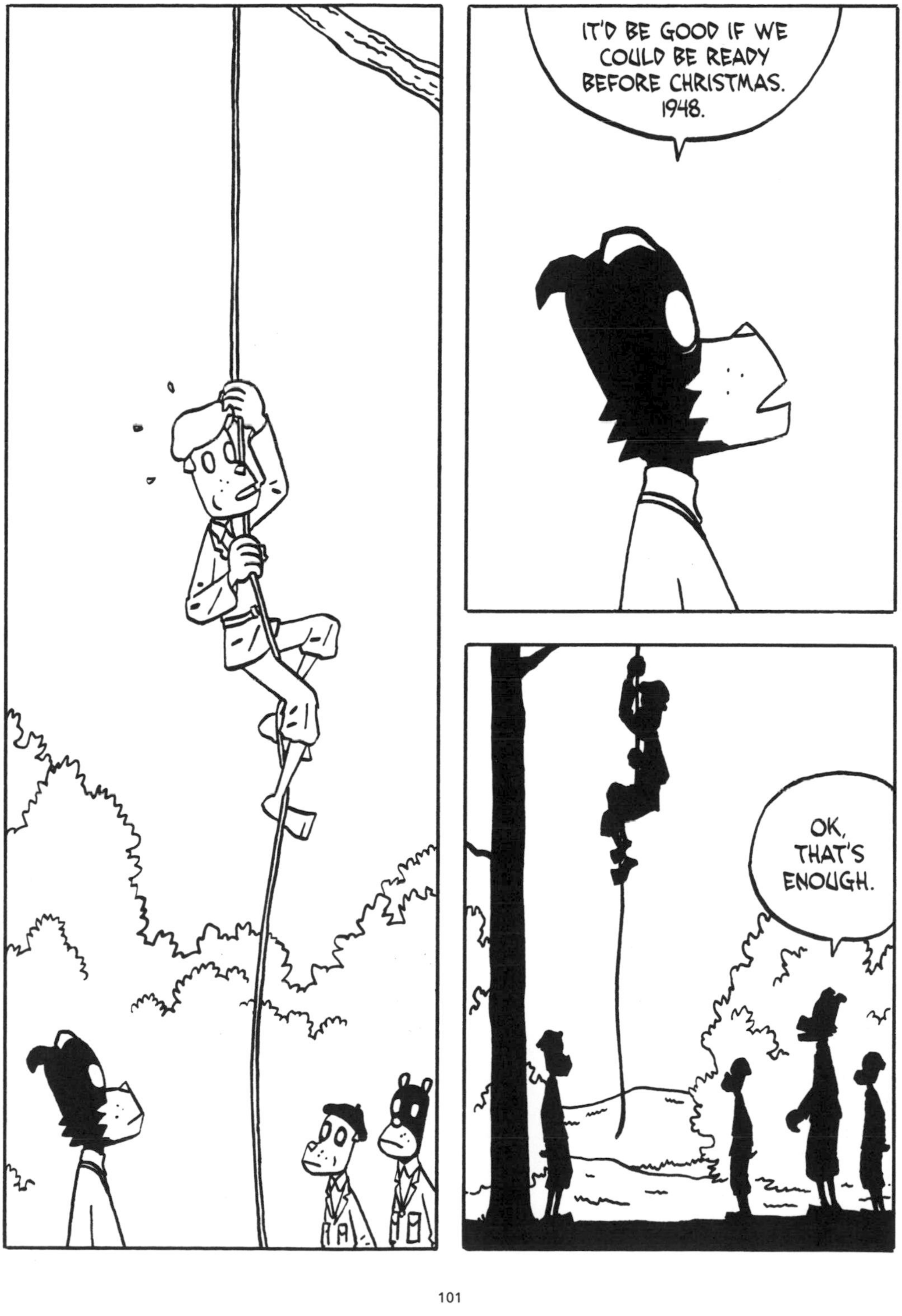
IT'D BE GOOD IF WE COULD BE READY BEFORE CHRISTMAS. 1948.
OK, THAT'S ENOUGH.

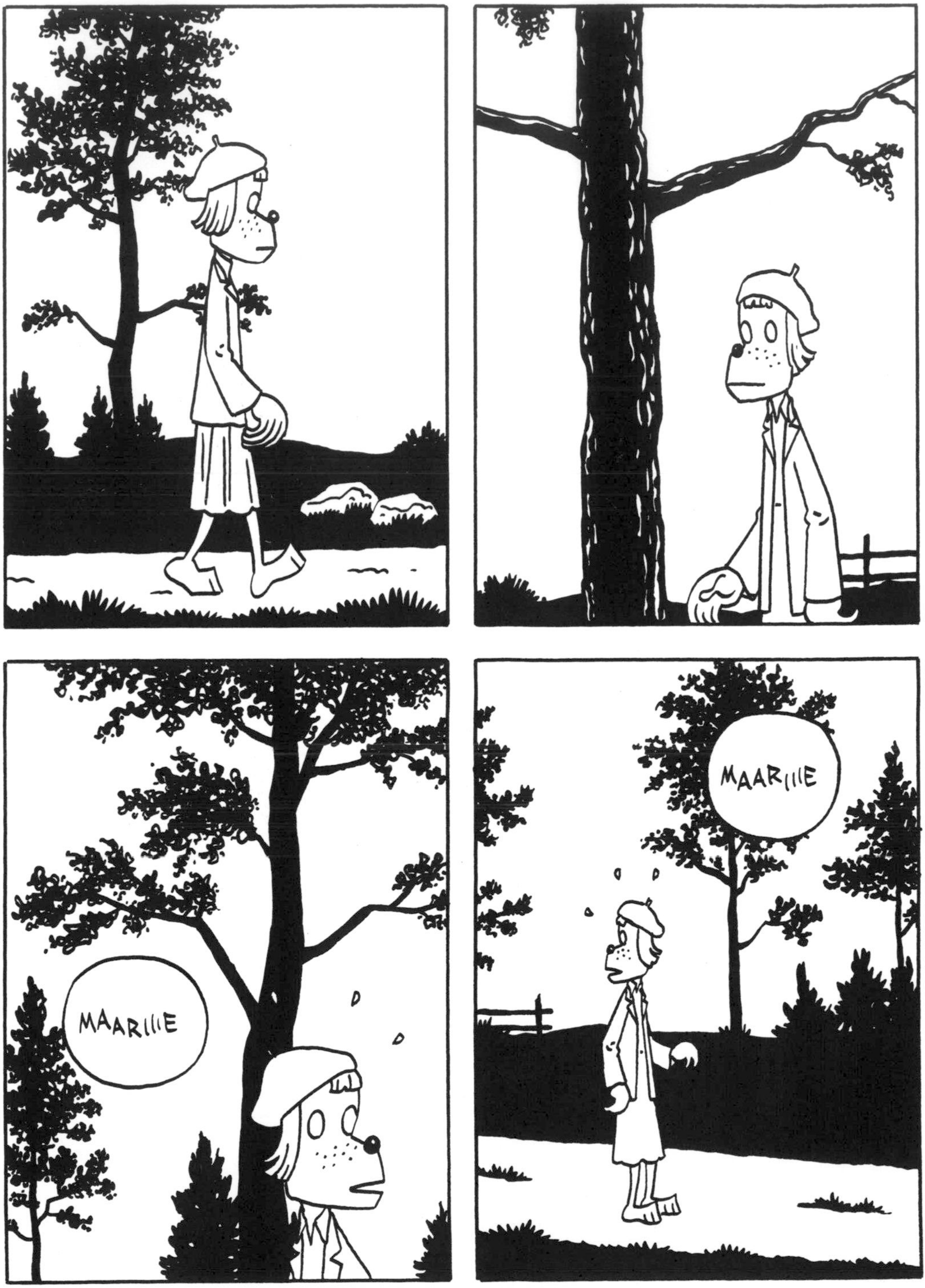
MAARIIIE
MAARIIIE

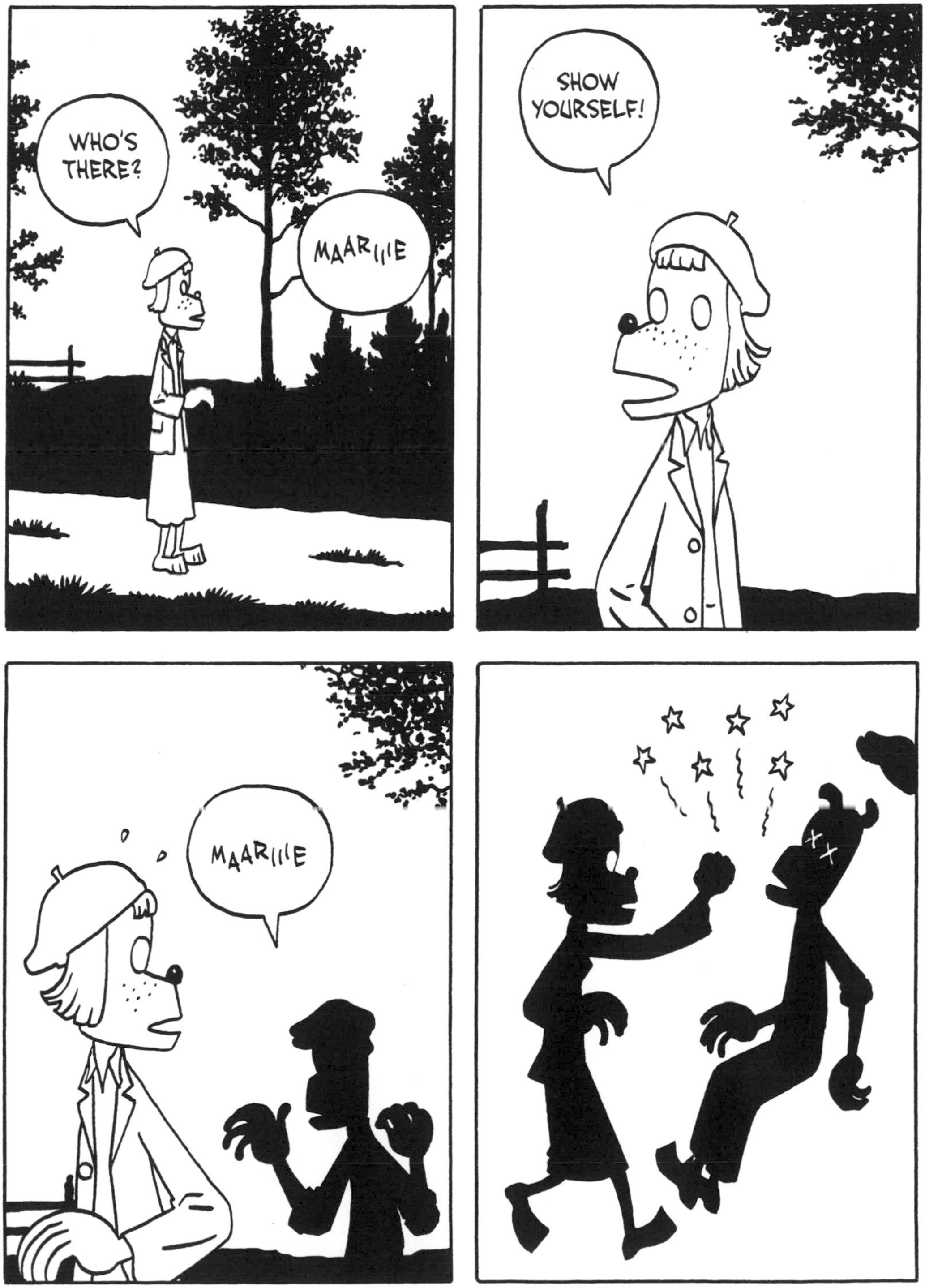
WHO'S THERE?
MAARIIIE
SHOW YOURSELF!
MAARIIIE

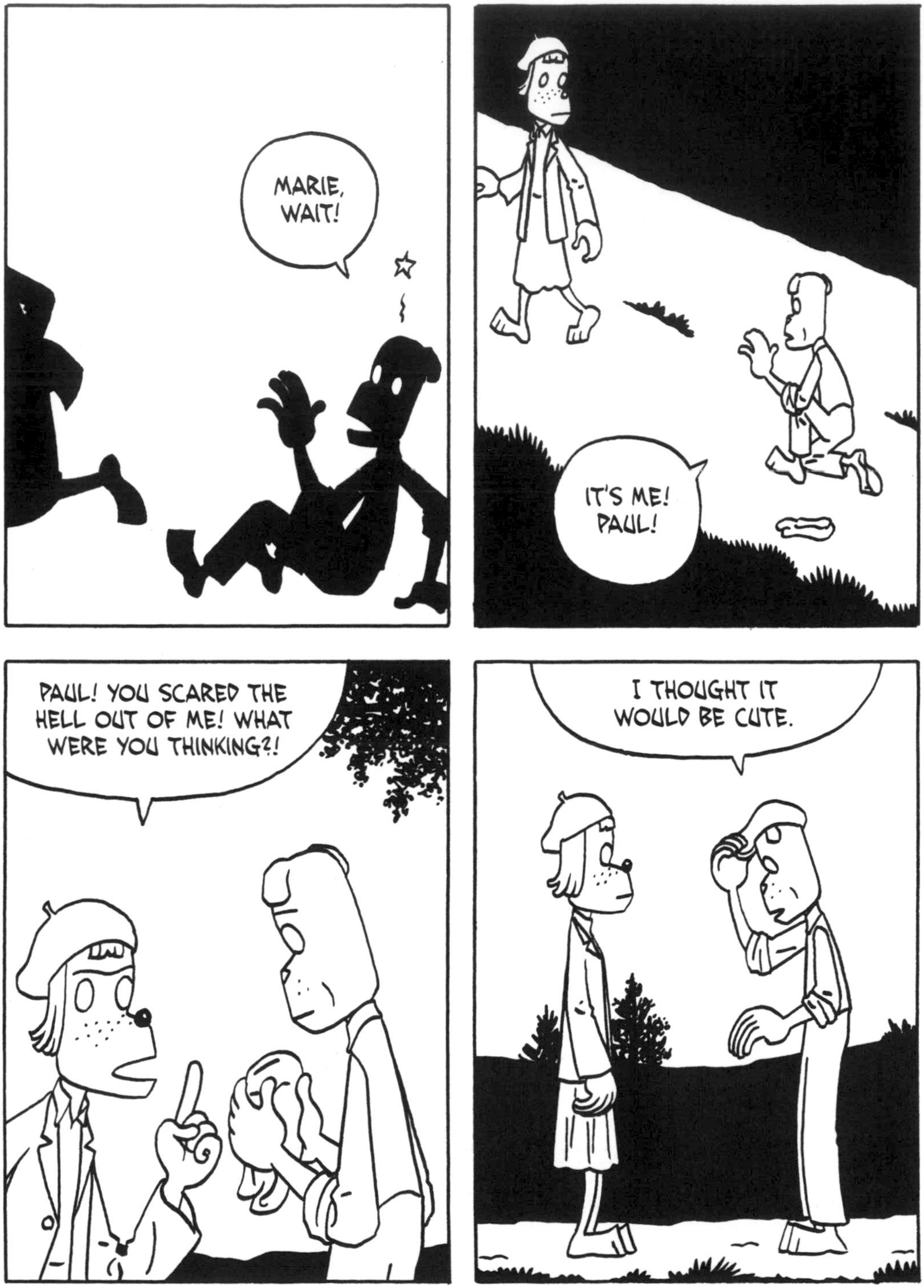
MARIE, WAIT!
IT'S ME! PAUL!
PAUL! YOU SCARED THE HELL OUT OF ME! WHAT WERE YOU THINKING?!
I THOUGHT IT WOULD BE CUTE.

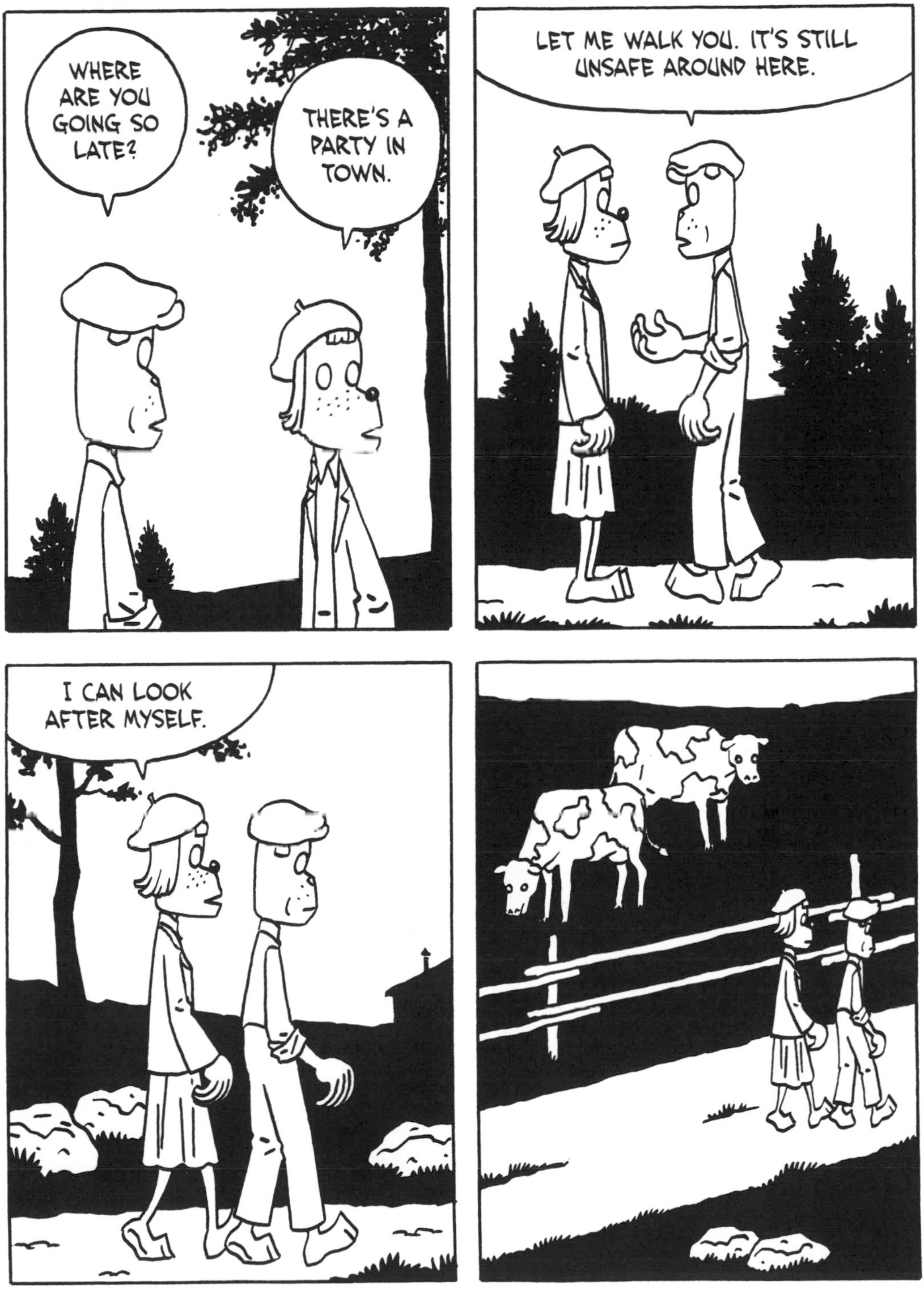
WHERE ARE YOU GOING SO LATE?
THERE'S A PARTY IN TOWN.
LET ME WALK YOU. IT'S STILL UNSAFE AROUND HERE.
I CAN LOOK AFTER MYSELF.

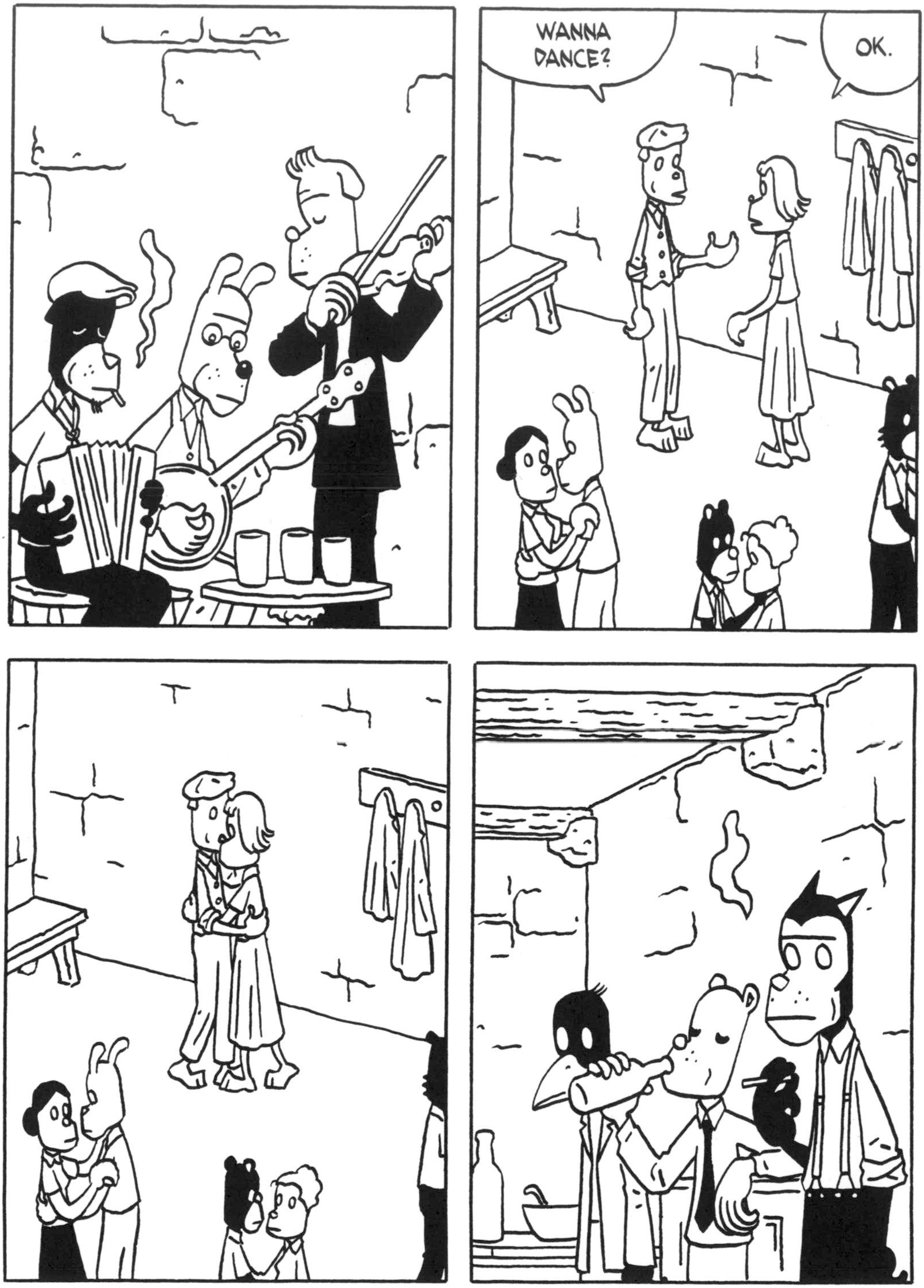
WANNA DANCE?
OK.

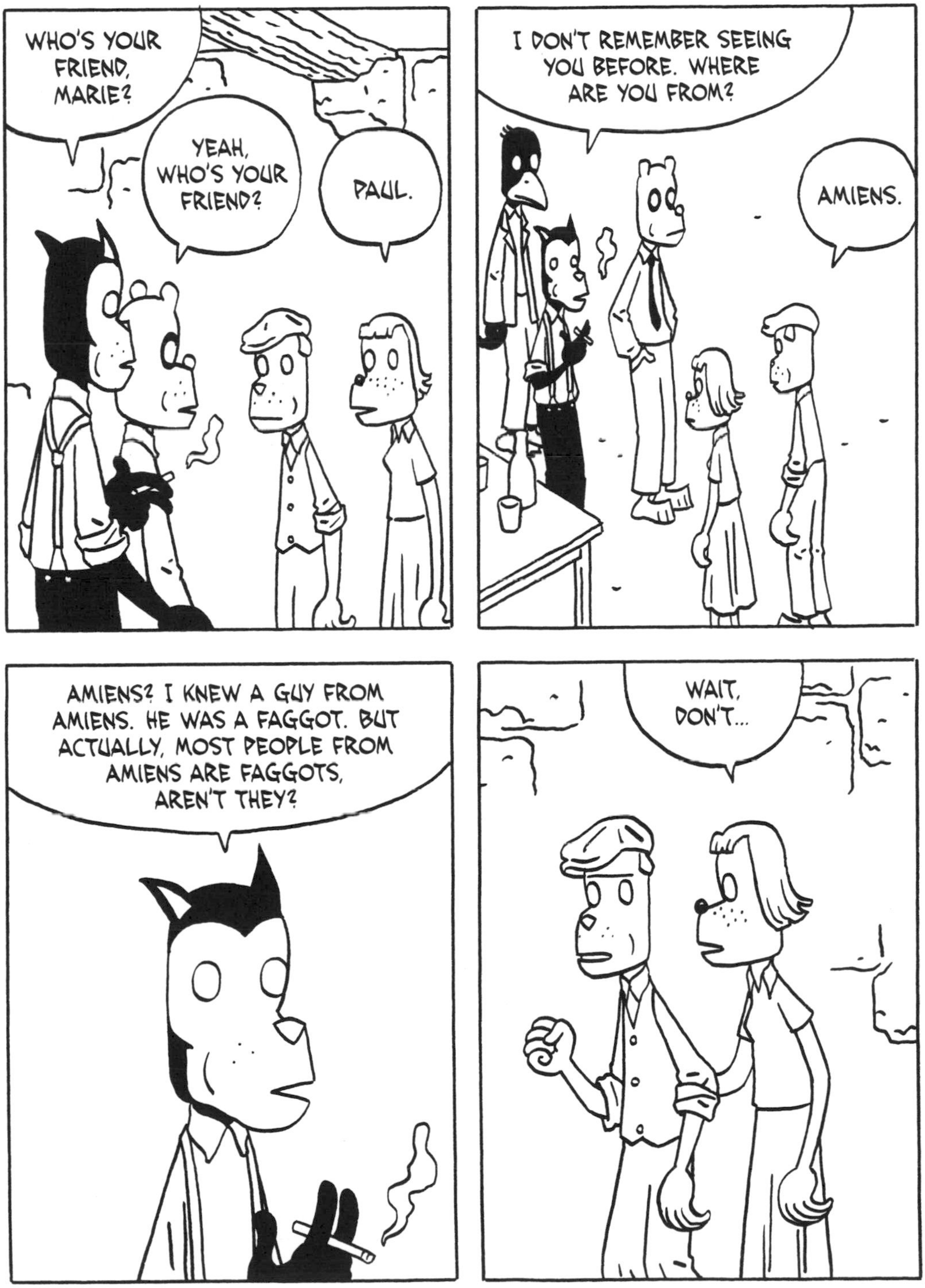
WHO'S YOUR FRIEND, MARIE?
YEAH, WHO'S YOUR FRIEND?
PAUL.
I DON'T REMEMBER SEEING YOU BEFORE. WHERE ARE YOU FROM?
AMIENS.
AMIENS? I KNEW A GUY FROM AMIENS. HE WAS A FAGGOT. BUT ACTUALLY, MOST PEOPLE FROM AMIENS ARE FAGGOTS, AREN'T THEY?
WAIT, DON'T...

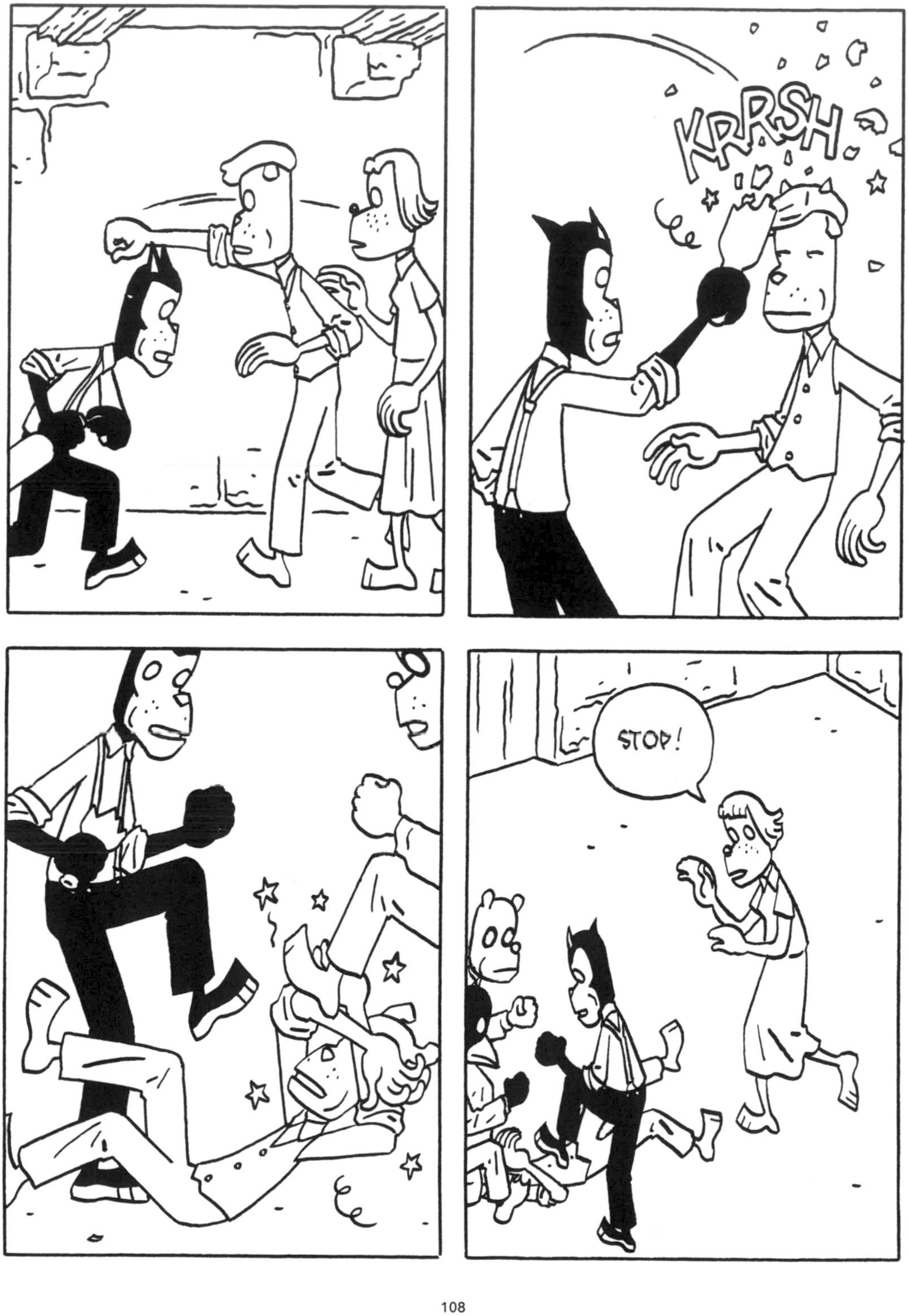
KRRSH
STOP!

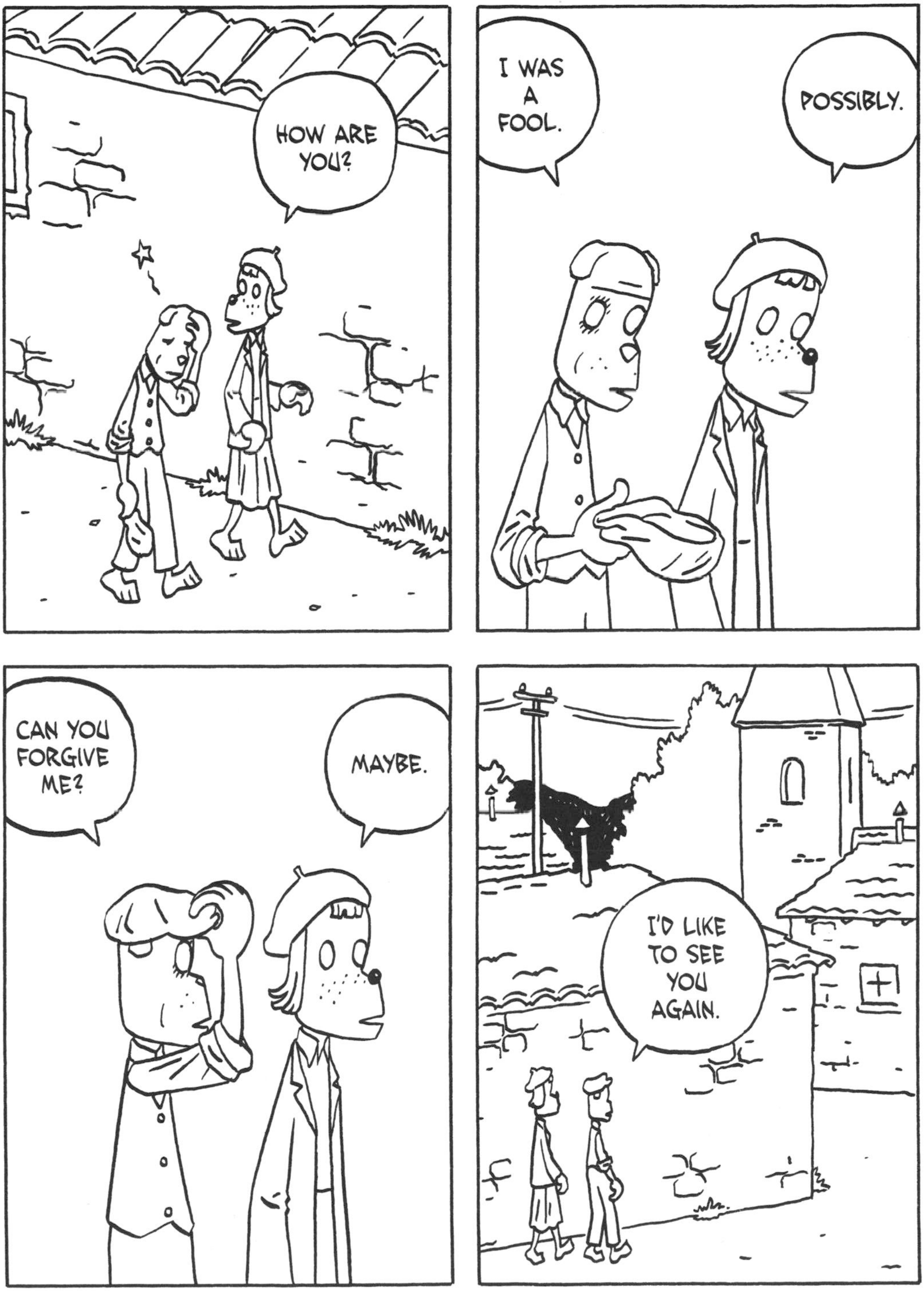
HOW ARE YOU?
I WAS A FOOL.
POSSIBLY.
CAN YOU FORGIVE ME?
MAYBE.
I'D LIKE TO SEE YOU AGAIN.

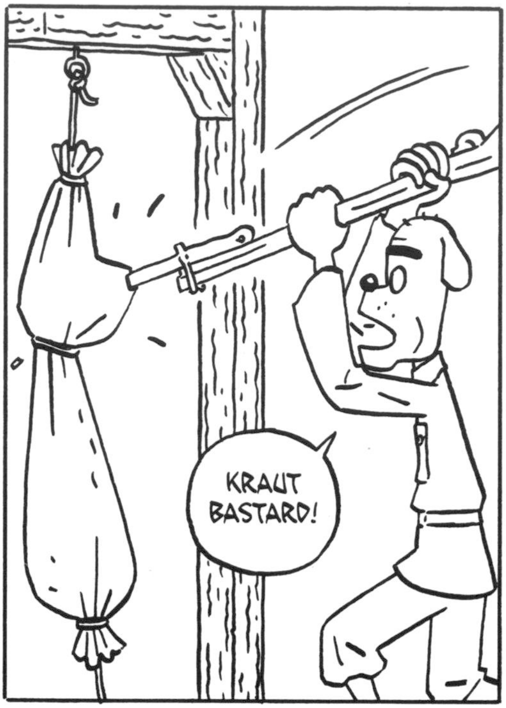
KRAUT BASTARD!

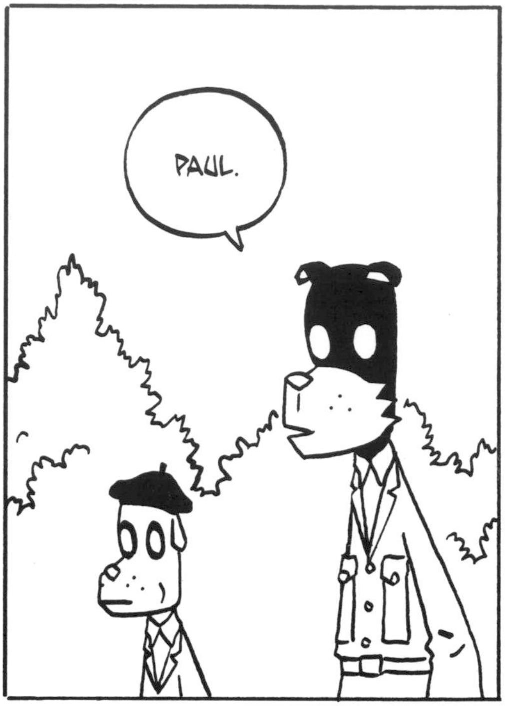
PAUL.

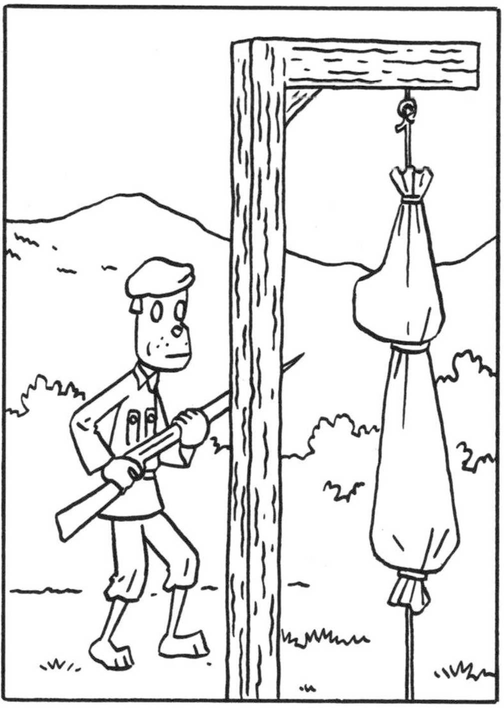

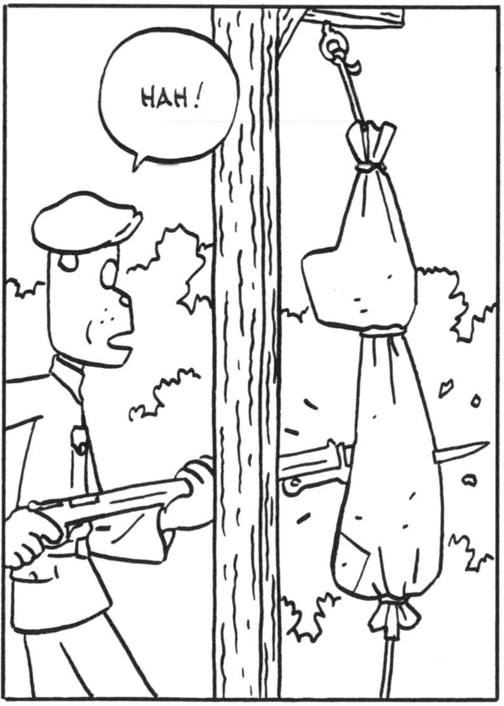
HAH!

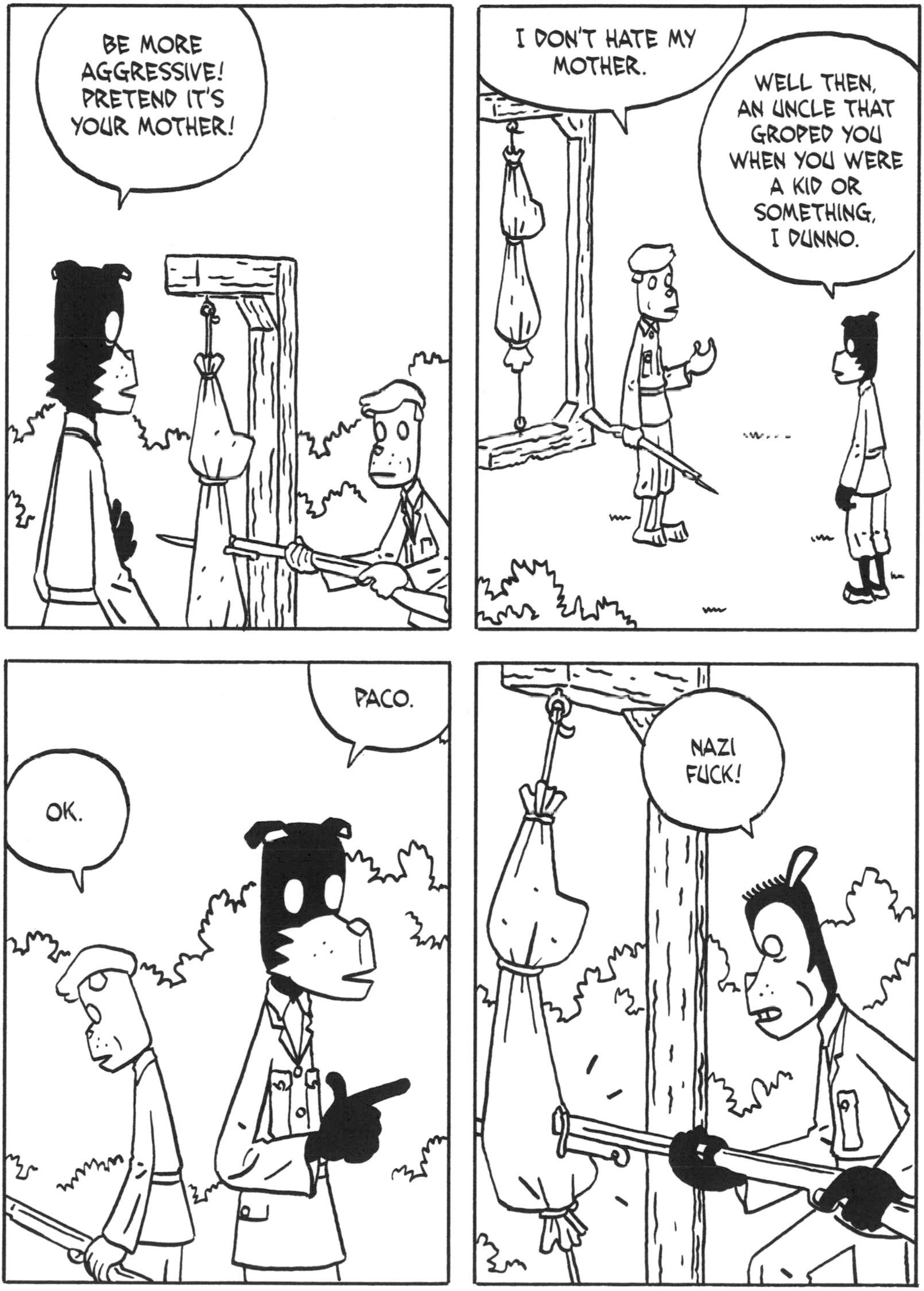
BE MORE AGGRESSIVE! PRETEND IT'S YOUR MOTHER!
I DON'T HATE MY MOTHER.
WELL THEN, AN UNCLE THAT GROPED YOU WHEN YOU WERE A KID OR SOMETHING, I DUNNO.
PACO.
OK.
NAZI FUCK!

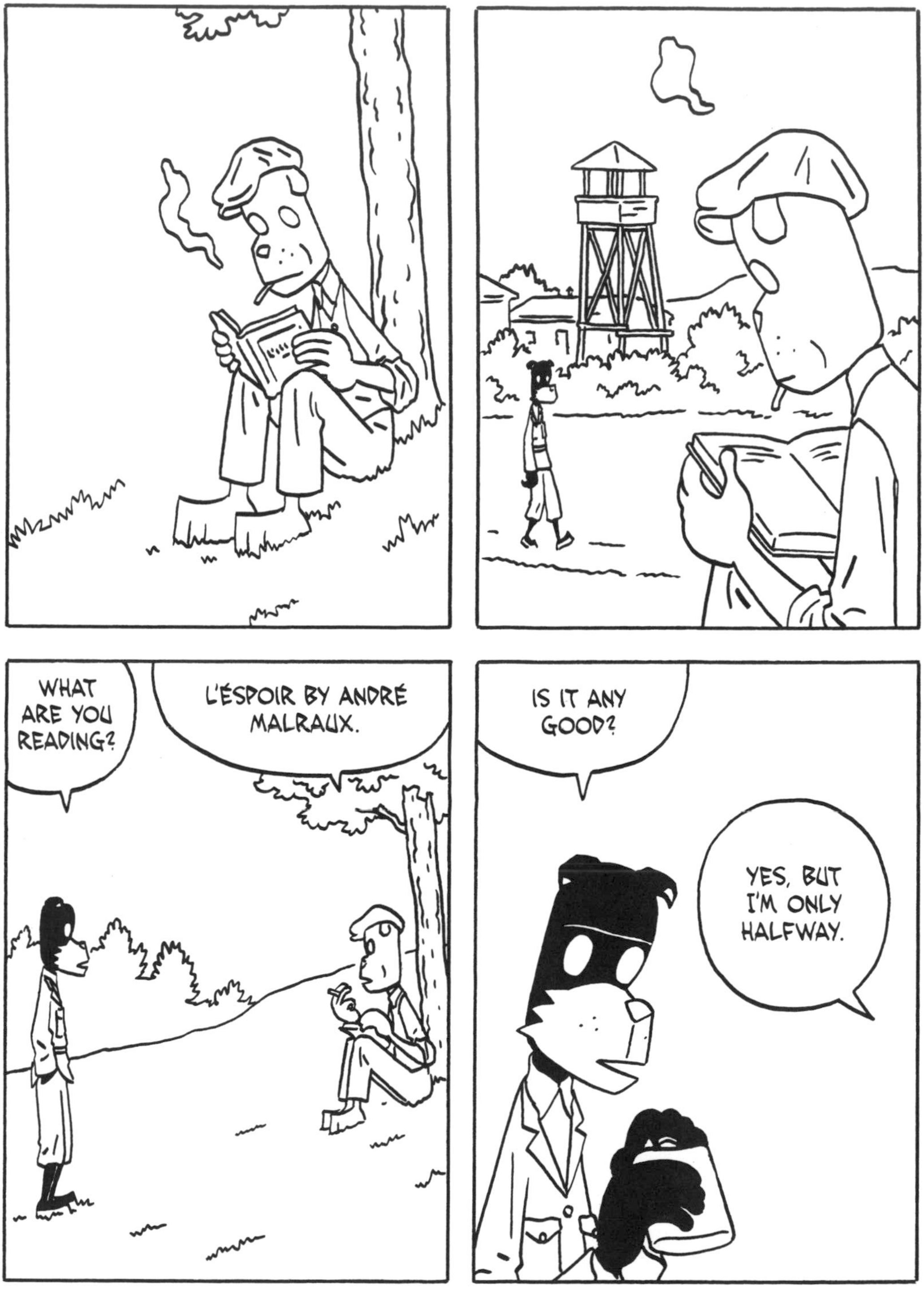
WHAT ARE YOU READING?
L'ESPOIR BY ANDRÉ MALRAUX.
IS IT ANY GOOD?
YES, BUT I'M ONLY HALFWAY.

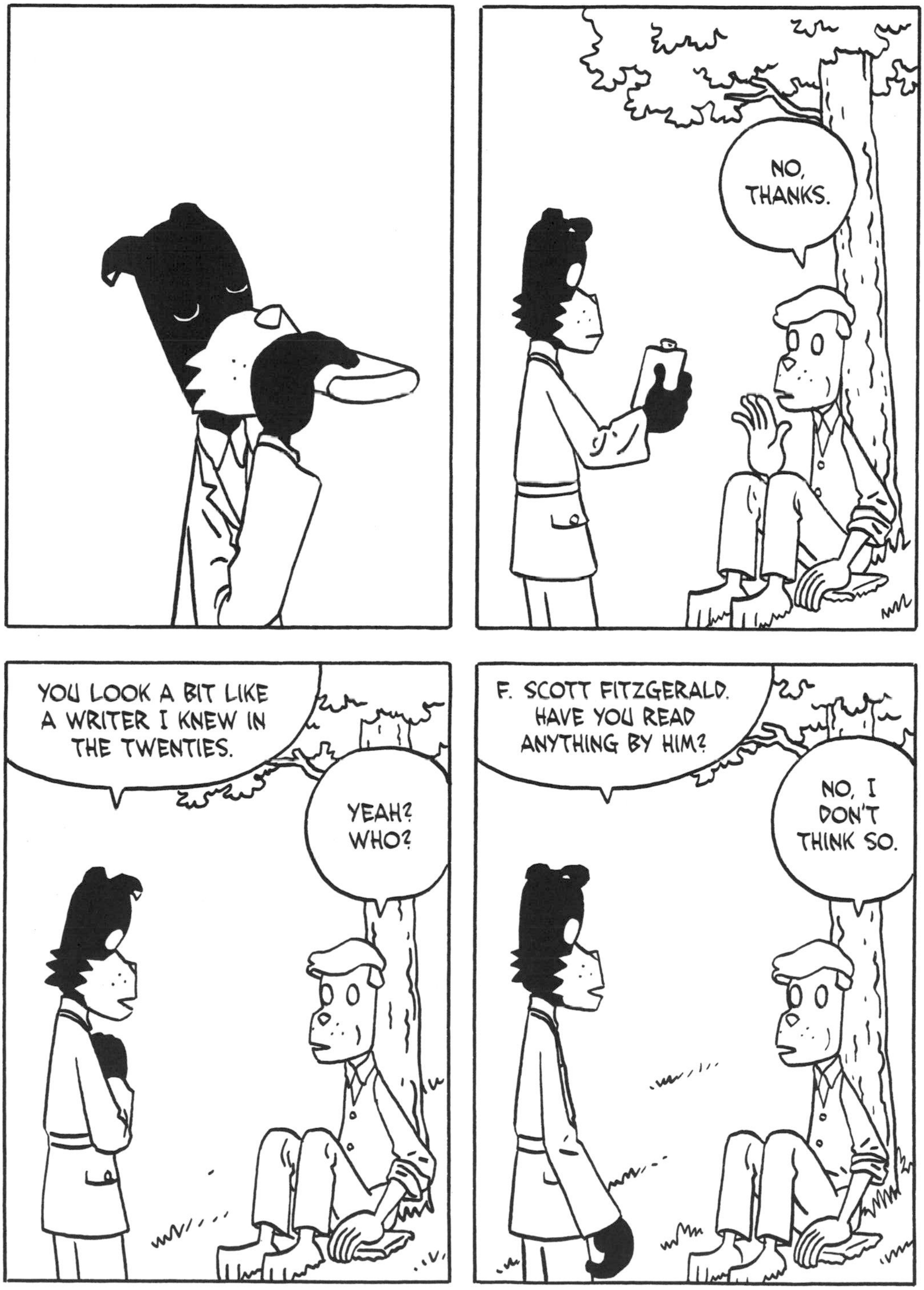
NO, THANKS.
YOU LOOK A BIT LIKE A WRITER I KNEW IN THE TWENTIES.
YEAH? WHO?
F. SCOTT FITZGERALD. HAVE YOU READ ANYTHING BY HIM?
NO, I DON'T THINK SO.

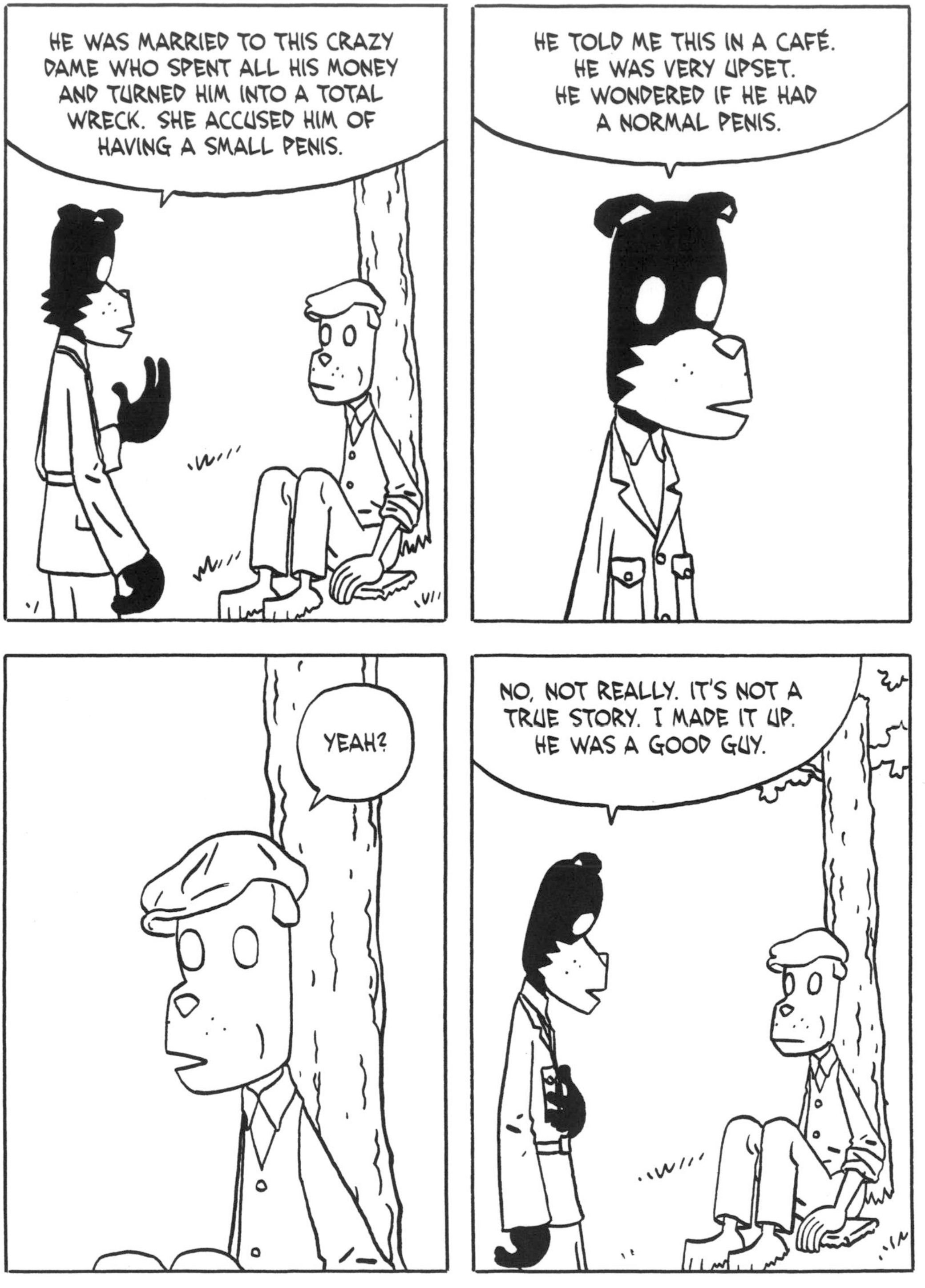
HE WAS MARRIED TO THIS CRAZY DAME WHO SPENT ALL HIS MONEY AND TURNED HIM INTO A TOTAL WRECK. SHE ACCUSED HIM OF HAVING A SMALL PENIS.
HE TOLD ME THIS IN A CAFÉ. HE WAS VERY UPSET. HE WONDERED IF HE HAD A NORMAL PENIS.
YEAH?
NO, NOT REALLY. IT'S NOT A TRUE STORY. I MADE IT UP. HE WAS A GOOD GUY.

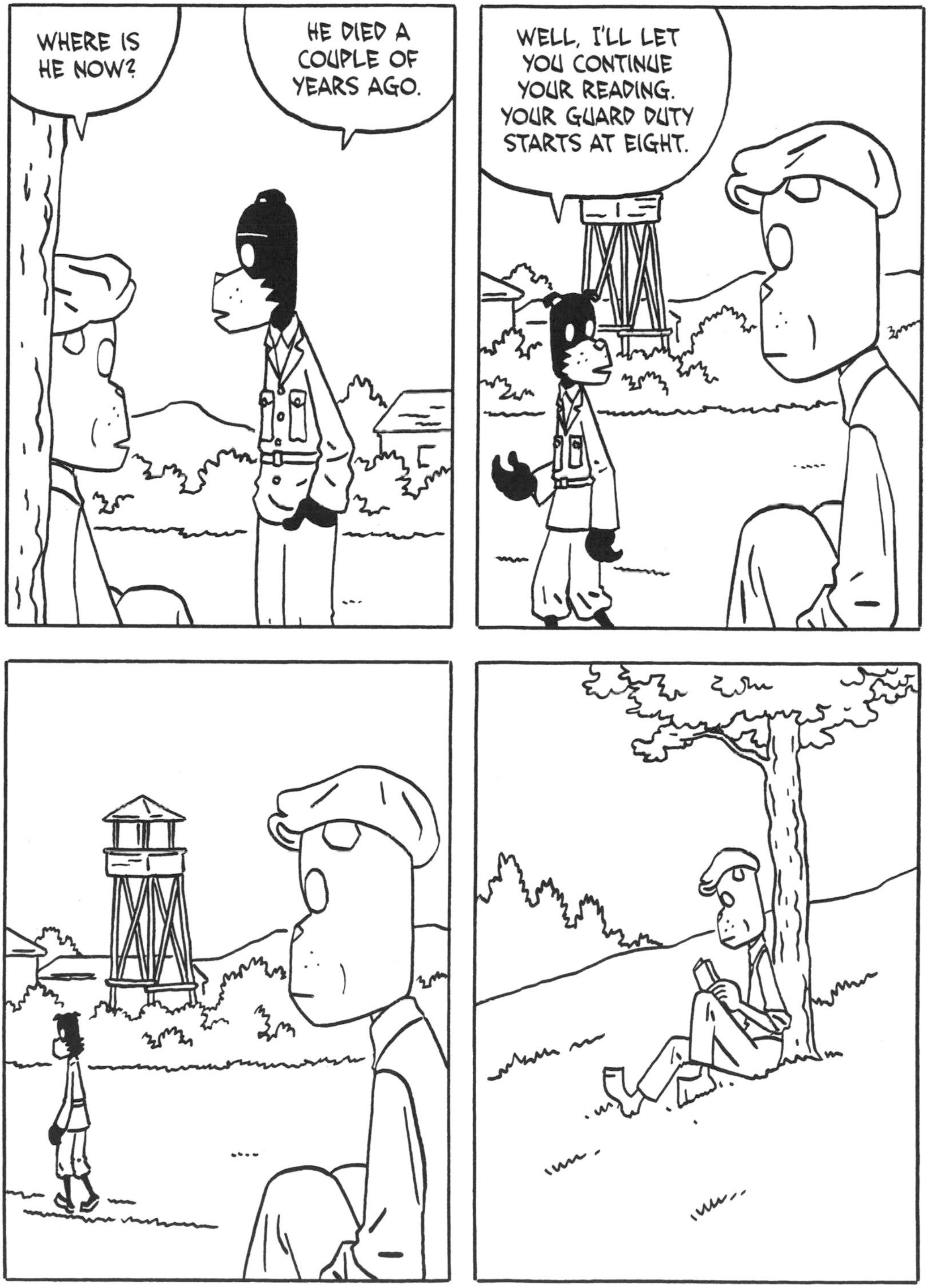
WHERE IS HE NOW?
HE DIED A COUPLE OF YEARS AGO.
WELL, I'LL LET YOU CONTINUE YOUR READING. YOUR GUARD DUTY STARTS AT EIGHT.

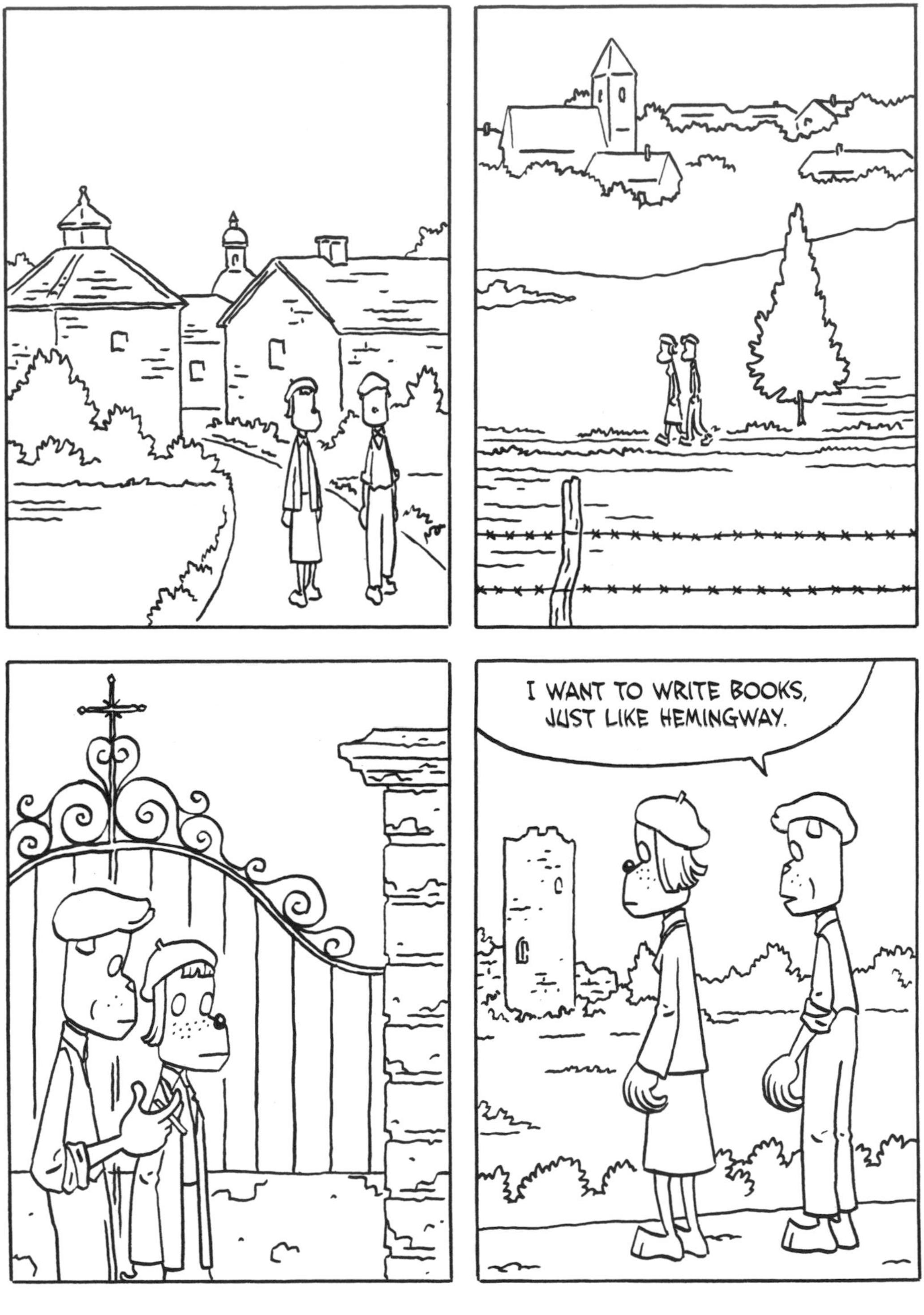
I WANT TO WRITE BOOKS, JUST LIKE HEMINGWAY.

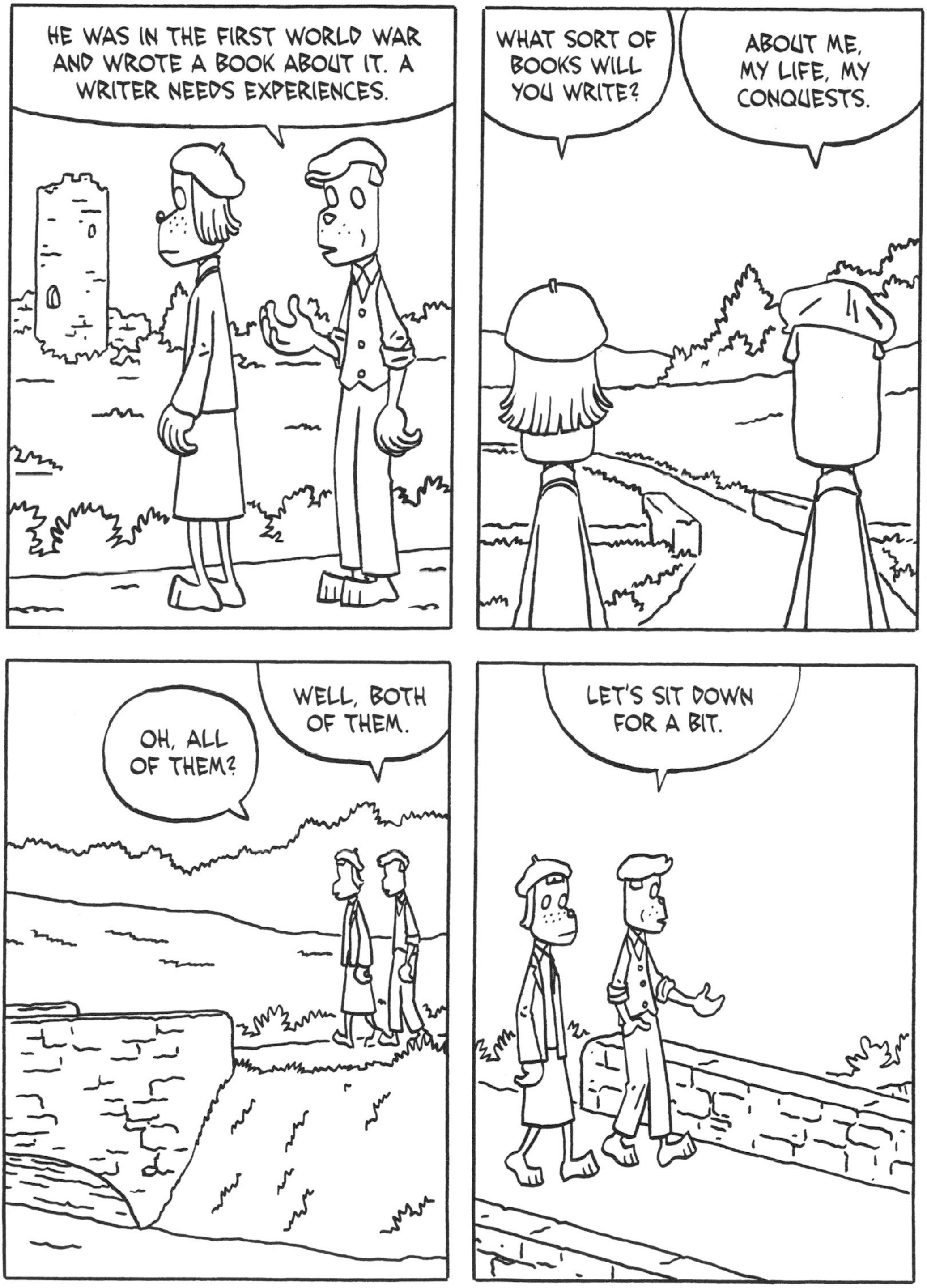
HE WAS IN THE FIRST WORLD WAR AND WROTE A BOOK ABOUT IT. A WRITER NEEDS EXPERIENCES.
WHAT SORT OF BOOKS WILL YOU WRITE?
ABOUT ME, MY LIFE, MY CONQUESTS.
OH, ALL OF THEM?
WELL, BOTH OF THEM.
LET'S SIT DOWN FOR A BIT.

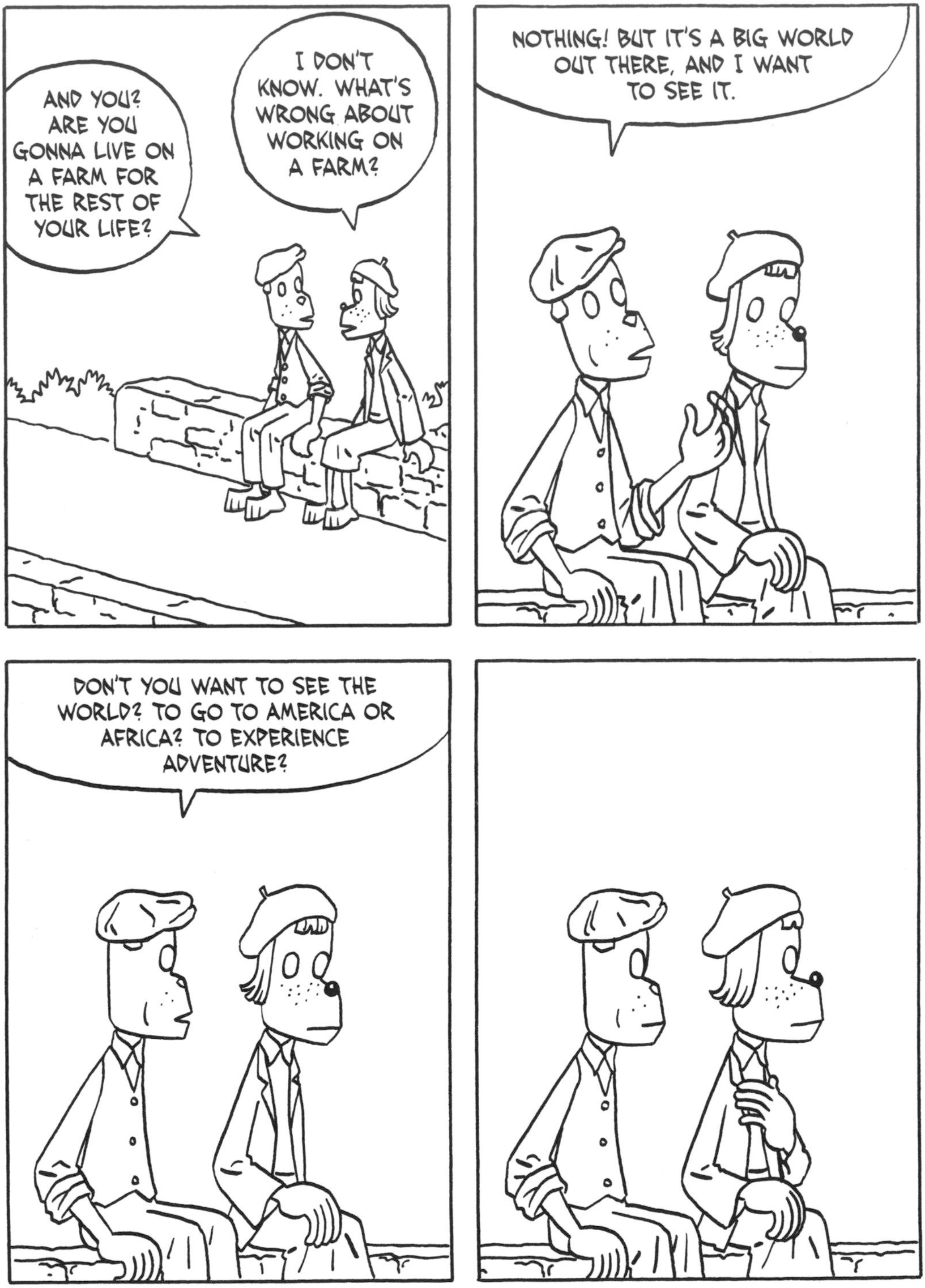
AND YOU? ARE YOU GONNA LIVE ON A FARM FOR THE REST OF YOUR LIFE?
I DON'T KNOW. WHAT'S WRONG ABOUT WORKING ON A FARM?
NOTHING! BUT IT'S A BIG WORLD OUT THERE, AND I WANT TO SEE IT.
DON'T YOU WANT TO SEE THE WORLD? TO GO TO AMERICA OR AFRICA? TO EXPERIENCE ADVENTURE?

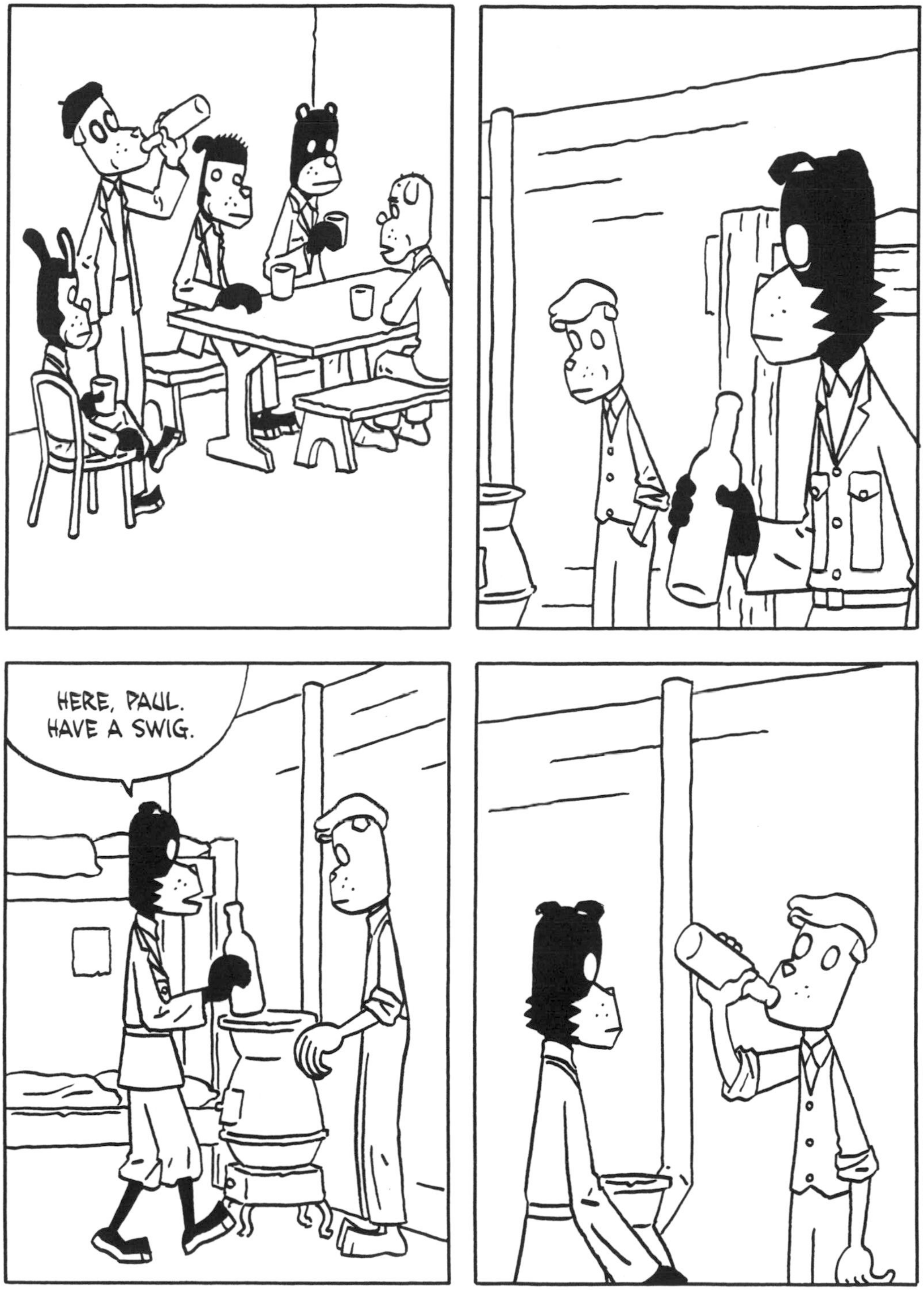
HERE, PAUL. HAVE A SWIG.

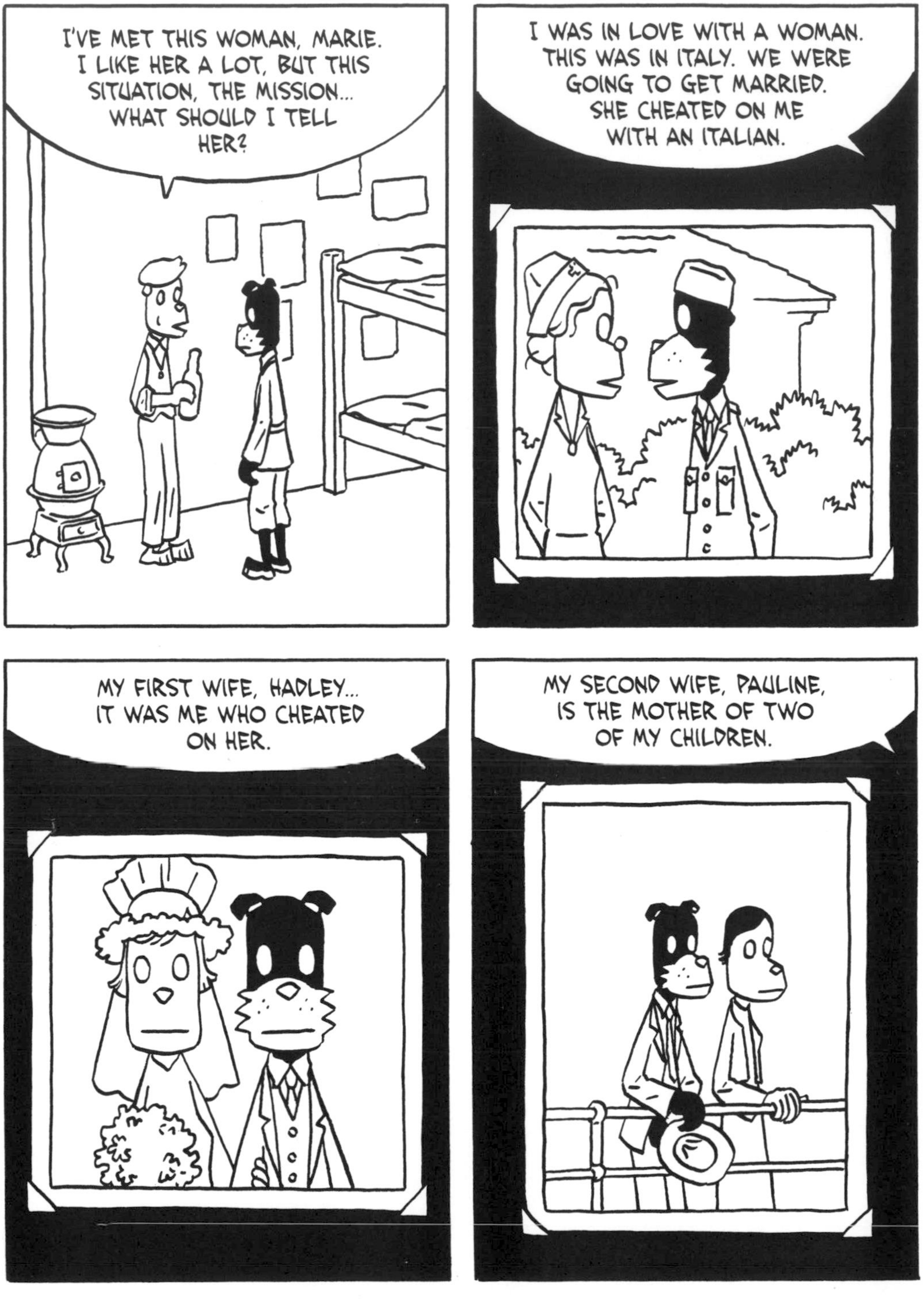
I'VE MET THIS WOMAN, MARIE. I LIKE HER A LOT, BUT THIS SITUATION, THE MISSION... WHAT SHOULD I TELL HER?
I WAS IN LOVE WITH A WOMAN. THIS WAS IN ITALY. WE WERE GOING TO GET MARRIED. SHE CHEATED ON ME WITH AN ITALIAN.
MY FIRST WIFE, HADLEY... IT WAS ME WHO CHEATED ON HER.
MY SECOND WIFE, PAULINE, IS THE MOTHER OF TWO OF MY CHILDREN.

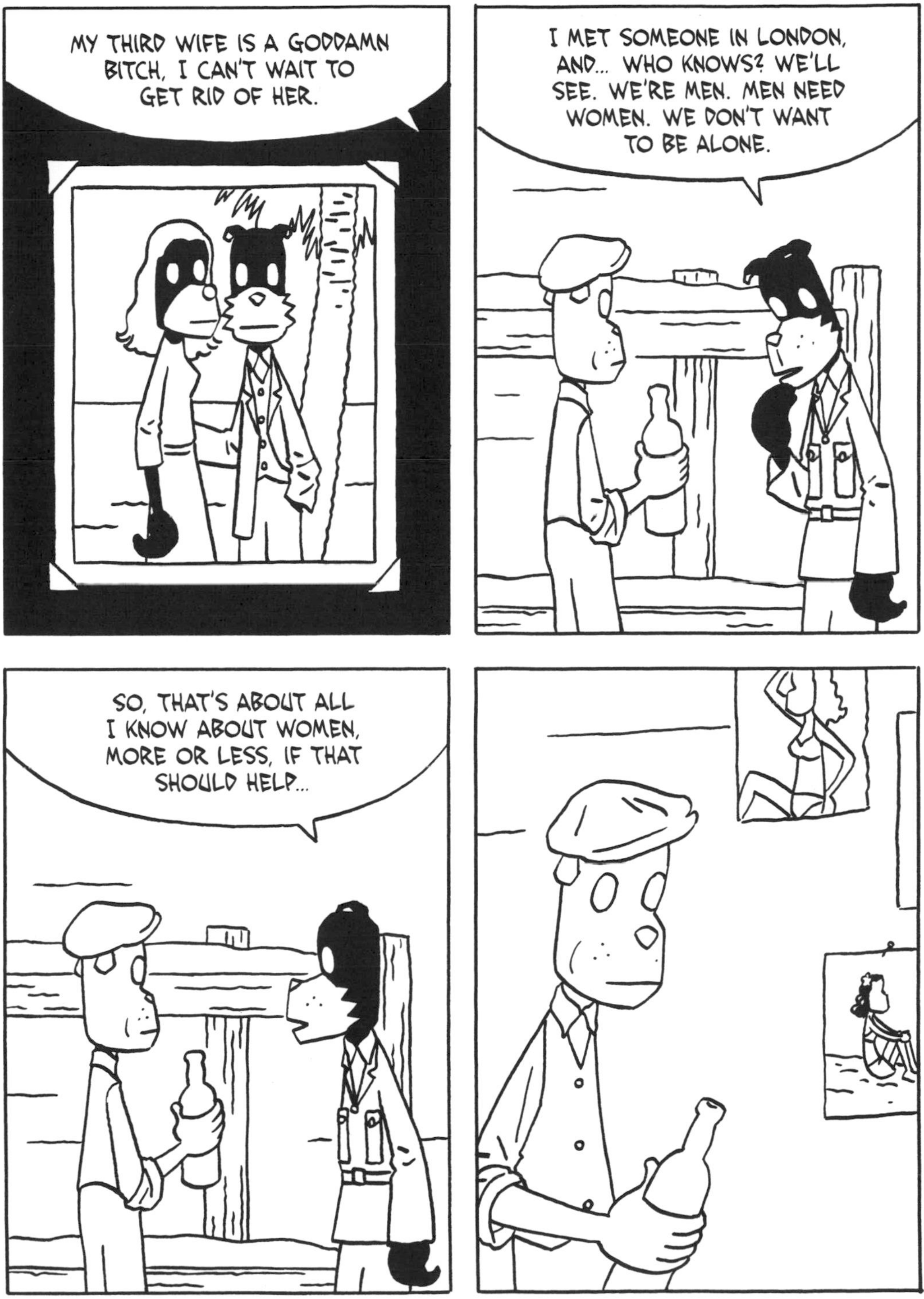
MY THIRD WIFE IS A GODDAMN BITCH, I CAN'T WAIT TO GET RID OF HER.
I MET SOMEONE IN LONDON, AND... WHO KNOWS? WE'LL SEE. WE'RE MEN. MEN NEED WOMEN. WE DON'T WANT TO BE ALONE.
SO, THAT'S ABOUT ALL I KNOW ABOUT WOMEN, MORE OR LESS, IF THAT SHOULD HELP...

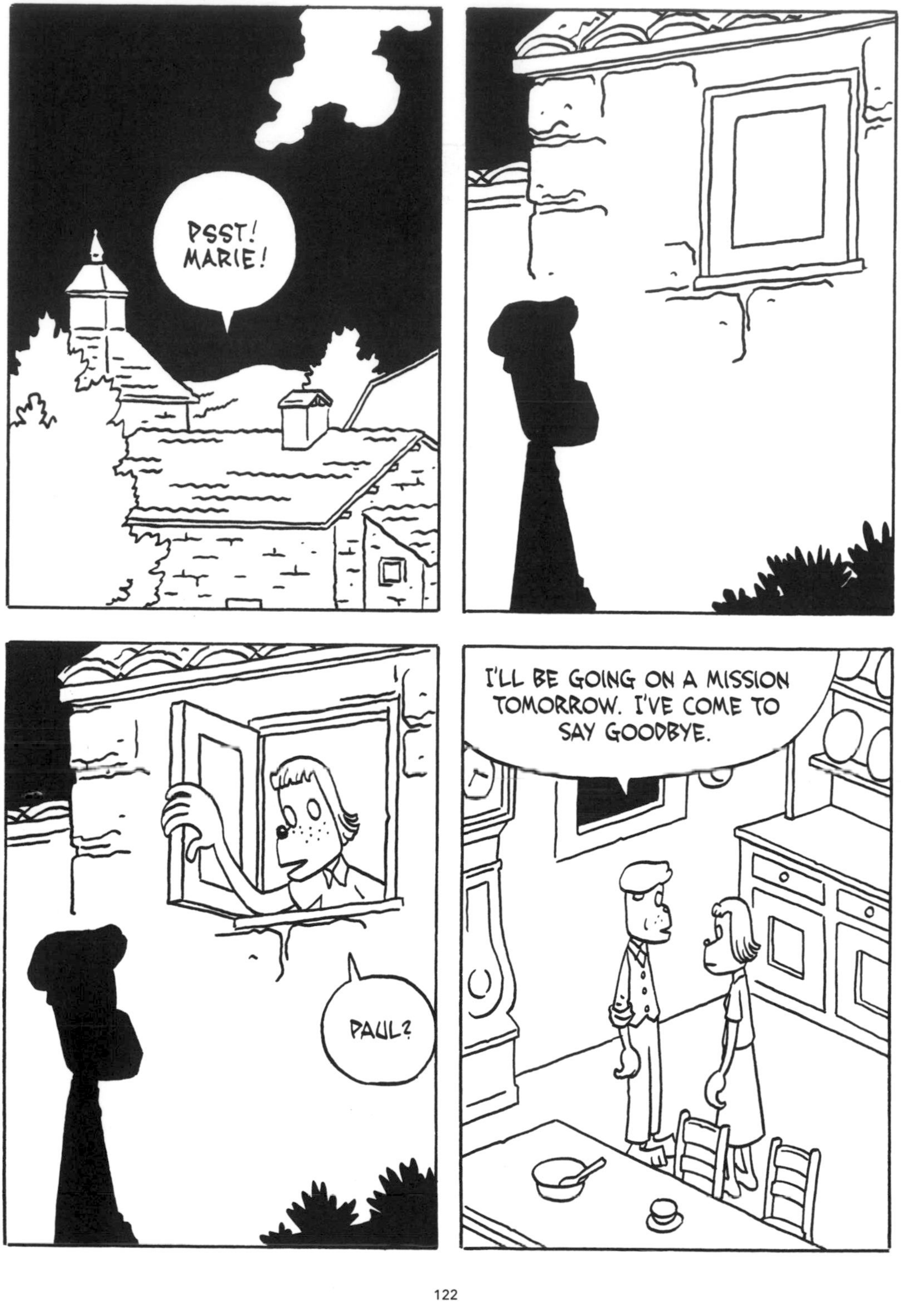
PSST! MARIE!
PAUL?
I'LL BE GOING ON A MISSION TOMORROW. I'VE COME TO SAY GOODBYE.

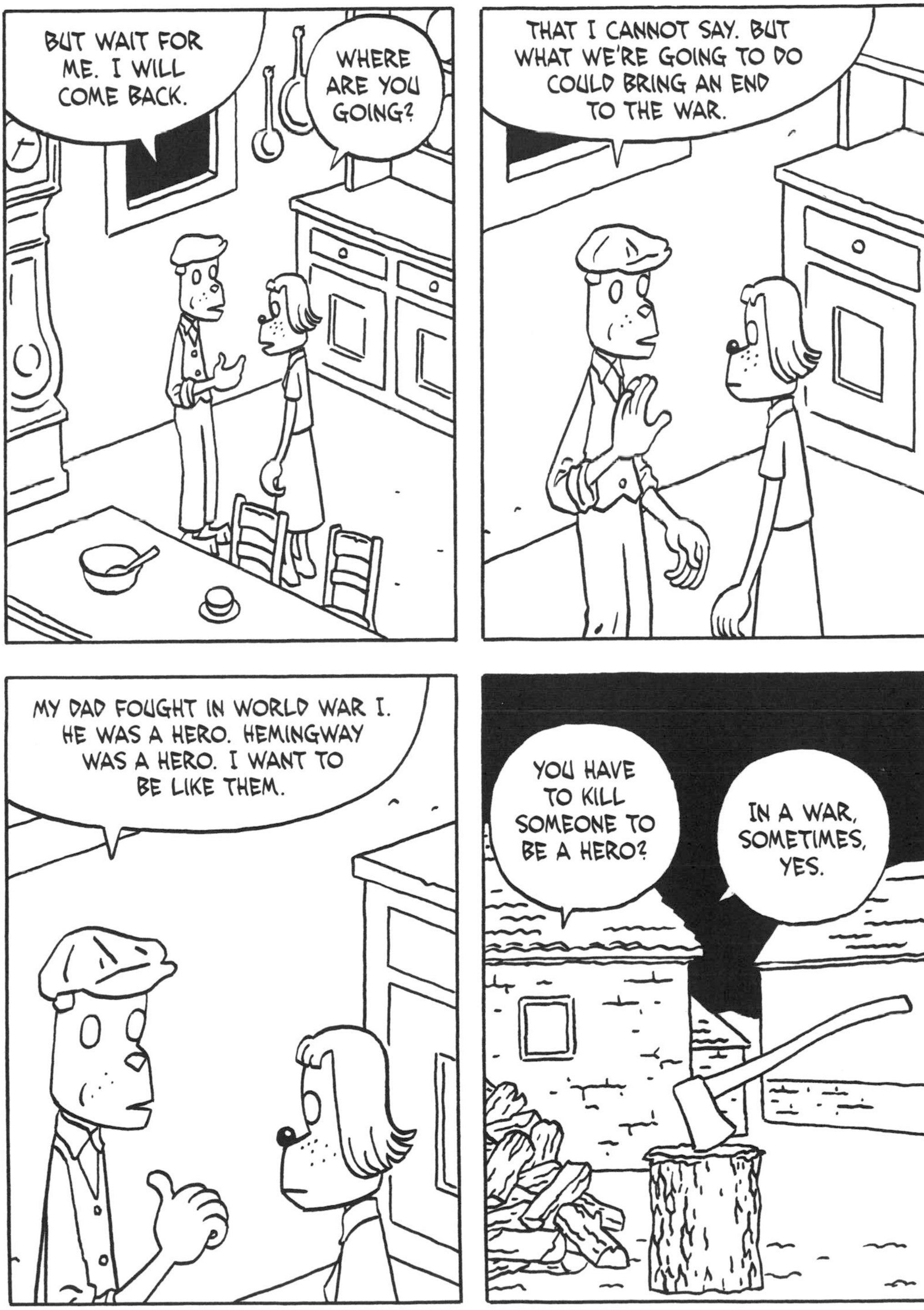
BUT WAIT FOR ME. I WILL COME BACK.
WHERE ARE YOU GOING?
THAT I CANNOT SAY. BUT WHAT WE'RE GOING TO DO COULD BRING AN END TO THE WAR.
MY DAD FOUGHT IN WORLD WAR I. HE WAS A HERO. HEMINGWAY WAS A HERO. I WANT TO BE LIKE THEM.
YOU HAVE TO KILL SOMEONE TO BE A HERO?
IN A WAR, SOMETIMES, YES.

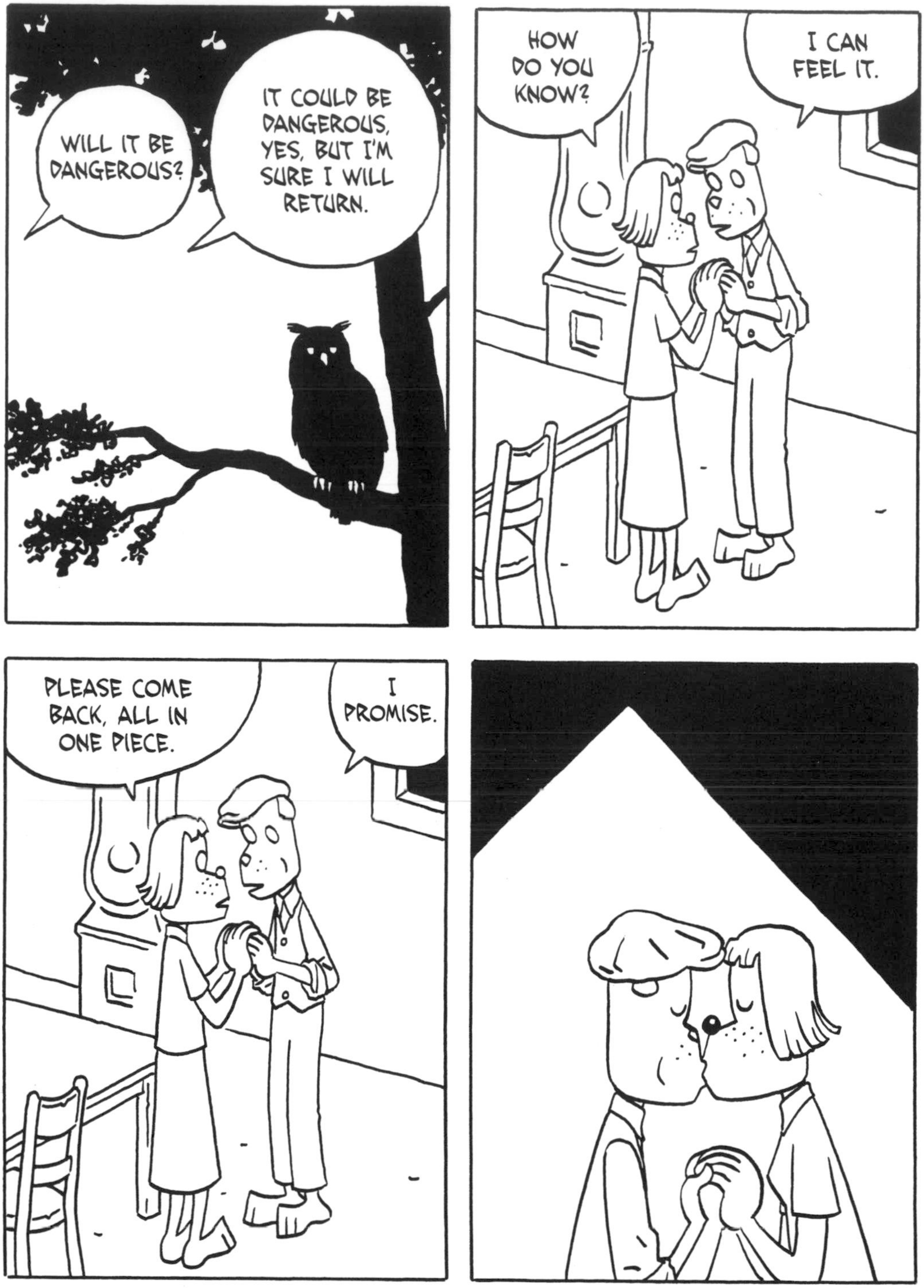
WILL IT BE DANGEROUS?
IT COULD BE DANGEROUS, YES, BUT I'M SURE I WILL RETURN.
HOW DO YOU KNOW?
I CAN FEEL IT.
PLEASE COME BACK, ALL IN ONE PIECE.
I PROMISE.

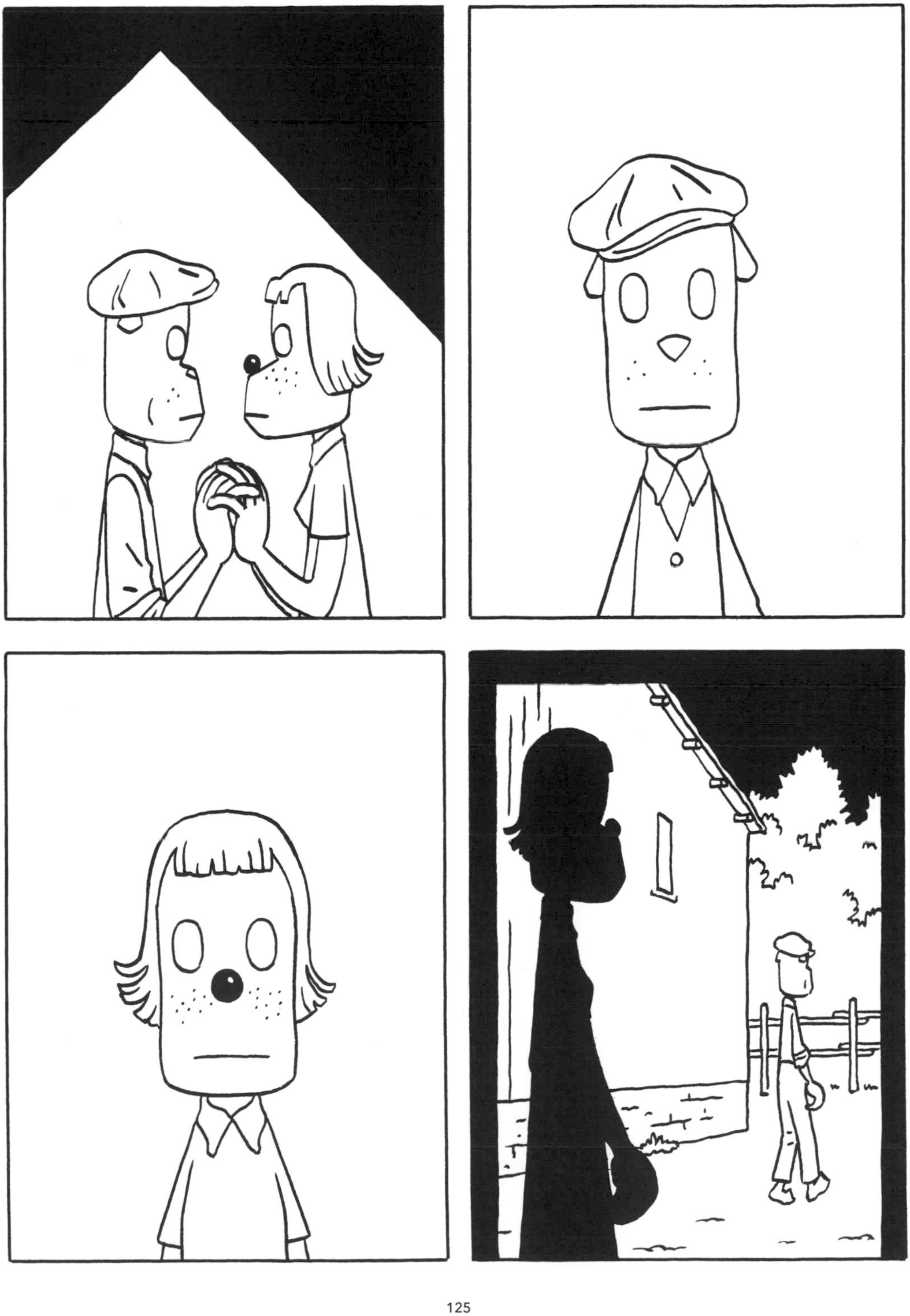

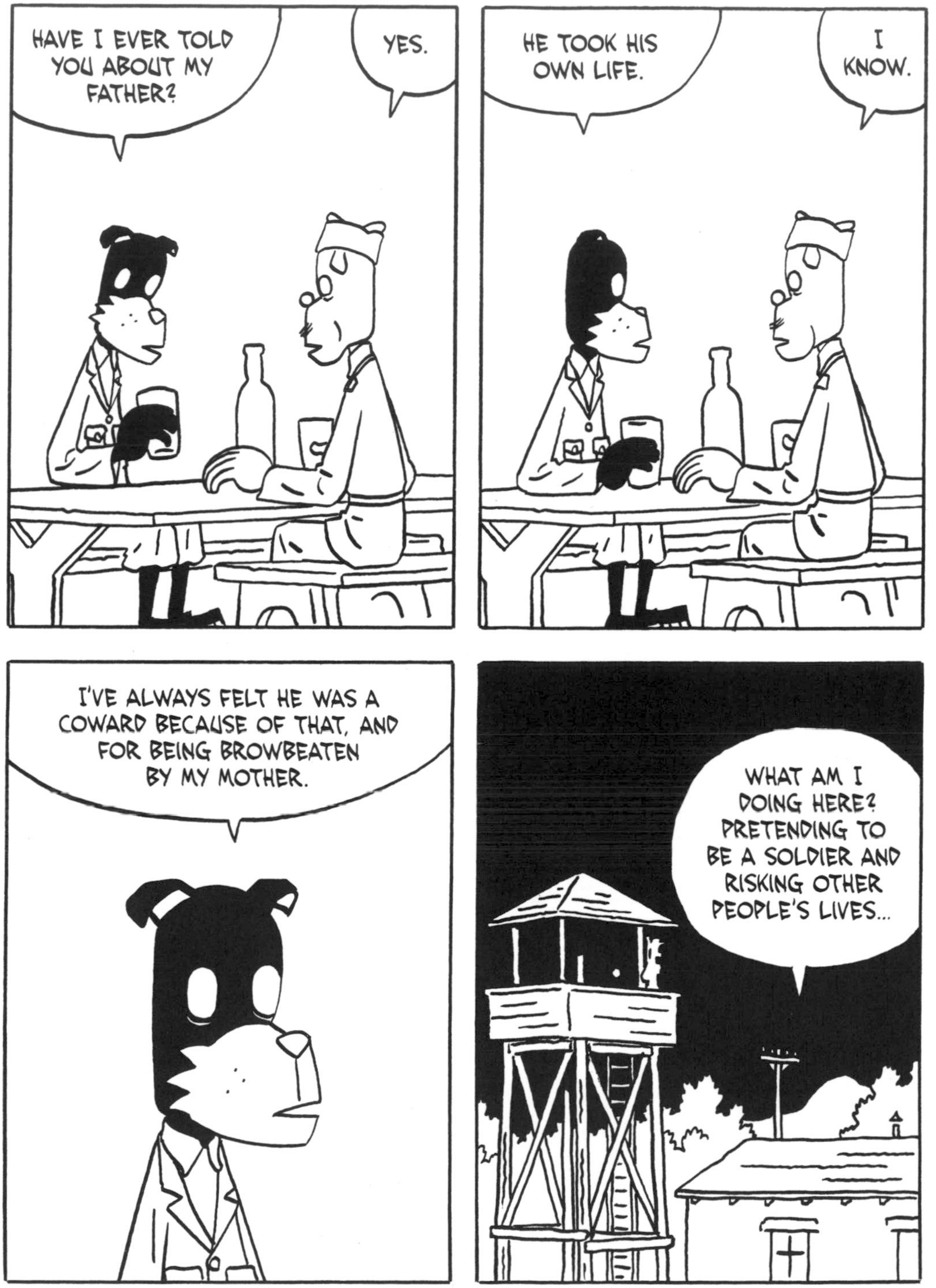
HAVE I EVER TOLD YOU ABOUT MY FATHER?
YES.
HE TOOK HIS OWN LIFE.
I KNOW.
I'VE ALWAYS FELT HE WAS A COWARD BECAUSE OF THAT, AND FOR BEING BROWBEATEN BY MY MOTHER.
WHAT AM I DOING HERE? PRETENDING TO BE A SOLDIER AND RISKING OTHER PEOPLE'S LIVES...

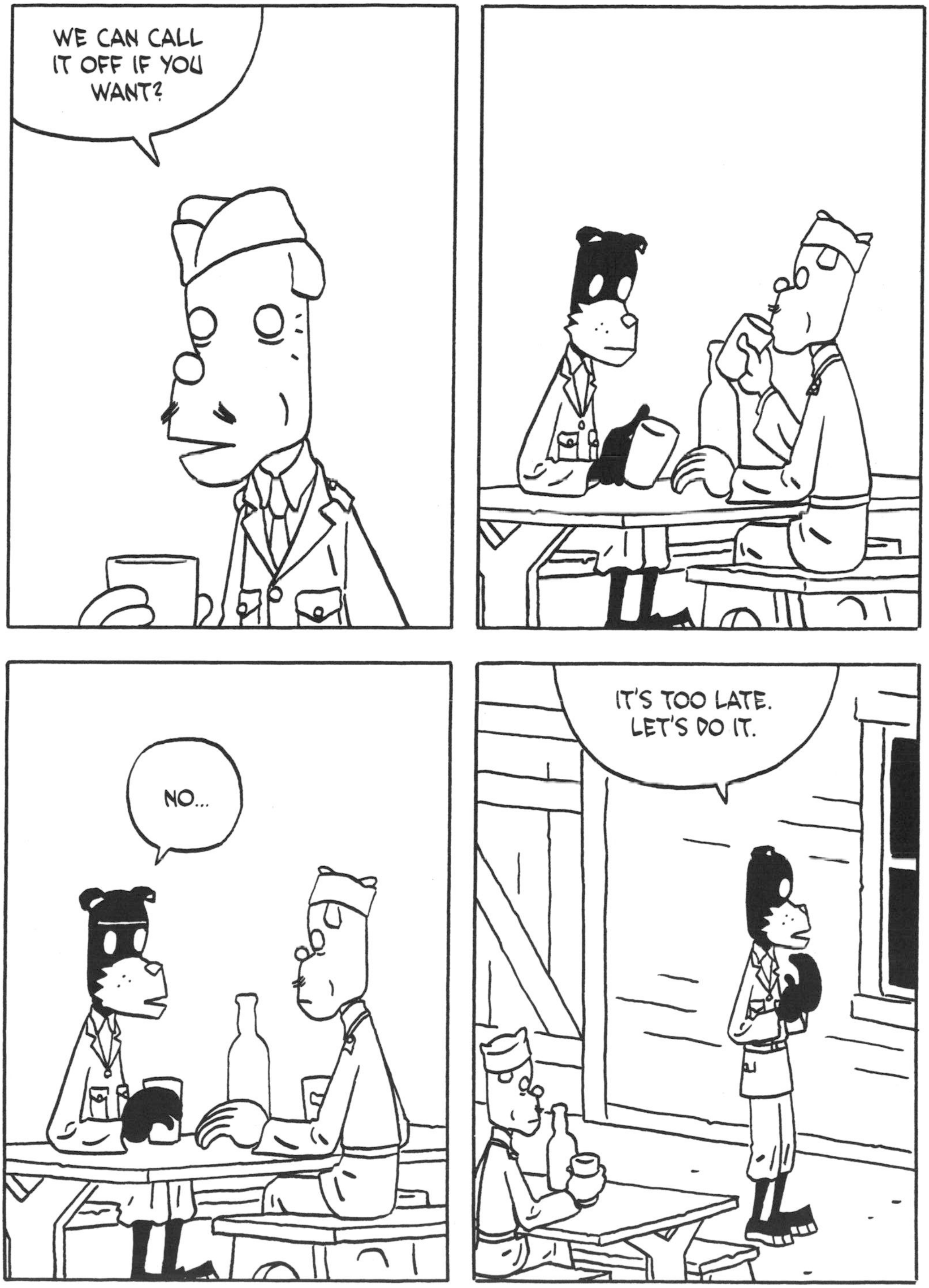
WE CAN CALL IT OFF IF YOU WANT?
NO...
IT'S TOO LATE. LET'S DO IT.

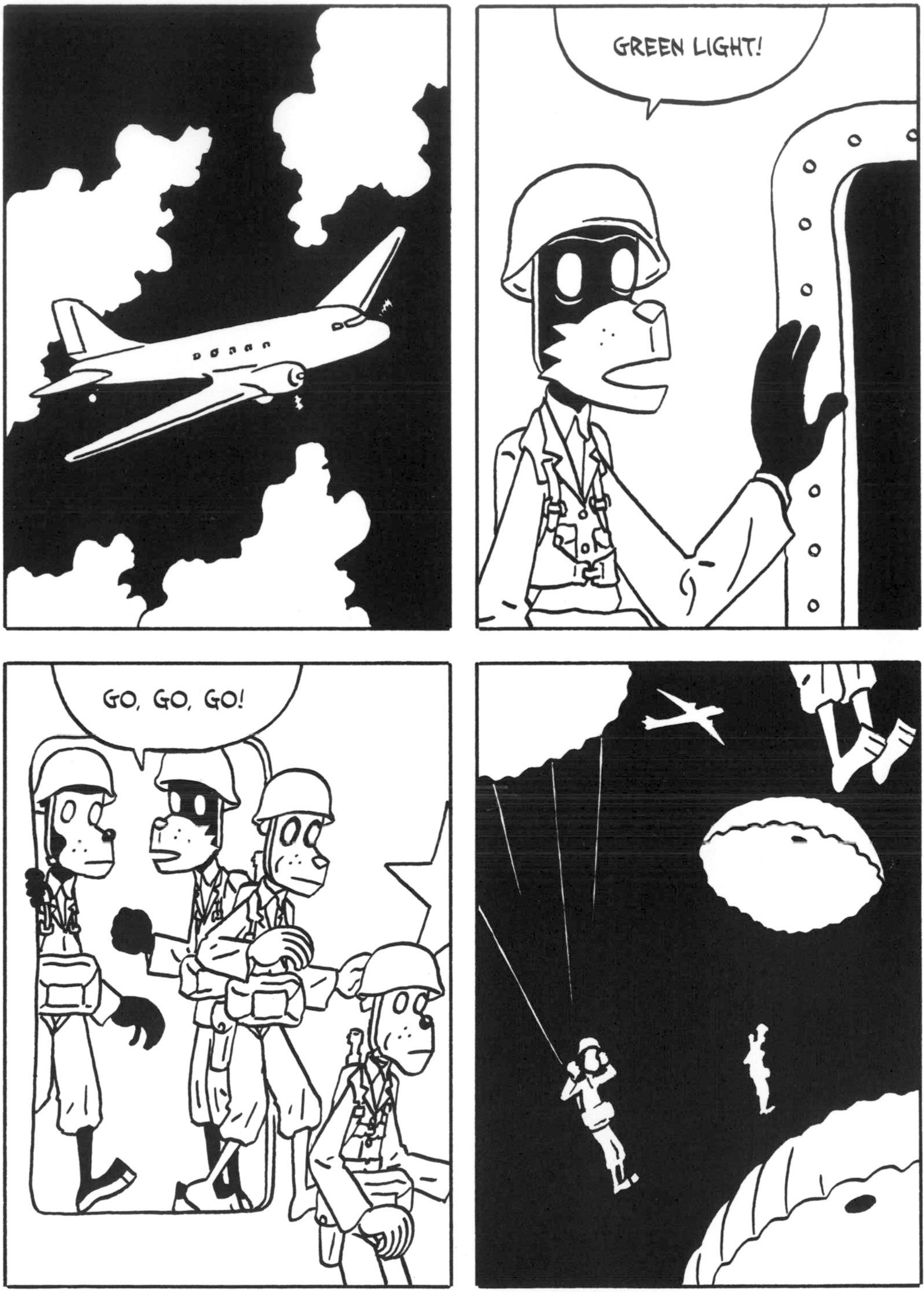
GREEN LIGHT!
GO, GO, GO!

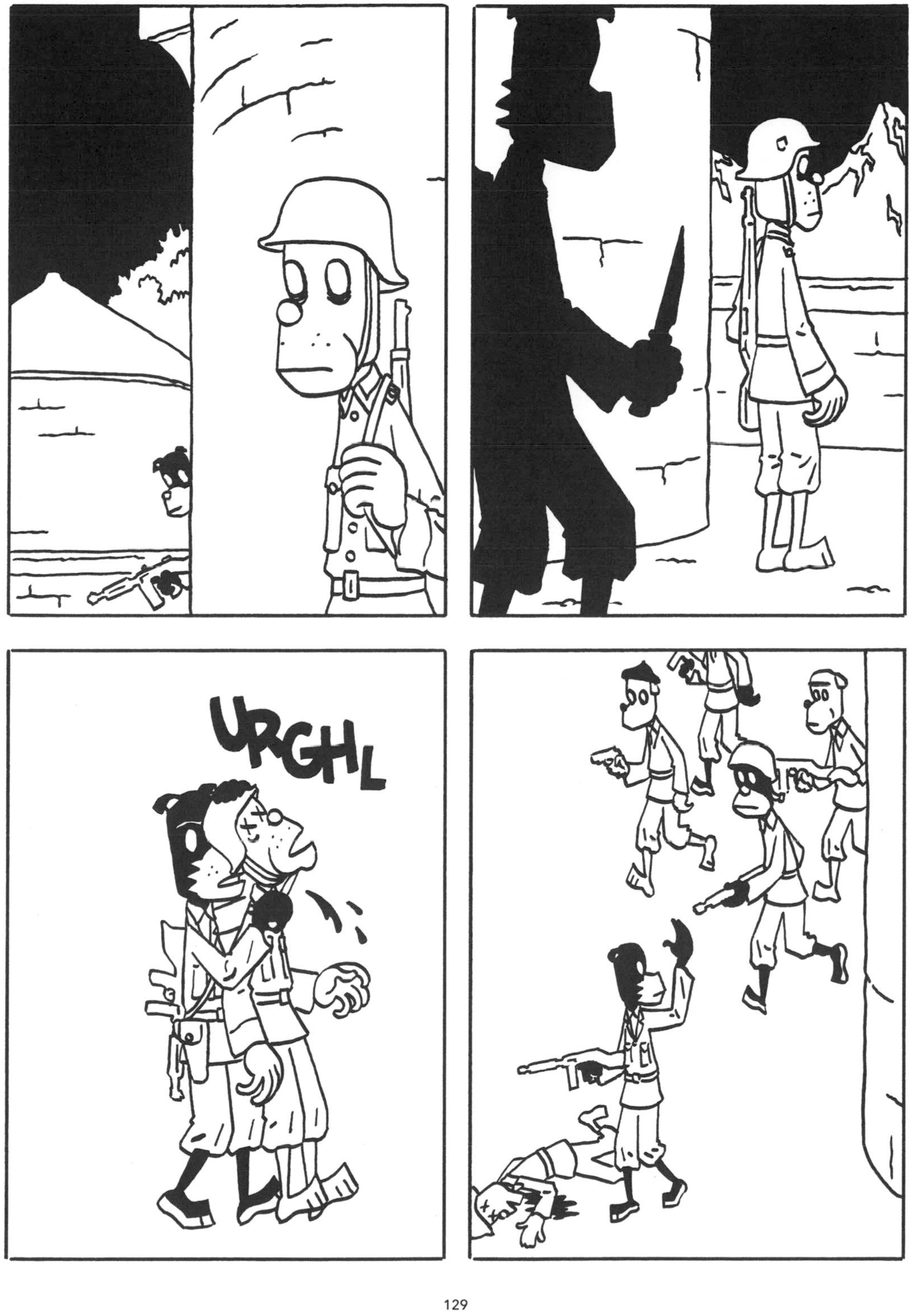
URGHL

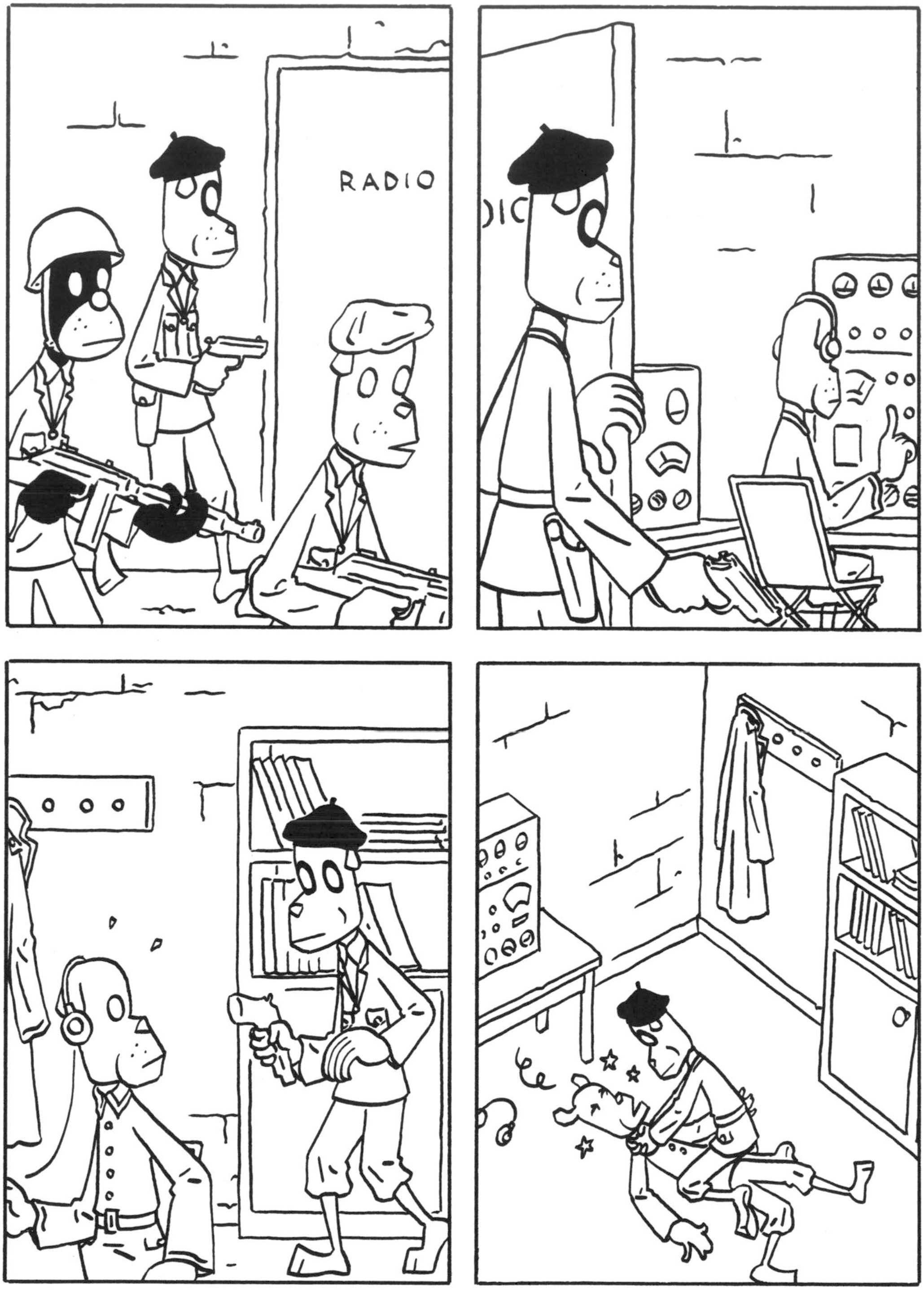
RADIO

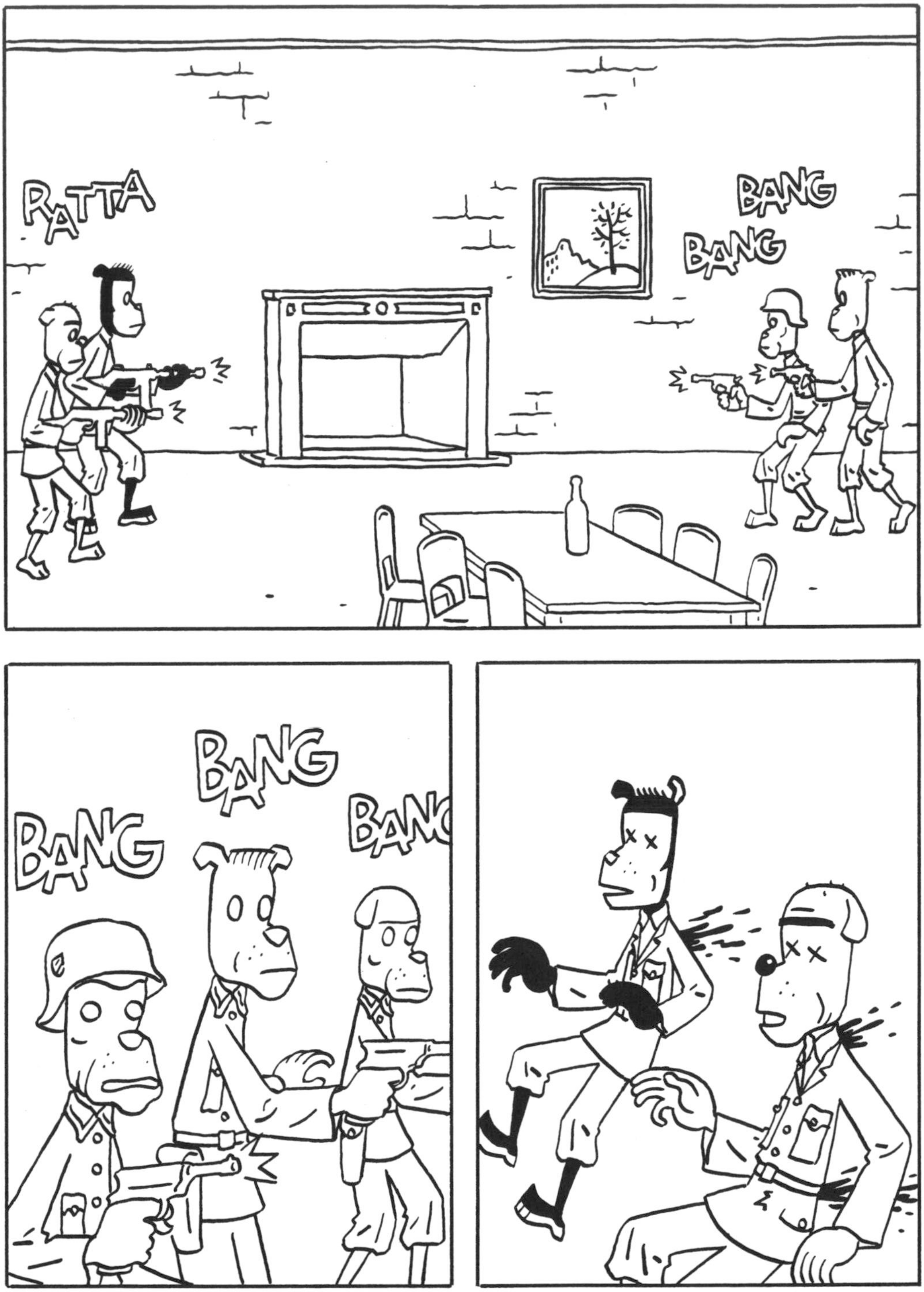
RATTA
BANG
BANG
BANG
BANG

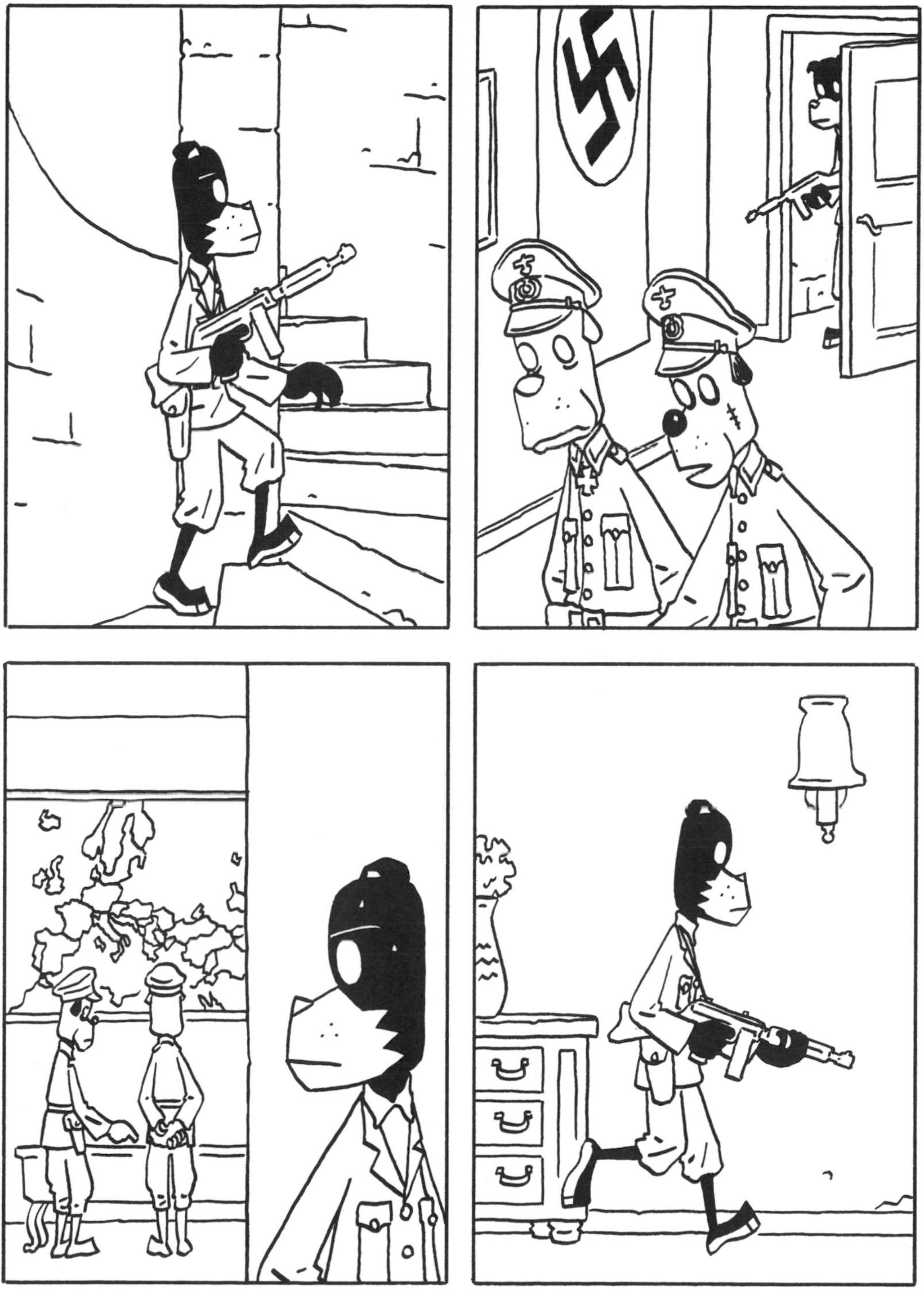

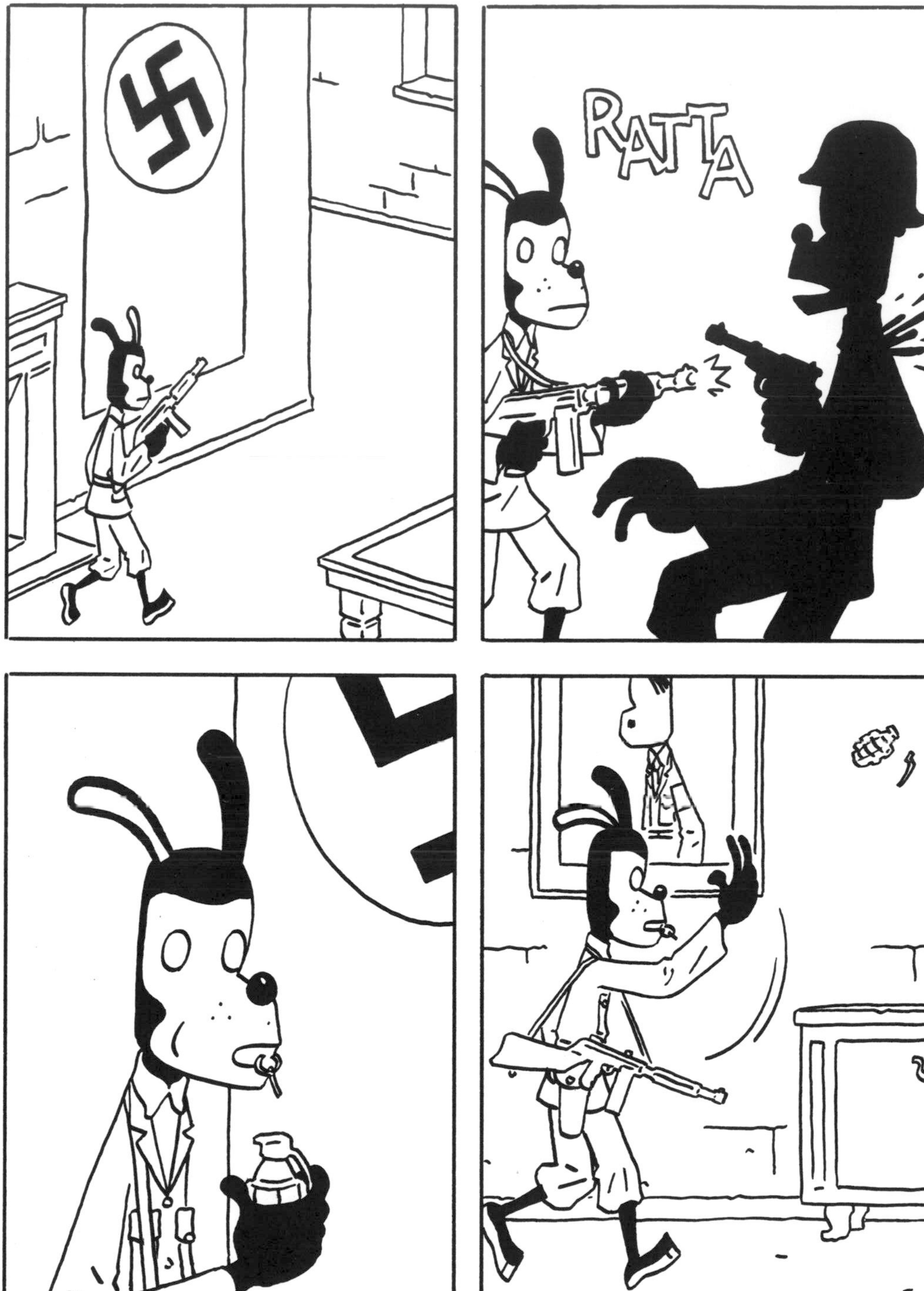
RATTA

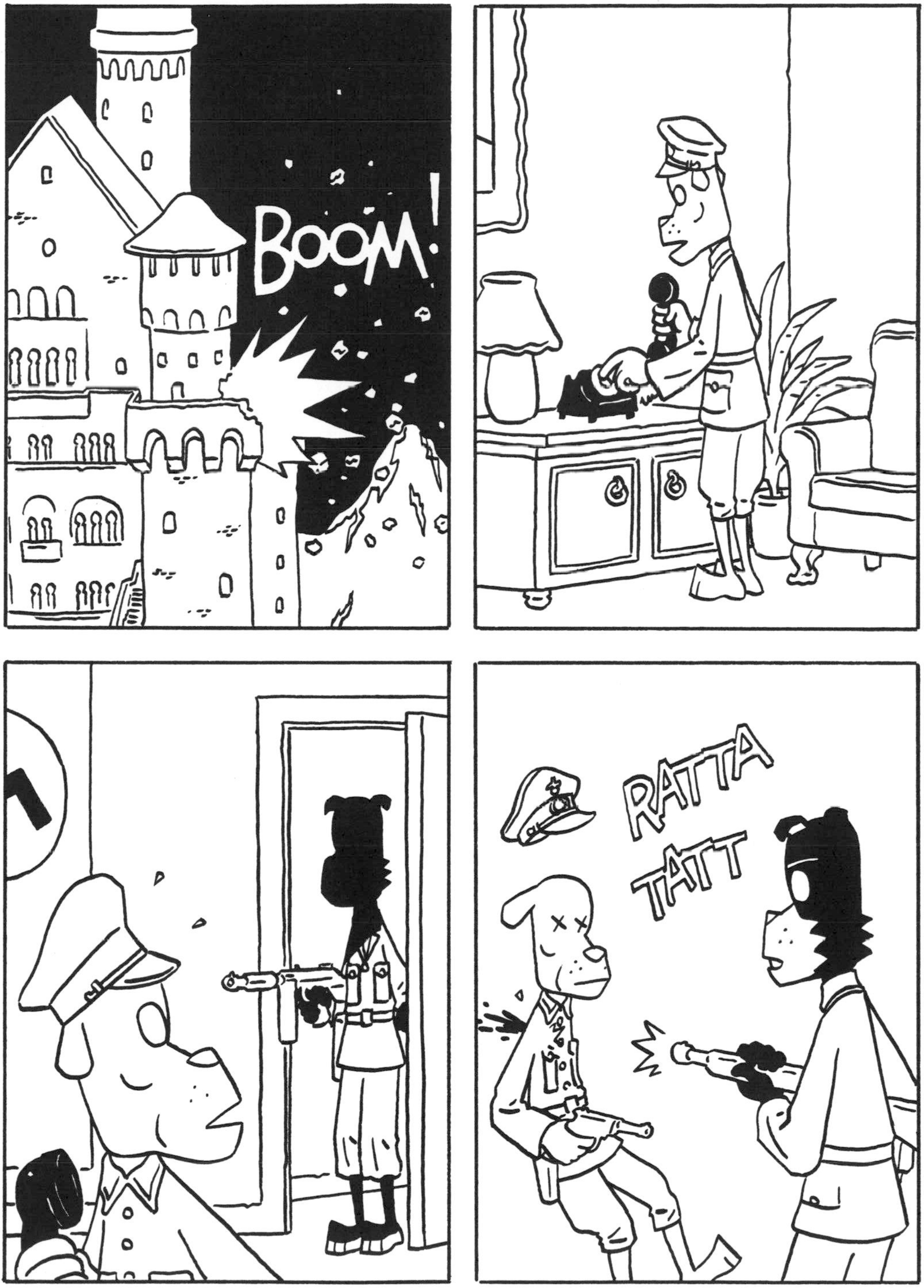
BOOM!
RATTA
TATT

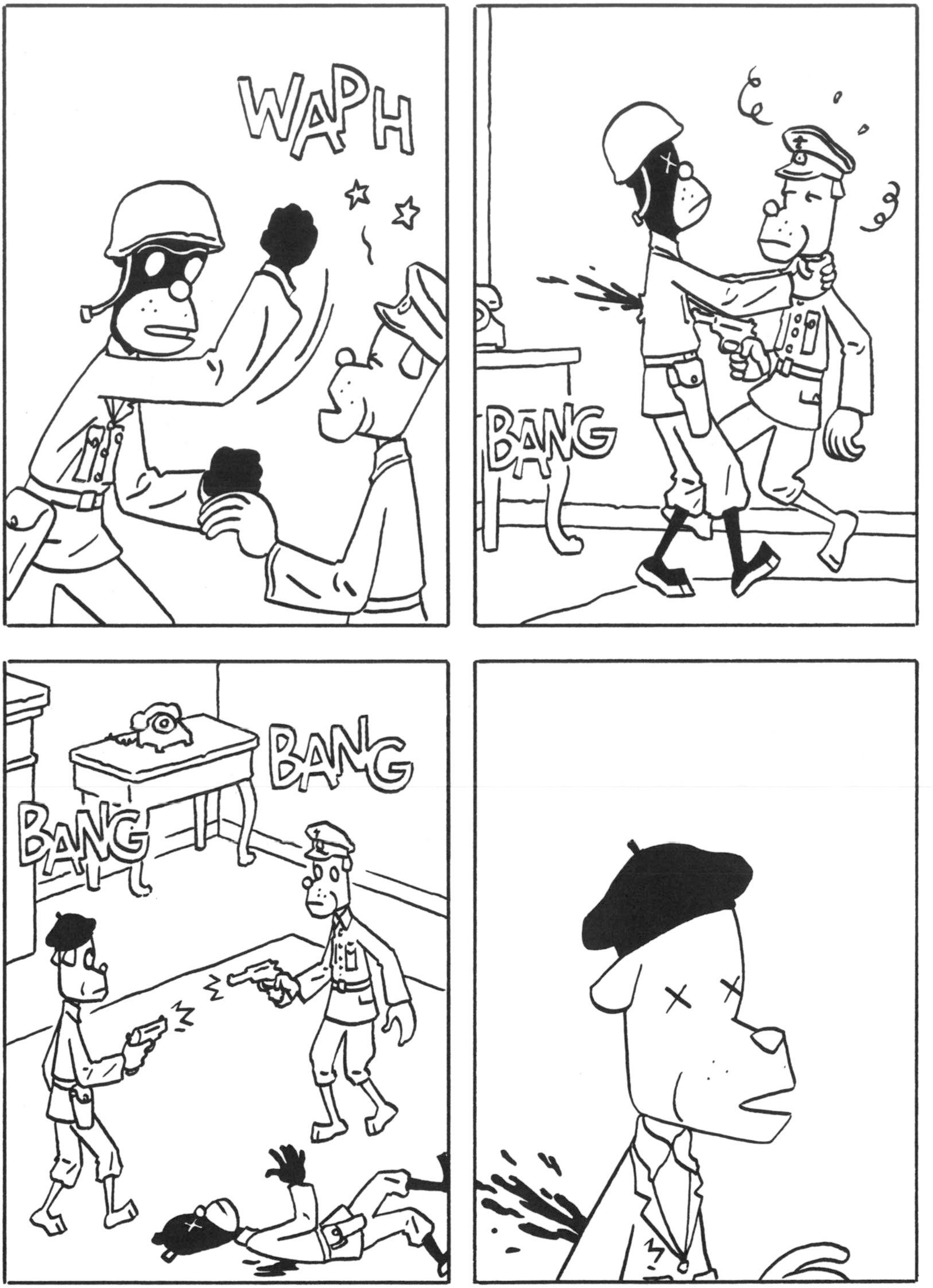
WAPH
BANG
BANG
BANG

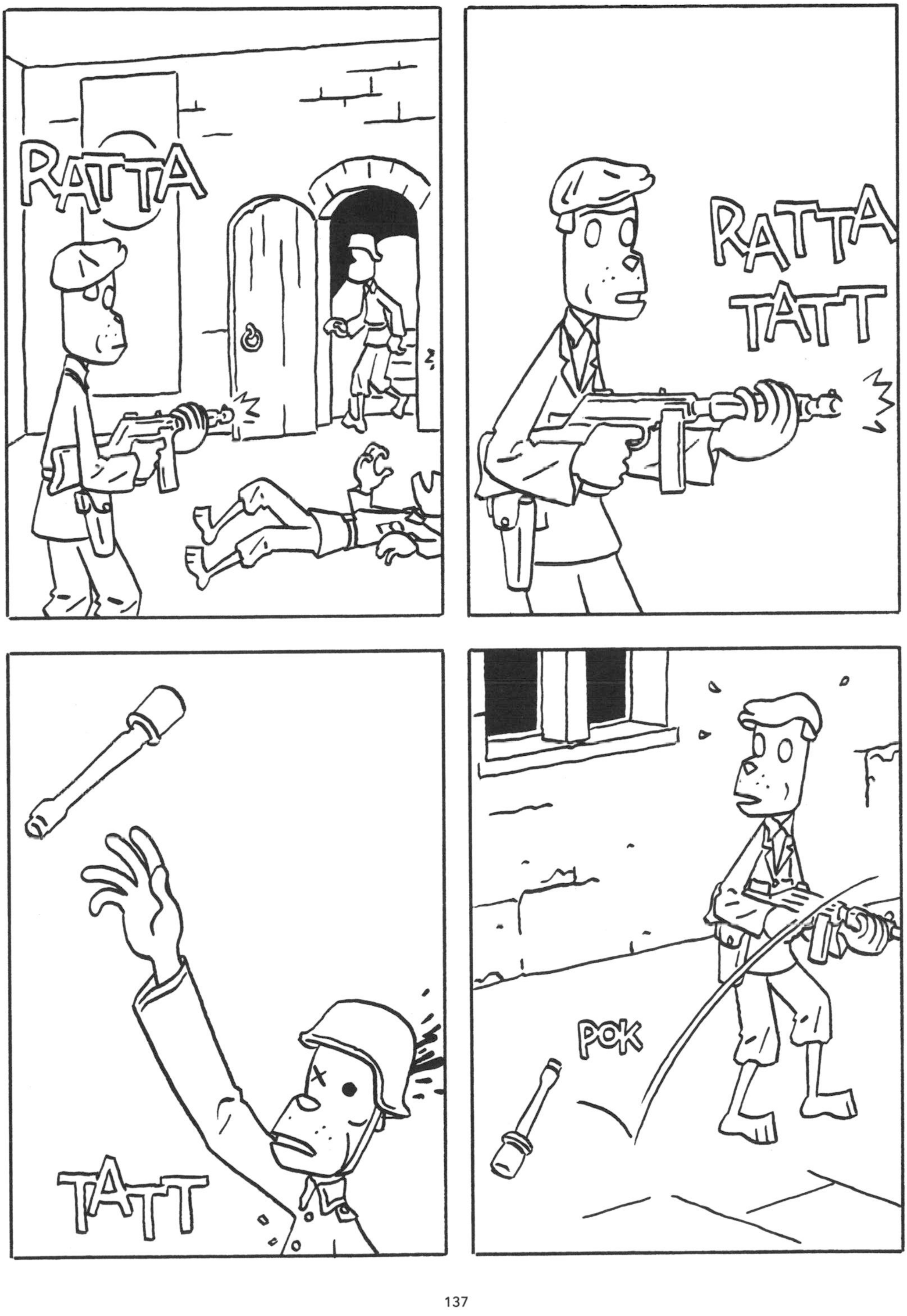
RATTA
RATTA
TATT
TATT
POK

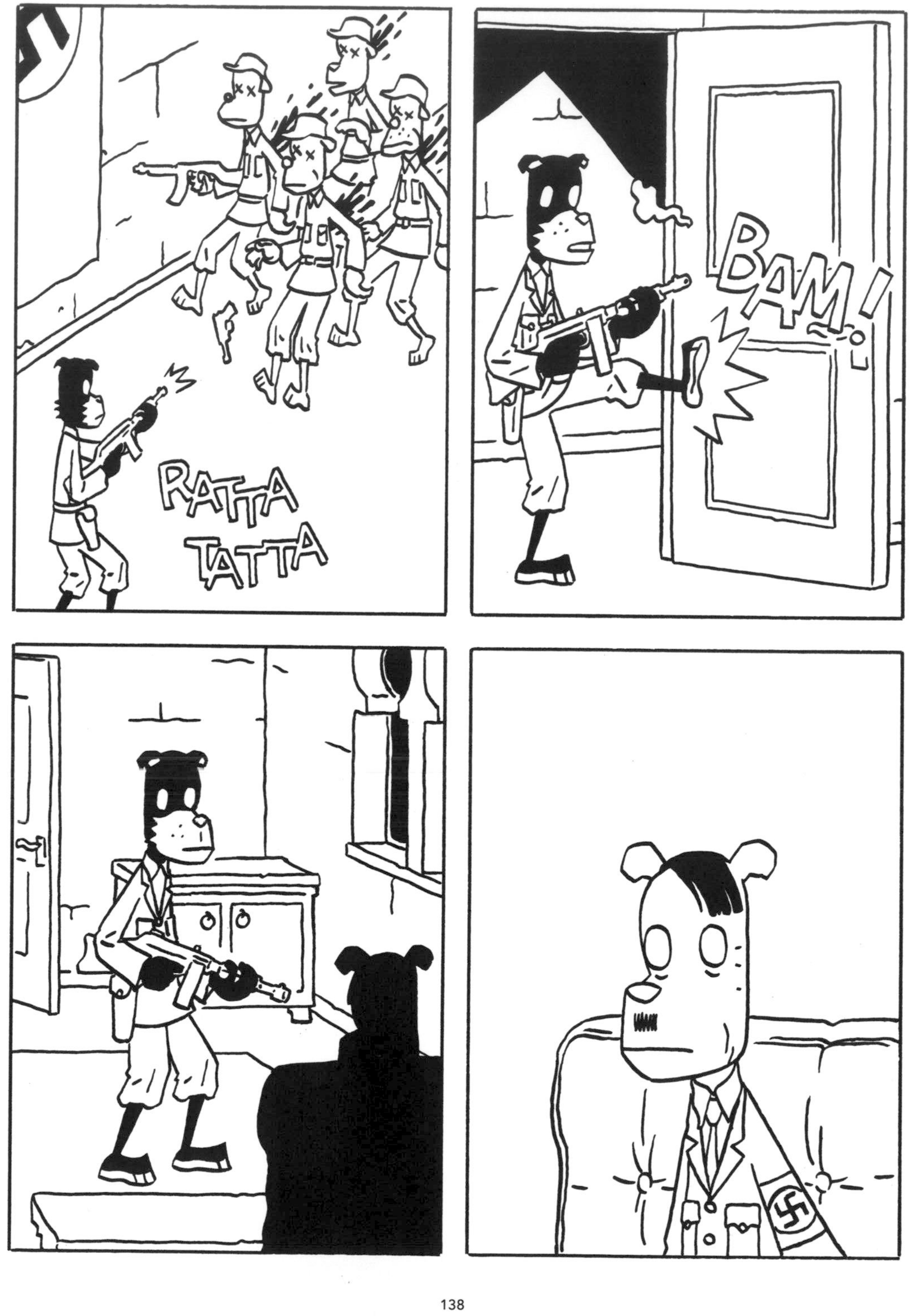
RATTA
TATTA
BAM!

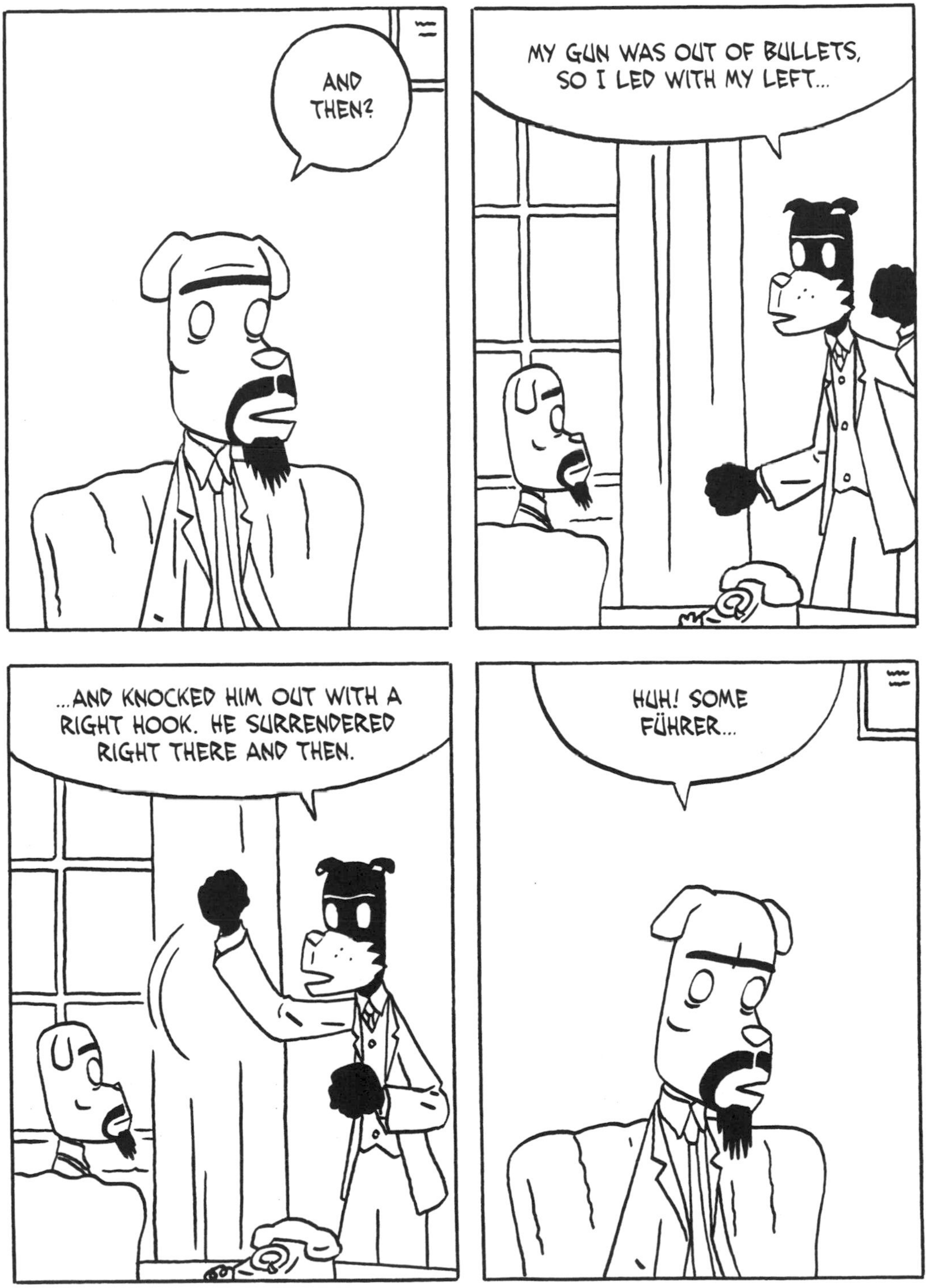
AND THEN?
MY GUN WAS OUT OF BULLETS, SO I LED WITH MY LEFT...
...AND KNOCKED HIM OUT WITH A RIGHT HOOK. HE SURRENDERED RIGHT THERE AND THEN.
HUH! SOME FÜHRER...

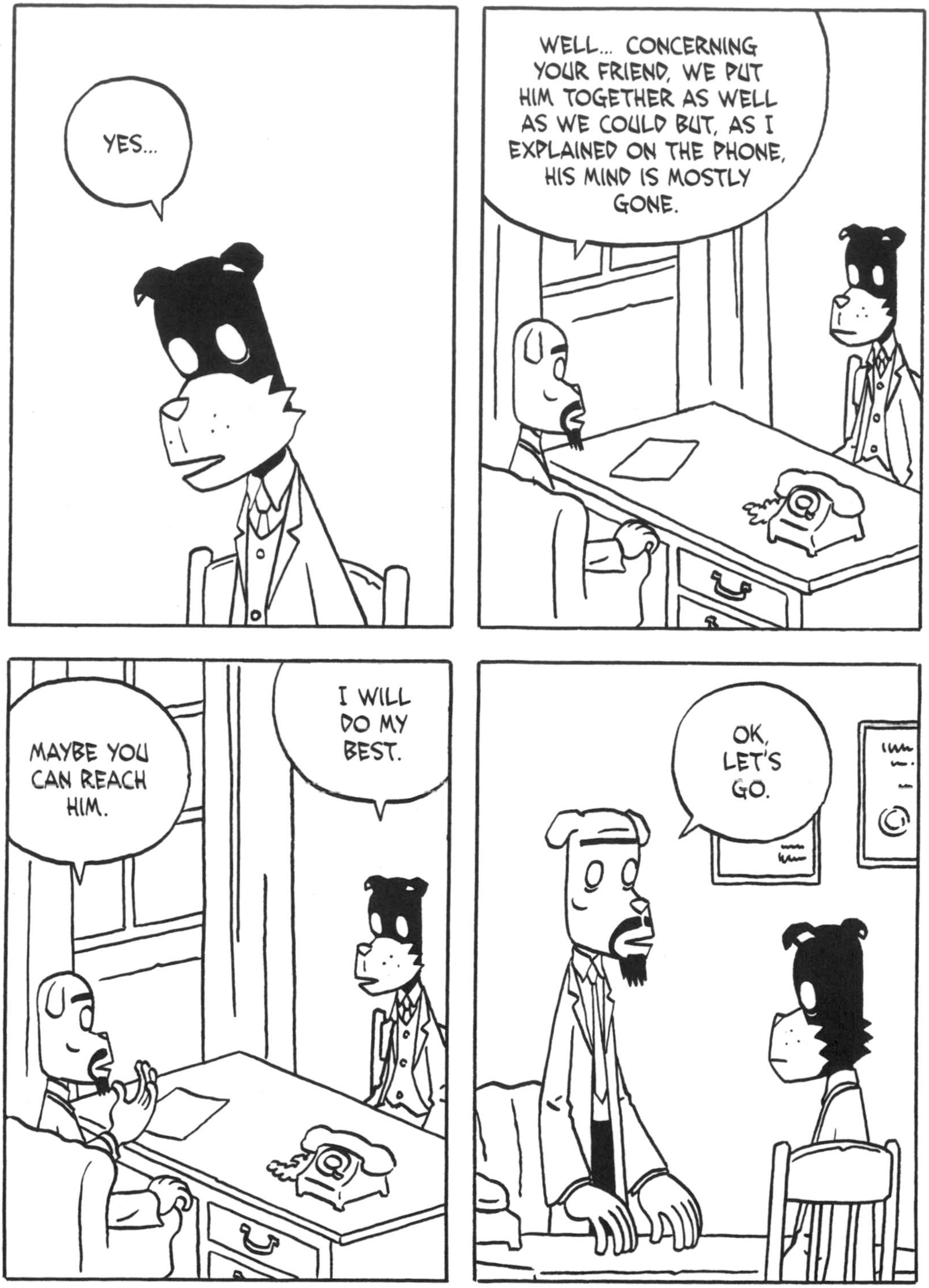
YES...
WELL... CONCERNING YOUR FRIEND, WE PUT HIM TOGETHER AS WELL AS WE COULD BUT, AS I EXPLAINED ON THE PHONE, HIS MIND IS MOSTLY GONE.
MAYBE YOU CAN REACH HIM.
I WILL DO MY BEST.
OK, LET'S GO.

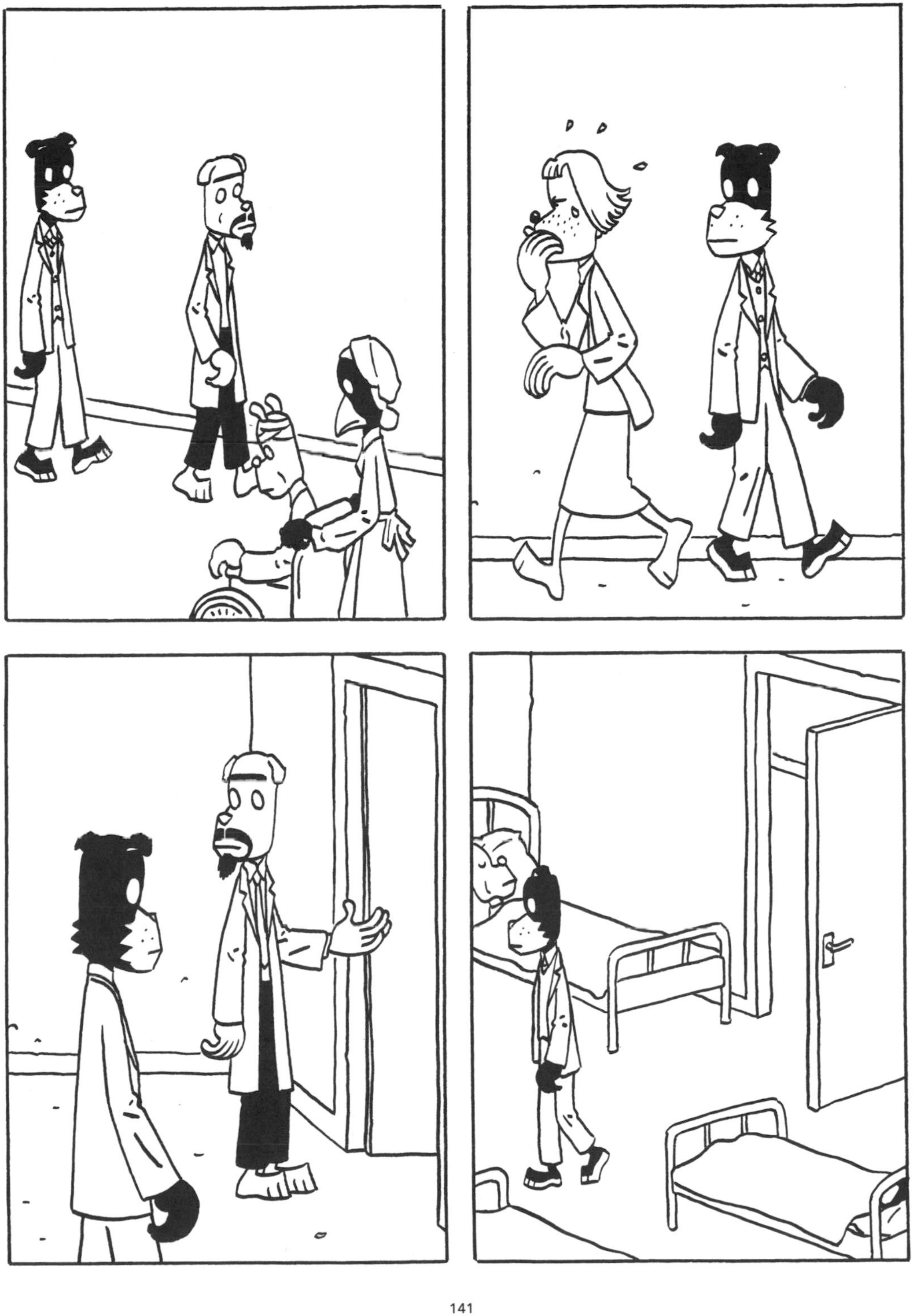

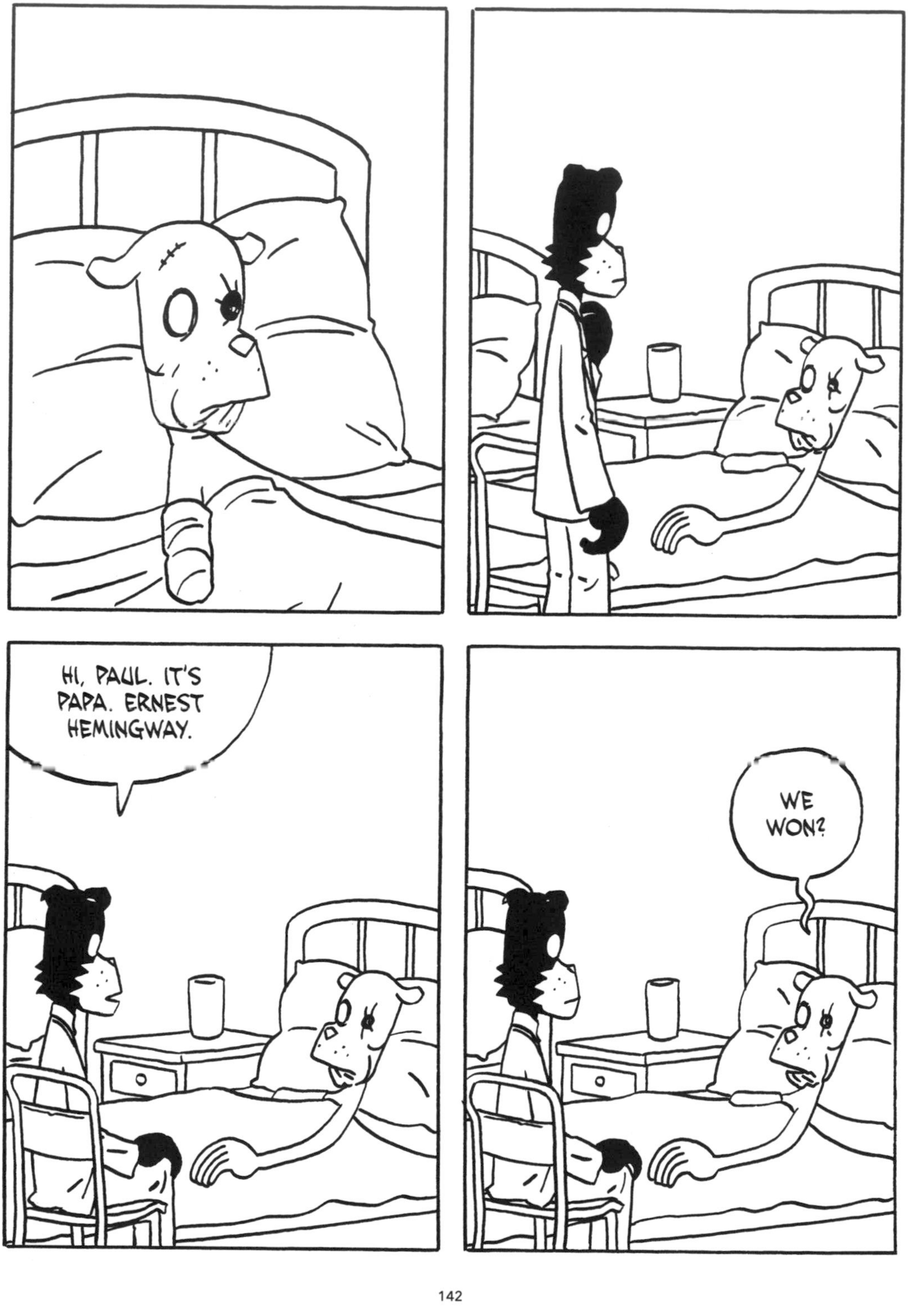
HI, PAUL. IT'S PAPA. ERNEST HEMINGWAY.
WE WON?

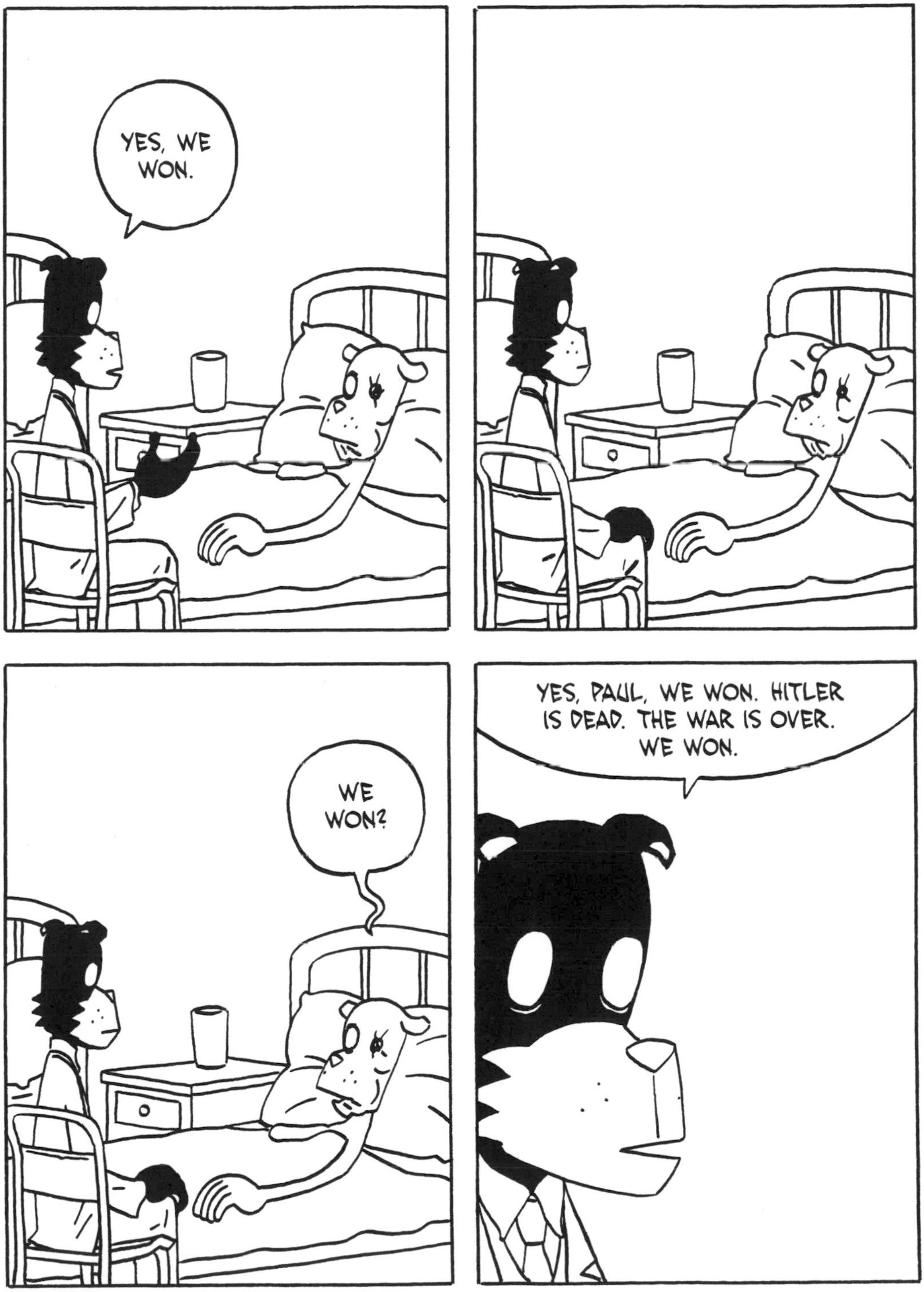
YES, WE WON.
WE WON?
YES, PAUL, WE WON. HITLER IS DEAD. THE WAR IS OVER. WE WON.

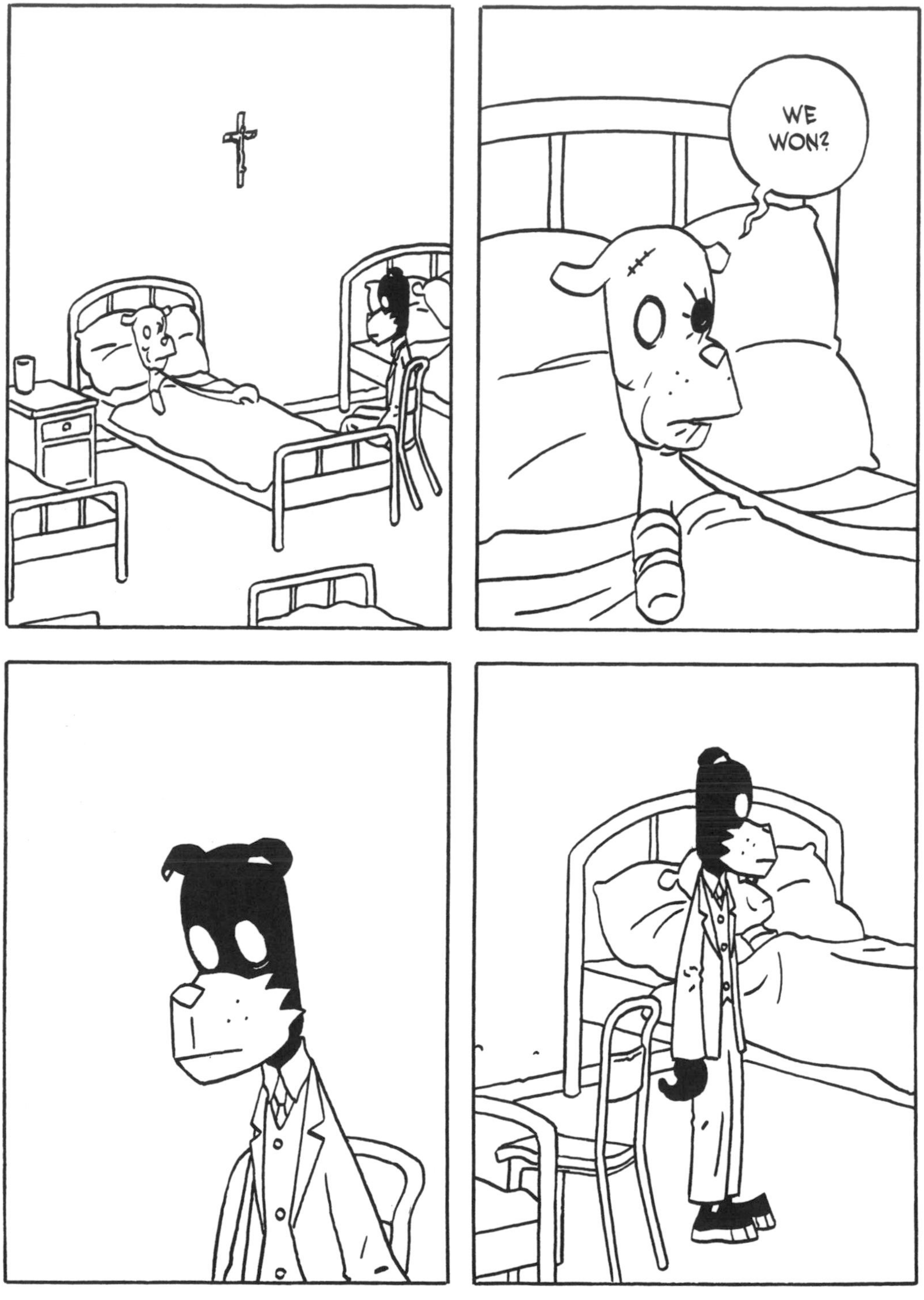
WE WON?

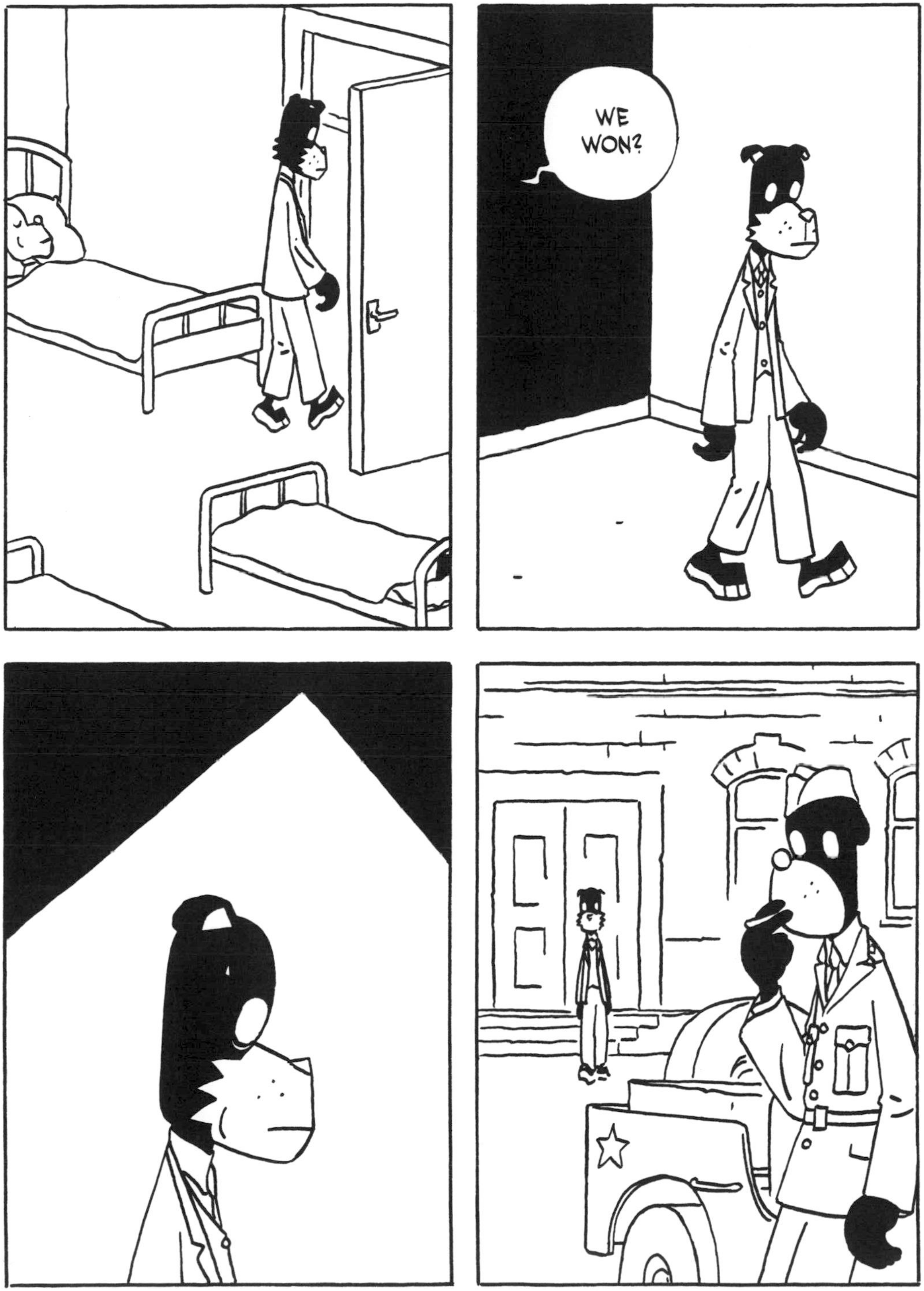
WE WON?

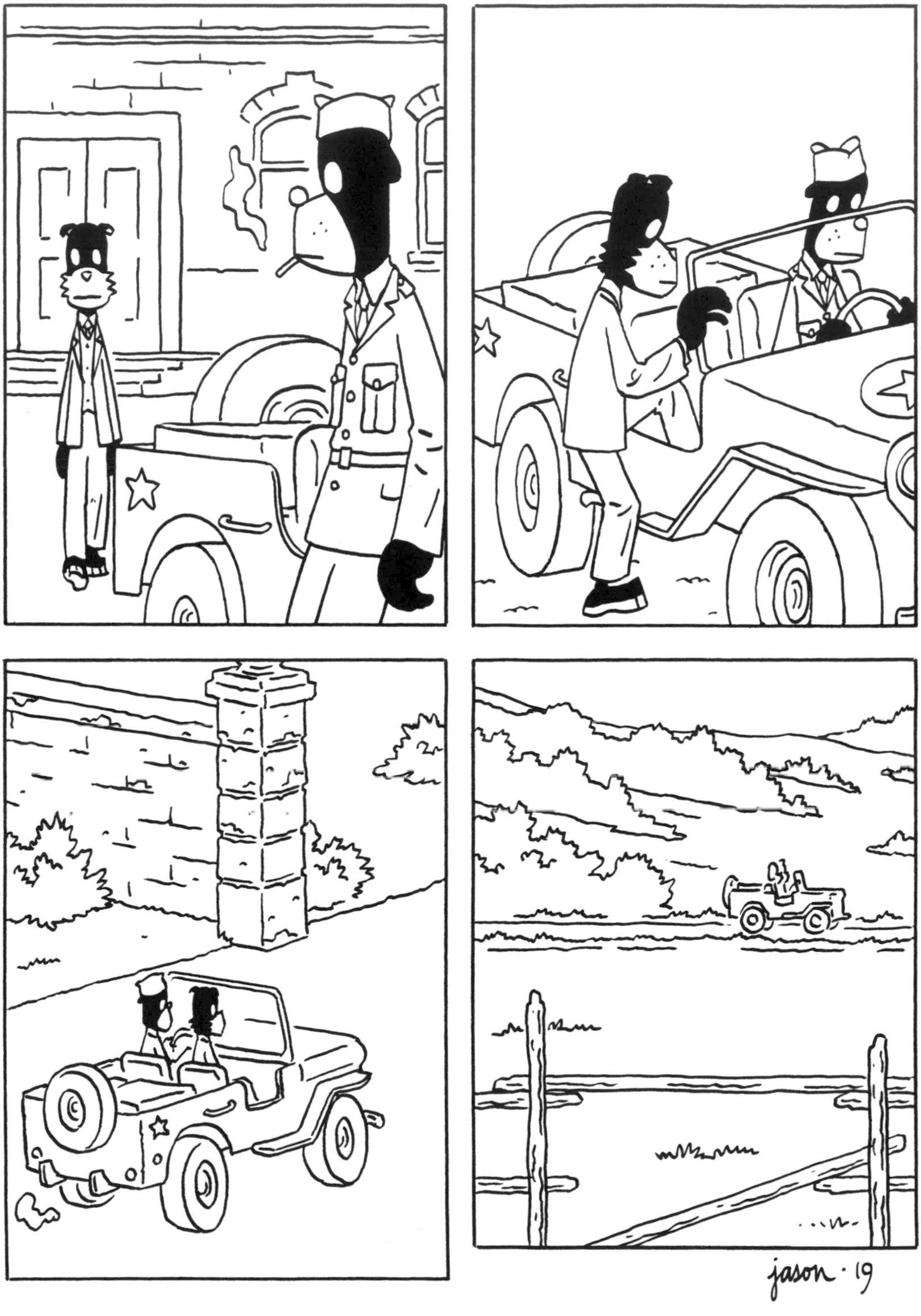
jason · 19

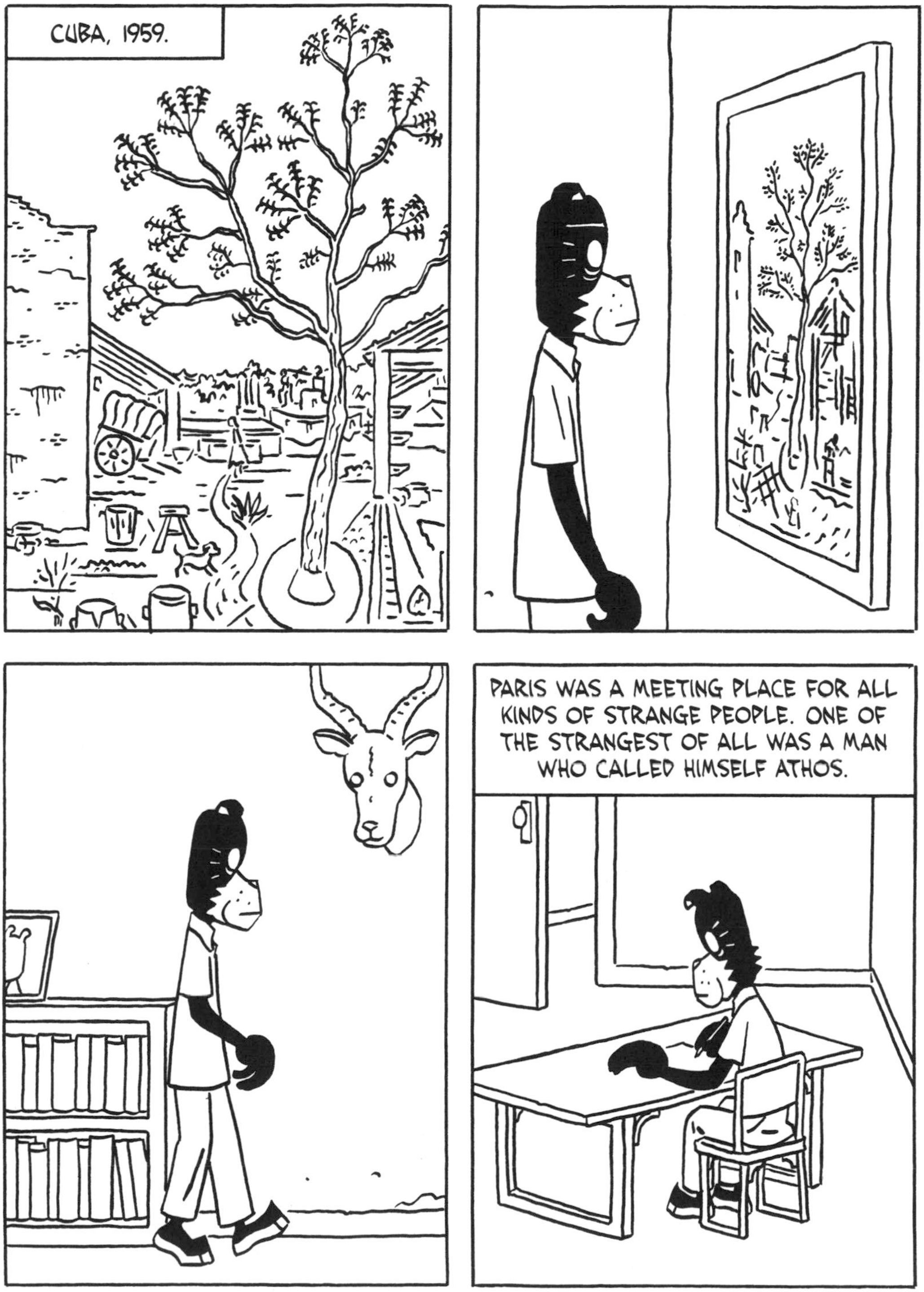
CUBA, 1959.
PARIS WAS A MEETING PLACE FOR ALL KINDS OF STRANGE PEOPLE. ONE OF THE STRANGEST OF ALL WAS A MAN WHO CALLED HIMSELF ATHOS.

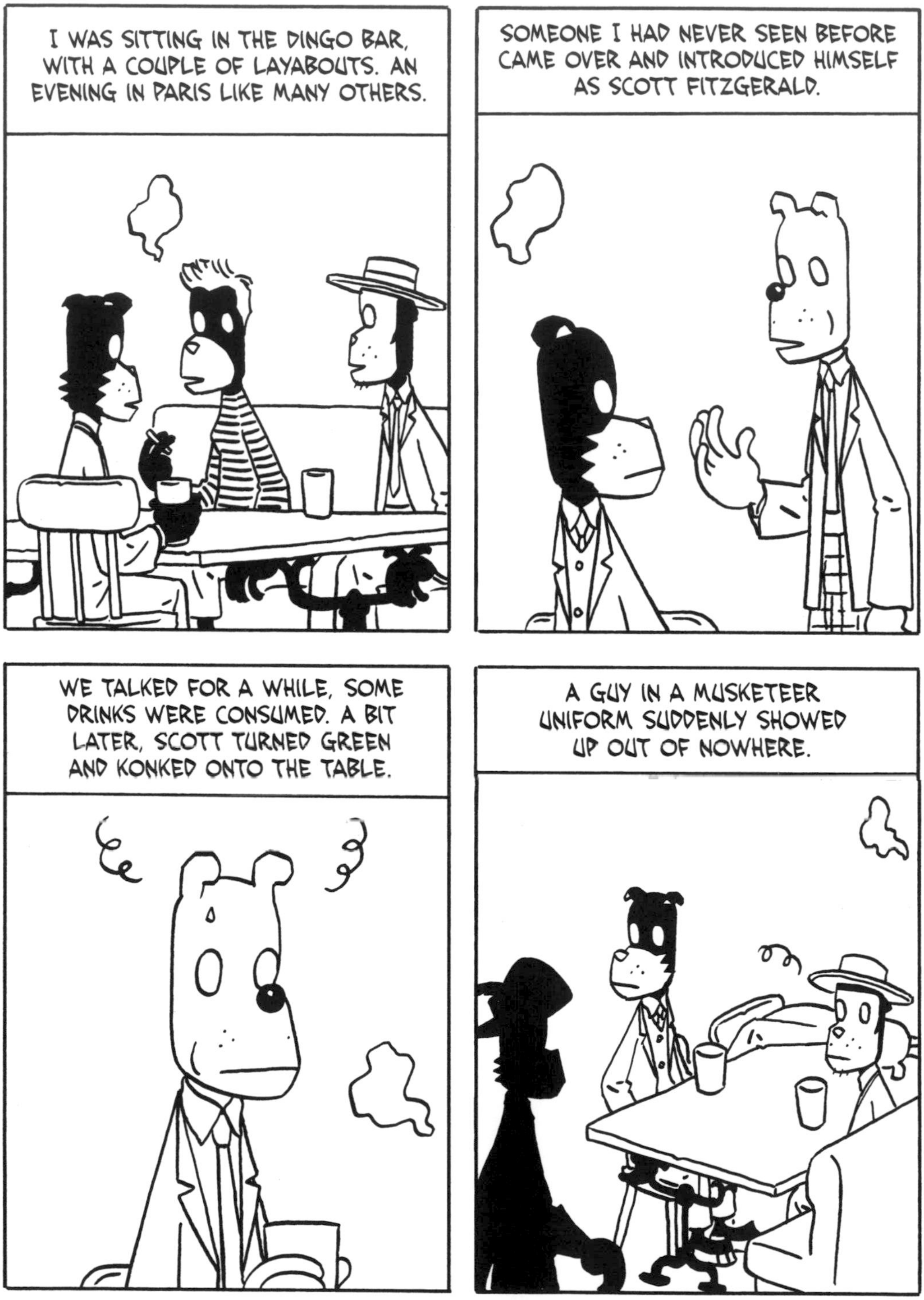
I WAS SITTING IN THE DINGO BAR, WITH A COUPLE OF LAYABOUTS. AN EVENING IN PARIS LIKE MANY OTHERS.
SOMEONE I HAD NEVER SEEN BEFORE CAME OVER AND INTRODUCED HIMSELF AS SCOTT FITZGERALD.
WE TALKED FOR A WHILE, SOME DRINKS WERE CONSUMED. A BIT LATER, SCOTT TURNED GREEN AND KONKED ONTO THE TABLE.
A GUY IN A MUSKETEER UNIFORM SUDDENLY SHOWED UP OUT OF NOWHERE.

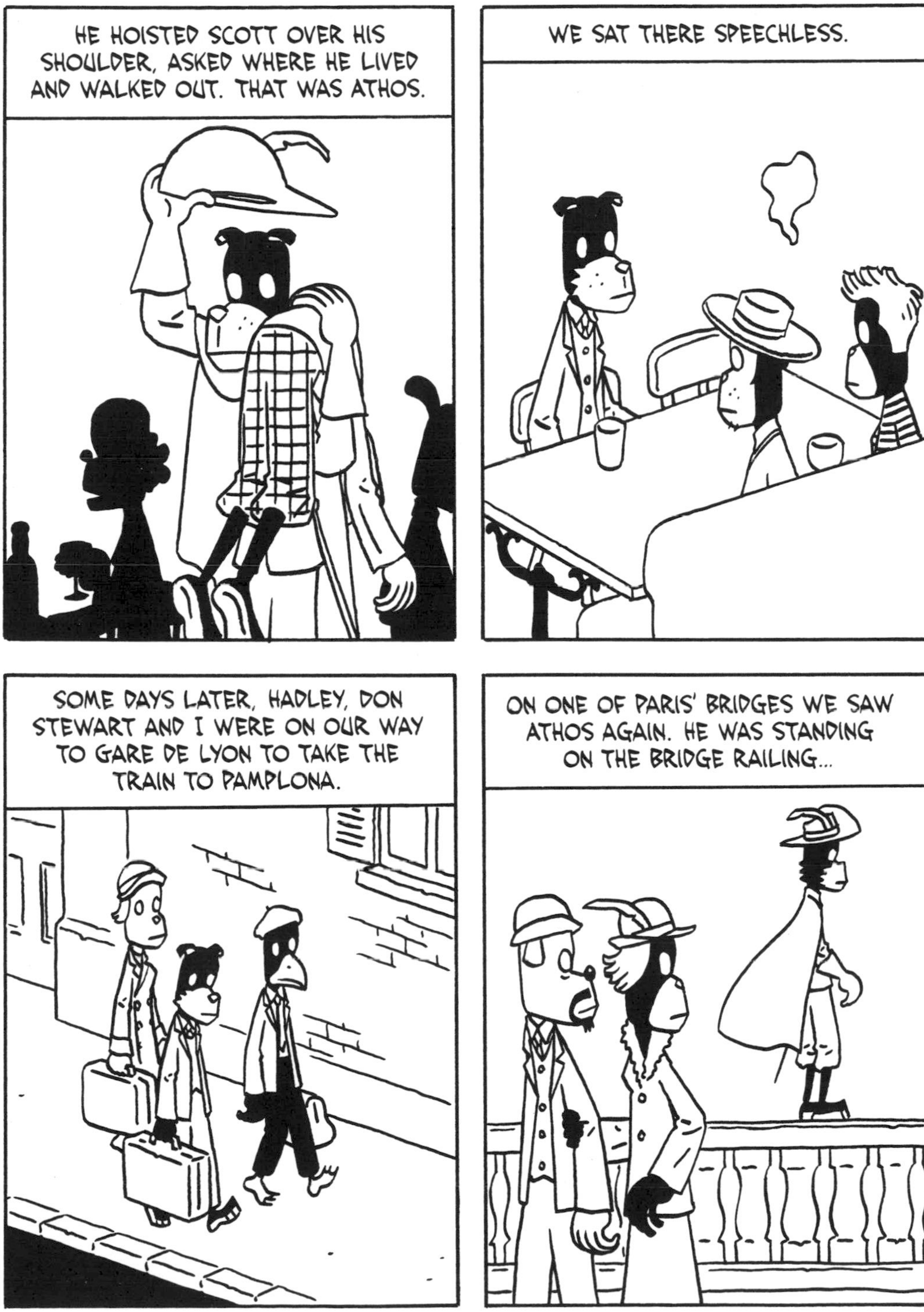
HE HOISTED SCOTT OVER HIS SHOULDER, ASKED WHERE HE LIVED AND WALKED OUT. THAT WAS ATHOS.
WE SAT THERE SPEECHLESS.
SOME DAYS LATER, HADLEY, DON STEWART AND I WERE ON OUR WAY TO GARE DE LYON TO TAKE THE TRAIN TO PAMPLONA.
ON ONE OF PARIS' BRIDGES WE SAW ATHOS AGAIN. HE WAS STANDING ON THE BRIDGE RAILING...

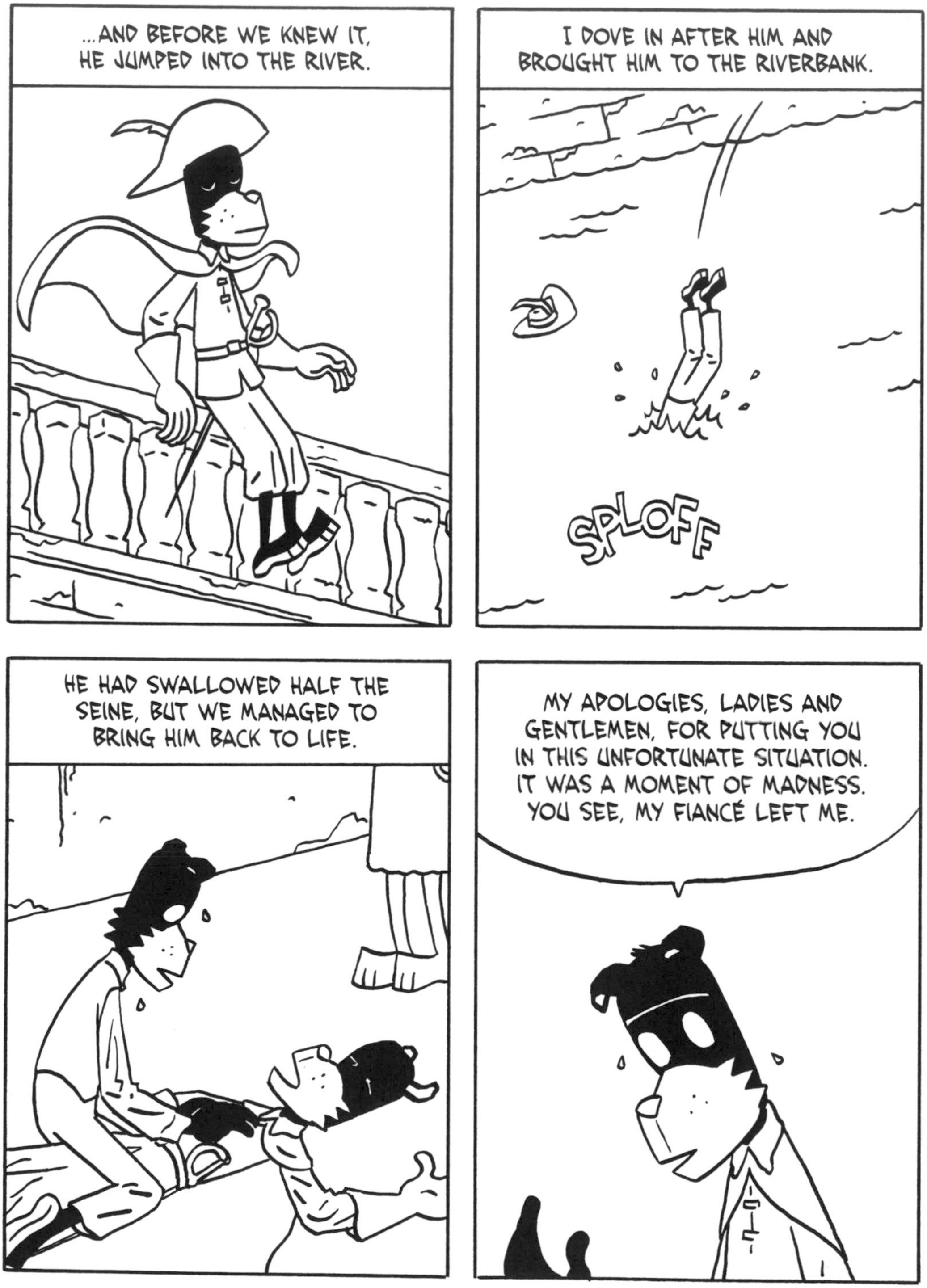
...AND BEFORE WE KNEW IT, HE JUMPED INTO THE RIVER.
I DOVE IN AFTER HIM AND BROUGHT HIM TO THE RIVERBANK.
SPLOFF
HE HAD SWALLOWED HALF THE SEINE, BUT WE MANAGED TO BRING HIM BACK TO LIFE.
MY APOLOGIES, LADIES AND GENTLEMEN, FOR PUTTING YOU IN THIS UNFORTUNATE SITUATION. IT WAS A MOMENT OF MADNESS. YOU SEE, MY FIANCÉ LEFT ME.

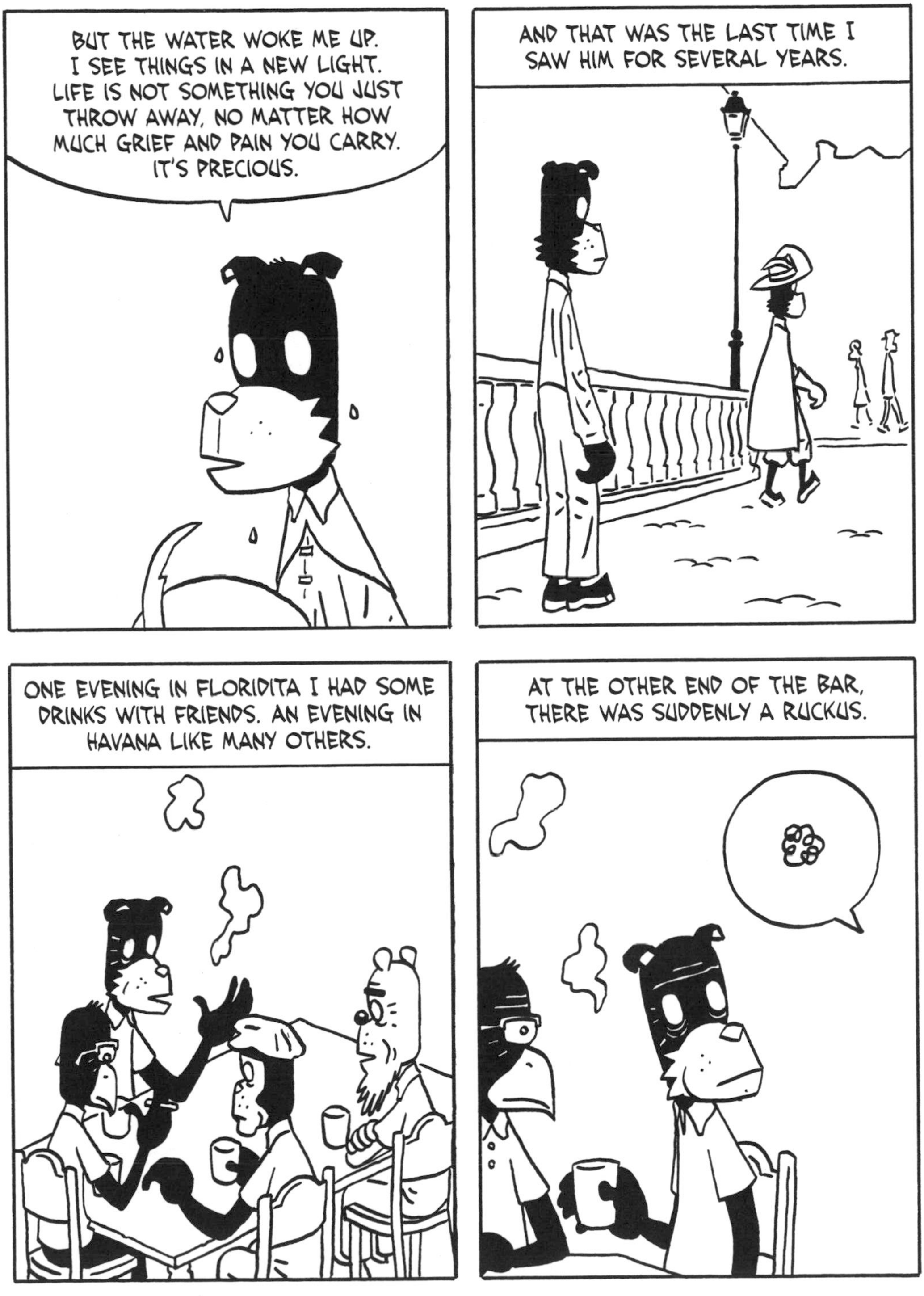
BUT THE WATER WOKE ME UP. I SEE THINGS IN A NEW LIGHT. LIFE IS NOT SOMETHING YOU JUST THROW AWAY, NO MATTER HOW MUCH GRIEF AND PAIN YOU CARRY. IT'S PRECIOUS.
AND THAT WAS THE LAST TIME I SAW HIM FOR SEVERAL YEARS.
ONE EVENING IN FLORIDITA I HAD SOME DRINKS WITH FRIENDS. AN EVENING IN HAVANA LIKE MANY OTHERS.
AT THE OTHER END OF THE BAR, THERE WAS SUDDENLY A RUCKUS.

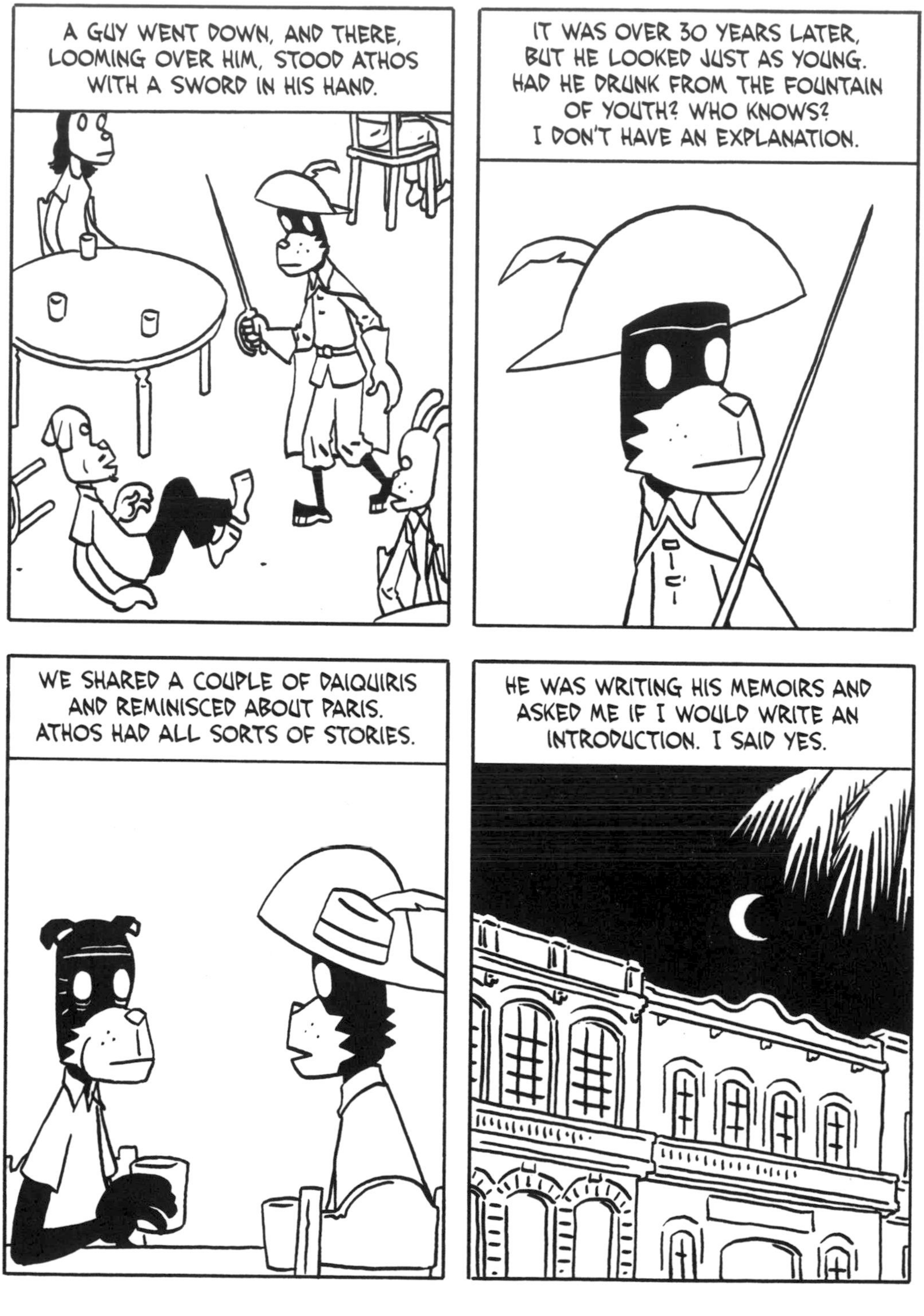
A GUY WENT DOWN, AND THERE, LOOMING OVER HIM, STOOD ATHOS WITH A SWORD IN HIS HAND.
IT WAS OVER 30 YEARS LATER, BUT HE LOOKED JUST AS YOUNG. HAD HE DRUNK FROM THE FOUNTAIN OF YOUTH? WHO KNOWS? I DON'T HAVE AN EXPLANATION.
WE SHARED A COUPLE OF DAIQUIRIS AND REMINISCED ABOUT PARIS. ATHOS HAD ALL SORTS OF STORIES.
HE WAS WRITING HIS MEMOIRS AND ASKED ME IF I WOULD WRITE AN INTRODUCTION. I SAID YES.

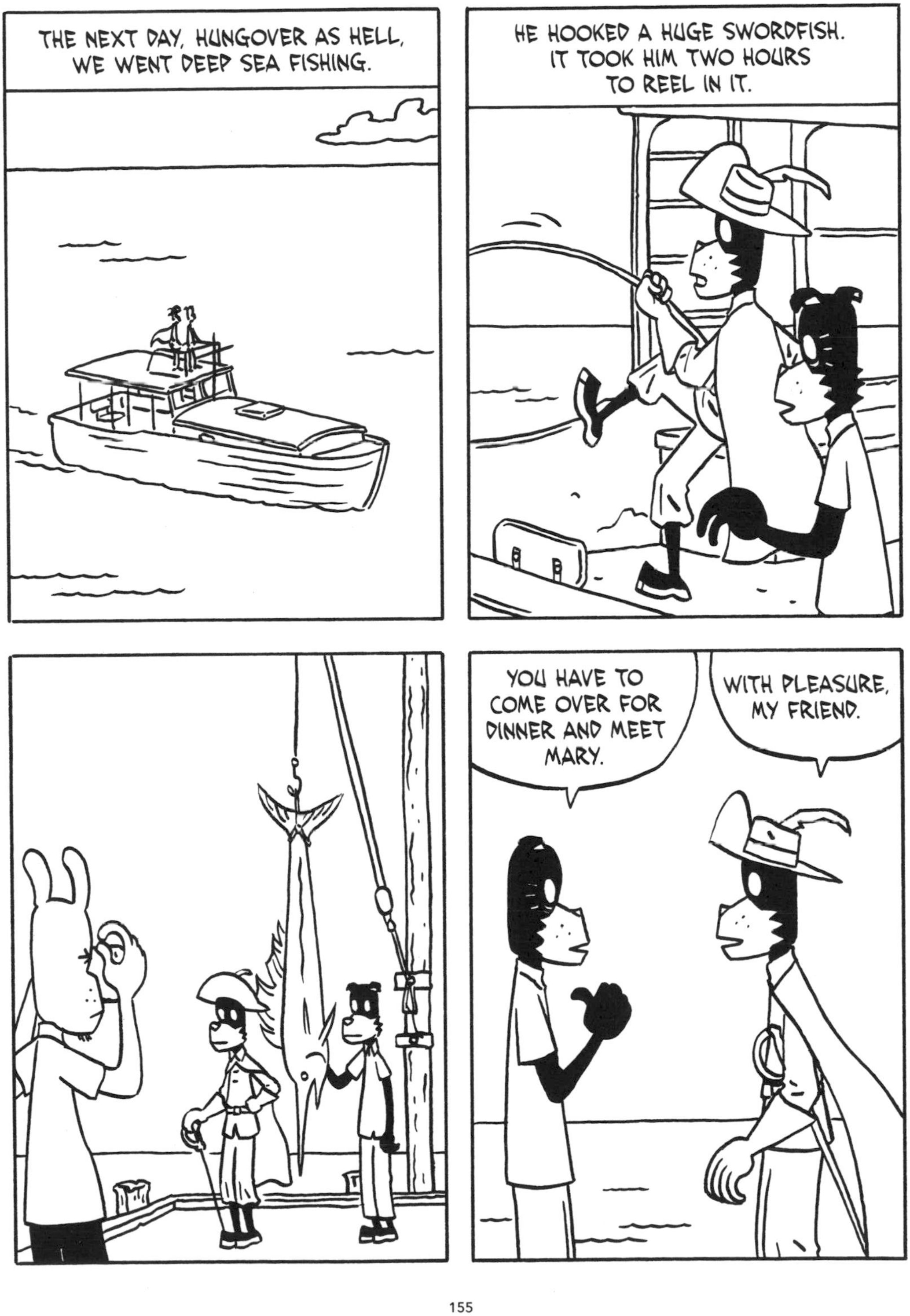
THE NEXT DAY, HUNGOVER AS HELL, WE WENT DEEP SEA FISHING.
HE HOOKED A HUGE SWORDFISH. IT TOOK HIM TWO HOURS TO REEL IN IT.
YOU HAVE TO COME OVER FOR DINNER AND MEET MARY.
WITH PLEASURE, MY FRIEND.

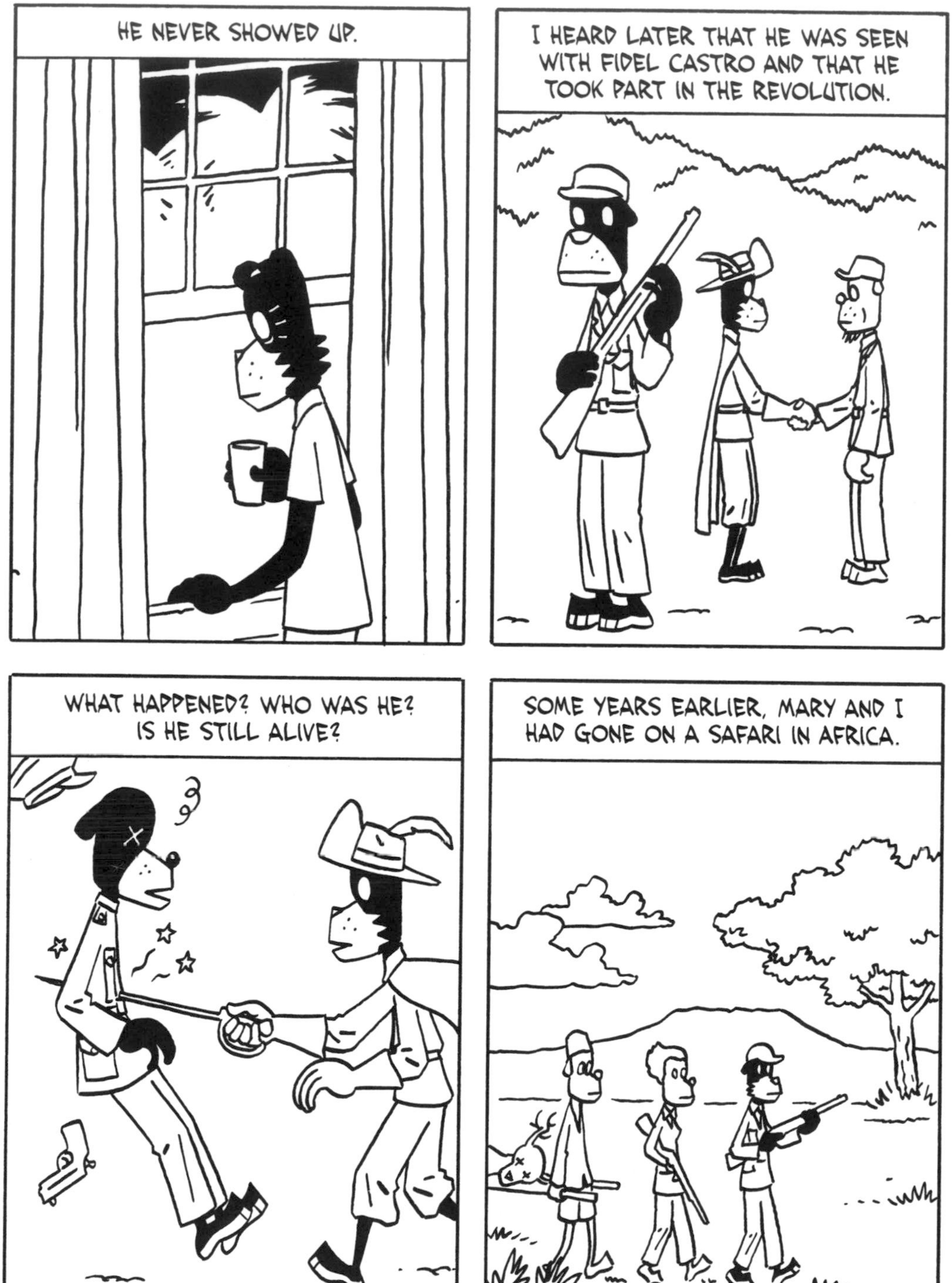
HE NEVER SHOWED UP.
I HEARD LATER THAT HE WAS SEEN WITH FIDEL CASTRO AND THAT HE TOOK PART IN THE REVOLUTION.
WHAT HAPPENED? WHO WAS HE? IS HE STILL ALIVE?
SOME YEARS EARLIER, MARY AND I HAD GONE ON A SAFARI IN AFRICA.

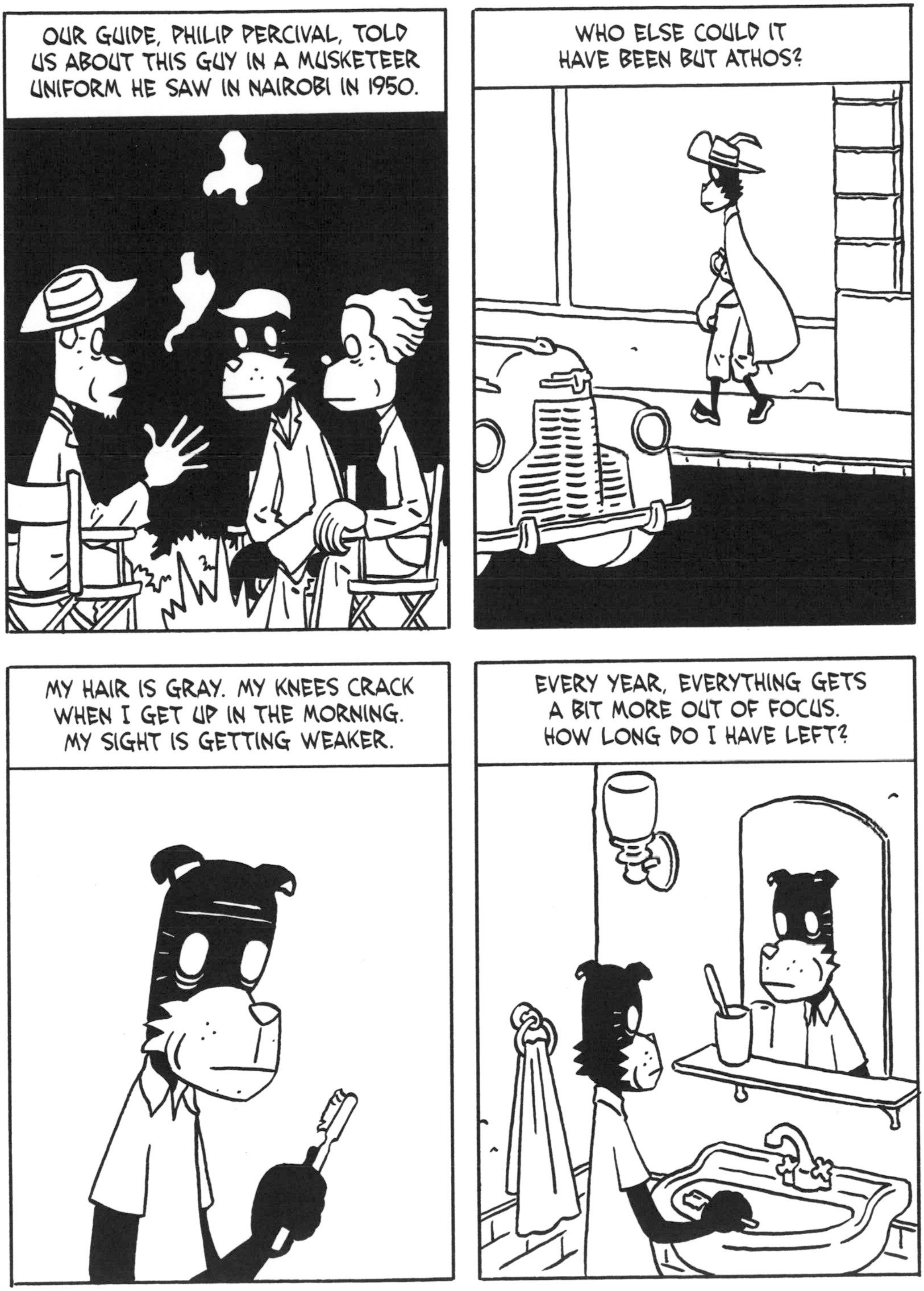
OUR GUIDE, PHILIP PERCIVAL, TOLD US ABOUT THIS GUY IN A MUSKETEER UNIFORM HE SAW IN NAIROBI IN 1950.
WHO ELSE COULD IT HAVE BEEN BUT ATHOS?
MY HAIR IS GRAY. MY KNEES CRACK WHEN I GET UP IN THE MORNING. MY SIGHT IS GETTING WEAKER.
EVERY YEAR, EVERYTHING GETS A BIT MORE OUT OF FOCUS. HOW LONG DO I HAVE LEFT?

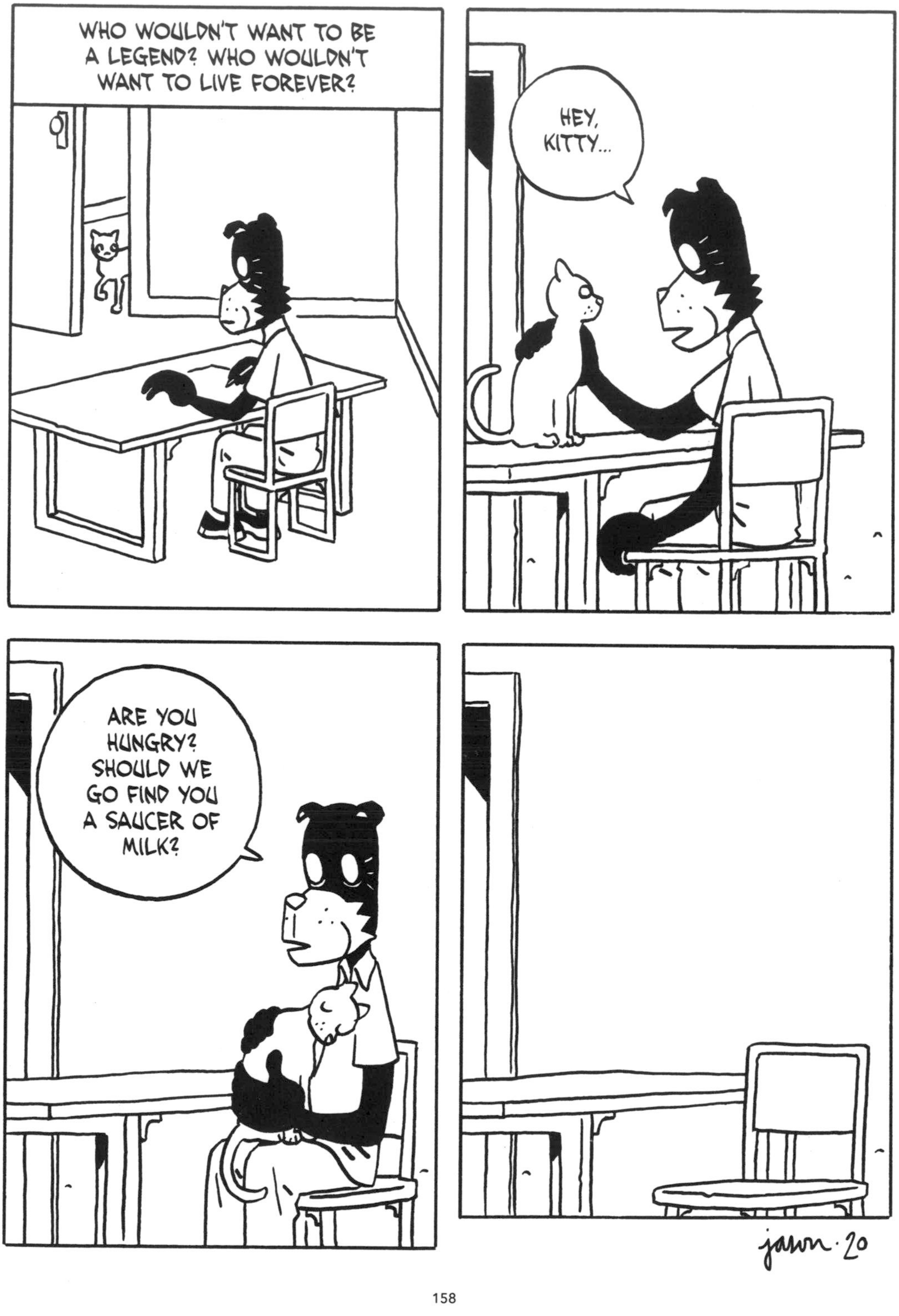
WHO WOULDN'T WANT TO BE A LEGEND? WHO WOULDN'T WANT TO LIVE FOREVER?
HEY, KITTY...
ARE YOU HUNGRY? SHOULD WE GO FIND YOU A SAUCER OF MILK?
jason · 20